HUSSERL AND THE QUESTION OF RELATIVISM

PHAENOMENOLOGICA

COLLECTION FONDÉE PAR H.L. VAN BREDA ET PUBLIÉE
SOUS LE PATRONAGE DES CENTRES D'ARCHIVES-HUSSERL

122

GAIL SOFFER

HUSSERL AND THE QUESTION OF RELATIVISM

Husserl and the Question
of Relativism

GAIL SOFFER

New School for Social Research,
New York, U.S.A.

KLUWER ACADEMIC PUBLISHERS
DORDRECHT / BOSTON / LONDON

Library of Congress Cataloging-in-Publication Data

```
Soffer, Gail.
   Husserl and the question of relativism / by Gail Soffer.
     p.   cm. -- (Phaenomenologica ; 122)
   Includes bibliographical references and index.
   ISBN 0-7923-1291-0 (alk. paper)
   1. Husserl, Edmund, 1859-1938.  2. Relativity--History.  3. Truth-
-History.   I. Title.  II. Series.
B3279.H94S59  1991
121'.092--dc20                                              91-17761
```

ISBN 0-7923-1291-0

Published by Kluwer Academic Publishers,
P.O. Box 17, 3300 AA Dordrecht, The Netherlands.

Kluwer Academic Publishers incorporates
the publishing programmes of
D. Reidel, Martinus Nijhoff, Dr W. Junk and MTP Press.

Sold and distributed in the U.S.A. and Canada
by Kluwer Academic Publishers,
101 Philip Drive, Norwell, MA 02061, U.S.A.

In all other countries, sold and distributed
by Kluwer Academic Publishers Group,
P.O. Box 322, 3300 AH Dordrecht, The Netherlands.

Printed on acid-free paper

Printed in The Netherlands

Νῦν δὲ περὶ ψυχῆς τὰ λεχθέντα συγκεφαλαιώσαντες,
εἴπωμεν πάλιν ὅτι ἡ φυχὴ τὰ ὄντα πώς ἐστι πάντα. ἢ
γὰρ αἰσθητὰ τὰ ὄντα ἢ νοητά, ἔστι δ᾽ ἡ ἐπιστήμη μὲν τὰ
ἐπιστητά πως, ἡ δ᾽αἴσθησις τὰ αἰσθητά· πῶς δὲ τοῦτο,
δεῖ ζητεῖν.

Aristotle, de Anima

Table of Contents

Acknowledgments

An earlier version of this work was presented as a dissertation at Columbia University under the sponsorship of Charles Parsons. I would like to express my gratitude to Professor Parsons for his encouragement of my study of Husserl over the course of several years and for the benefit of his counsel and judgment. My second reader, Charles Larmore, also provided many years of valuable comments and ideas, including especially useful indications of the relation of Husserl to other thinkers. Many thanks also to J.N. Mohanty, David Carr, and Richard Bernstein for helpful conversations and written remarks during the later stages of this project. I have profited not only from their penetrating thematic insights but also from their special wisdom and mentorship.

A research stay at the Husserl-Archives of Cologne was made possible by a grant from the Deutscher Akademischer Austauschdienst. I am indebted to Elisabeth Ströker, Ursula Panzer and Reinhold Smid for their kind assistance during this stay. Thanks are also due to Samuel IJsseling, Philip Buckley, Ullrich Melle, and Rudolf Bernet of the Husserl-Archives of Leuven. I greatly appreciated their support of my project and the very stimulating discussions during my visit to Leuven.

My greatest debt of gratitude remains to my family and friends, without whose special participation this work would not have been possible.

Preface

The question of relativism is a perennial one, and as fundamental and far-reaching as the question of truth itself. Is truth absolute and universal, the same everywhere and for everyone? Or is truth historically, culturally, biologically, or otherwise relative, varying from one epoch or species to another?

Although the issues surrounding relativism have attracted especially intense interest of late, they continue to spark heated controversies and to pose problems lacking an obvious resolution. On the side of one prevalent form of relativism, it is argued that we must finally recognize the historical and cultural contingency of our available means of cognition, and therefore abandon as naïve the absolute conception of truth dear to traditional philosophy. According to this line of thinking, even if there were universally valid principles, knowledge of them would not be possible for us, and thus an absolute conception of truth must be rejected in light of the demands of critical epistemology.

However, when truth is accordingly relativized to some contingent subjective cognitive background, new difficulties arise. One of the most infamous of these is the logical inconsistency of the resulting thesis of relativism itself. Yet an even more serious problem is that the relativization of truth makes truth itself contingent, thereby undermining the motivation for preferring one belief or value to another, or even to its opposite. For if all our beliefs are true only given, for example, the prevailing norms, values and modes of reasoning of this society, and if these latter are not themselves true, but simply elements of the cognitive background that happens to be in effect, then there is no rational ground for the affirmation that our beliefs are superior to the contrary beliefs of others, beliefs which are equally valid given some other contingent background. Of course it can be granted that we do in fact prefer our own beliefs, and perhaps in straightforward everyday living and choosing cannot do otherwise. However, in moments of critical reflection it must be conceded that this preference is itself no more than a contingent fact, rather than an authentically justifiable one. Thus a consequent relativism results in an extreme pessimism about the possibility of any rational thought or action.

Husserl is one of the few major thinkers of the 20th century for whom the problem of relativism is of utmost importance. Writings such as "Philosophy as Rigorous Science" and the *Crisis* make clear the magnitude of what, according to Husserl, is at stake: not merely the resolution of a narrowly technical philosophical issue, but the intellectual, ethical and spiritual well-being of human civilization as a whole. The overcoming relativism stands as a veritable quest for Husserl, and can be seen to be a guiding motive for the entire development of his phenomenology. A major contribution of a phenomenological approach to this issue is that it provides the means for a *positive* defense of an absolute conception of truth, a defense which demonstrates that and the extent to which knowledge of such truth is possible. However, the same phenomenological approach which makes possible an epistemic justification of non-relative truth makes possible a justification of relative truth as well. Thus the attempt to employ phenomenology to overcome relativism in the most conclusive way possible ultimately results in an affirmation and reconciliation of both a relative and a non-relative conception of truth.

This work presents a reconstruction and evaluation of Husserl's evolving position in relation to relativism. The main focus is upon the question of the relativity of truth. Husserl's responses to this question are analyzed in three main moments: his critique of relativism; his positive defense of absolute truth by way of a phenomenological reinterpretation of it; and his ultimate attempt to reconcile both a relative and a non-relative conception of truth in light of the analysis of the lifeworld. Thus I argue that despite Husserl's early virulent opposition to relativism, and his subsequent efforts to develop an epistemically sound conception of absolute truth, Husserl's own phenomenology itself leads to a limited affirmation of relativism. However, contrary to critical attacks in the literature suggesting that a consistently phenomenological approach should have led Husserl to a complete abandonment of an absolute notion of truth, I maintain that Husserl's phenomenology shows the reconcilability and defensibility of both relativity and the absolute.

Chapter One is devoted to the critique of relativism in the *Prolegomena* to the *Logical Investigations*. The general approach in this early writing is a formal one: the thesis of relativism is shown to contain paradoxes and contradictions, and to depend upon equivocal uses of language. Although Husserl himself eventually realized the inability of formal argumentation to provide a conclusive overcoming of relativism, the *Prolegomena* critique remains of interest both as a starting-point and in light of contemporary discussions of relativism in the analytic literature, many of which are carried out wholly at this formal level. Thus the analysis of the *Prolegomena* in this chapter provides an occasion for examining the relation between Husserl and the contemporary analytic tradition, as well as for a general evaluation of the adequacy of formal approaches to relativism. The demonstration of the limited success of such approaches highlights the motivation for the more complex phenomenological strategy adopted by Husserl later on.

Ultimately, Husserl's overriding concern is to justify a non-relative conception of truth for the sciences, and for 'science' in the form of philosophy above all. Accordingly, the second chapter takes up the defense of a 'scientific', non-relative philosophy in "Philosophy as Rigorous Science." The analysis of this chapter falls into two parts. The first part examines the *Logos* critique of historicism, a critique which complements and amplifies the argumentation of the *Prolegomena*. The second part addresses the *Logos* essay's first beginnings of a *positive* justification of non-relative truth, a justification mounted in terms of a 'philosophy as rigorous science'. In addition to elucidating the notions of 'science' and 'scientific philosophy', and evaluating the positive *Logos* arguments in their behalf, here I discuss the relation between Husserl's approach to relativism and his foundationalist epistemic project as a whole.

Chapter Three turns to Husserl's properly phenomenological analysis and its implications for the relativism problematic. The central contribution of this analysis is its conception of truth, a conception which is to overcome both the skepticism engendered by the traditional correspondence theory on the one side, and the relativism of coherence and Kantian-style theories on the other. This chapter contains a reconstruction of the phenomenological theory of truth in its historical development in the *Prolegomena*, the Sixth Logical Investigation, and *Ideas I*, as well as a comparison of Husserl's position to those of his primary philosophical antecedents, Descartes, Locke, Berkeley, and Kant. According to the principle of critical epistemology of decisive importance for both Kant and Husserl, a theory of truth (and one of 'absolute' truth in particular) is justified only insofar as knowledge of such truth is possible. Here I argue that Cartesian objectivism falls prey to the epistemic critique and so degenerates into skepticism. By contrast, Kant does indeed successfully address the epistemic critique and avoid skepticism, but only at the cost of affirming or at least engendering an untenable relativism. Here I emphasize that unlike Descartes on the one side and Kant on the other, Husserl's phenomenological analysis of truth is responsive to the concerns of critical epistemology while preserving truth's non-relativity.

Chapter Four is devoted to a critical evaluation of the Husserlian claim that phenomenology itself attains the 'absolute'. In light of the epistemic critique and its demand for a justification of the possibility of knowledge, any overcoming of relativism can be no stronger than the overcoming of skepticism that supports it. Yet it is in the analysis of the *Evidenz* attained by phenomenology that the Husserlian response to the epistemic critique reaches its high point, and thus it is upon its success that the overcoming of skepticism ultimately depends. The discussion of this chapter begins with a reconstruction of the essential elements of the phenomenological method, including the epoché and noetic-noematic analysis. This then makes possible an elucidation of the sense in which the results produced by this method are 'absolute', both in terms of certainty or apodicticity (against skepticism) and intersubjectivity (against relativism). The Husserlian transcendental foundation of knowledge is once again contrasted with the Kantian one and shown to avoid the hidden relativism of this latter.

The fifth and final chapter takes up Husserl's confrontation with relativism in the context of his analysis of the lifeworld. The discussion presented in this chapter has two main strands. First, it is shown how the analysis of the lifeworld leads to an affirmation of a limited version of relativism, i.e., at the level of the concrete lifeworld. Thus contrary to the prevalent interpretation holding that Husserl conceived of the lifeworld as single and universal, it is maintained that the lifeworld is culturally and historically relative: even according to Husserl's own explicit analysis, there is not one concrete lifeworld but a plurality of them, each relative to a limited intersubjective community. However, at the same time as Husserl affirms the relativity of the lifeworld, and develops an alternate conception of truth adapted to it, he attempts to employ the lifeworld in a new effort to give a final justification to claims by phenomenology and the sciences to attain truths of universal intersubjective intelligibility and verifiability. Thus in the concluding section of this chapter I argue that phenomenology makes possible a reconciliation and a positive defense of both a relative and a non-relative notion of truth.

The interpretation of Husserl presented in this work is based upon both published and unpublished writings. My reading of *Nachlaß* manuscripts of the 1920's and 1930's was especially decisive for the realization that the later Husserl is sympathetic to and attempts to defend a limited version of relativism. However, in the present work I have for the most part avoided lengthy citations and detailed exegesis of these manuscripts. This is because I found that once one has become clear about Husserl's later sympathy to relativism, it is possible to find evidence of it in published materials as well. It seemed desirable to ground the interpretation in published writings wherever possible, given their general availability.

A few further remarks about the methodology employed in this work may be of use. The treatment of Husserl's evolving position in relation to relativism presented here is both historical and systematic. In addition to tracing the various phases of Husserl's thought, I also seek to provide a resolution of the problem of relativism which has merit in its own right. However, the interest in achieving a systematic resolution of the question of relativism had certain implications for the historical analysis as well. The method of historical interpretation employed here could be termed 'positive reconstruction': its aim is to present not so much what a thinker actually thought or wrote as what he should have done so, given the dominant tendencies and possibilities of his own analysis. Thus in some places the interpretation presented here smoothes over inconsistencies, introduces changes in emphasis, and develops lines of thought beyond what can be found in the texts themselves. However, in using this approach I do not mean to agree with Gadamer that there is no distinction between understanding and application, nor to hold that the interpretation which everywhere is determined by the question of truth or by the principle of charity is also the most historically accurate one. To the contrary, the effort to produce a positive reconstruction only heightened my awareness of the difference between it and a literal reading, and increased my conviction that a decisive systematic interest does not lead to the most historically accurate interpretation. Perhaps one could wish for a more detailed account of the differences between Husserl's thought as positively and as literally reconstructed than is to be found here, but such an account lies outside the scope of this work, with its predominating systematic interest.

It is my hope that the present work will be accessible not only to the specialist but also to the general philosophical reader. My guiding intention in writing it was to presuppose as little specialized knowledge of Husserl's thought and writings as possible. It is true that I did not always follow this principle in practice, especially when to do so would have added excessively to the expository sections of the work and detracted from the main line of argument. The resulting compromise may still seem elementary in places to the expert, but there is so much debate surrounding even the most basic of Husserl's doctrines that I believed it better to err on the side of completeness.

List of Abbreviations

(Note: For complete publication information, see the Bibliography.)

BDH	"Der Briefwechsel Dilthey-Husserl".
CM	*Cartesianische Meditationen.*
EU	*Erfahrung und Urteil. Untersuchungen zur Genealogie der Logik.*
FTL	*Formale und transzendentale Logik.*
Hua	*Husserliana.*
Id I	*Ideen zu einer reinen Phänomenologie und phänomenologischen Philosophie, Erstes Buch.*
K	*Die Krisis der europäischen Wissenschaften und die transzendentale Phänomenologie.*
LU	*Logische Untersuchungen, Zweiter Band. Untersuchungen zur Phänomenologie und Theorie der Erkenntnis.*
P	*Logische Untersuchungen, Erster Band. Prolegomena zur reinen Logik*

CHAPTER ONE

The Critique of Relativism in the *Prolegomena* to the *Logical Investigations*

Husserl presents his first thoroughgoing critique of relativism in Chapter 7 of the *Prolegomena* to the *Logical Investigations*. This critique takes place within the broader context of the central argument of the *Prolegomena*, the refutation of psychologism. One line of argumentation within this refutation is: relativism is incoherent and self-refuting, psychologism is a form of relativism, therefore ... In accordance with its function within this main argument, the critique addresses first and foremost relativism in the form of psychologism, i.e., the form in which *what* is relativized is the validity of the fundamental principles of logic; and that *to which* this is relativized is the psychological constitution of a given species. Yet while this particular form of relativism is the primary target of the critique, relativism in a more general form falls within its range, as Husserl himself remarks upon several occasions.

The general approach to the question of relativism adopted by Husserl in this early writing is a formal one. Relativism is reconstructed, and then its central thesis is shown to give rise to paradoxes and contradictions, and to depend upon equivocal uses of language. The conclusion drawn is that the thesis itself must be rejected. The limitations of the refutation set out in the *Prolegomena* were eventually realized by Husserl himself, who returned to the question of relativism again and again in his later writings. One of the main failings of the *Prolegomena* approach is that it does not undertake an investigation of the motives of relativism – or better, of the views and worries of those who come to be branded as 'relativist' – but rather begins curtly with a ready-made formulation of the relativist thesis. How is this formulation reached, if not as a result of an inquiry into what actual 'relativists' hold as a position, and what leads them to hold this position? It appears that the formulation is adopted unreflectively from traditional discussions, discussions which are aimed more at demonstrating the incoherence of relativism than at understanding what relativism is.

The standard definition of relativism is of the absolutists' making. Thus even once relativism as reconstructed by its opponents has been shown to be incoherent, the question of whether the reconstruction itself is an accurate one, or whether the views of the so-called relativists have been adequately addressed, still remains.

Husserl's own treatment of the question moves well beyond this merely formal approach in his subsequent writings. However, the *Prolegomena* critique remains of interest both as a starting-point for a full analysis of the question of relativism, and in light of the continued prevalence of formal approaches in contemporary discussions of relativism. Our analysis of the *Prolegòmena* will highlight certain additions and refinements which Husserl brings to the standard formal arguments, as well as providing an occasion for evaluation of the overall adequacy of what remains a widespread approach to this question. The limited success of this approach shows the motivation for the more complex phenomenological strategy subsequently adopted by Husserl.

1. THE *PROLEGOMENA* CRITIQUE

Husserl gives a preliminary characterization of relativism by way of a gloss on the famous dictum of Protagoras:

"The measure of all truth is the individual person. What is true for a person is what appears to **him** to be true; one thing to one person, the opposite to another, if it so appears to him."[1]

Husserl also gives the briefer formulation: "All truth (and knowledge) is relative – relative to the contingently judging **subject**."[2] A number of points are decisive for this general conception of relativism. First, relativism takes the form of an assertion: it is a thesis. Further, Husserl conceives of relativism primarily as a thesis concerning the nature of truth. A position according to which knowledge or justification is relative, but truth is absolute – quite apart from any question of the coherence or acceptability of such a position – would not be relativism in the sense understood by Husserl. Finally, relativism is the thesis that the truth of a judgment is 'relative to' (i.e., a function of) certain *contingent* features of the judging subject. 'Contingent' here means that the feature is not a universal and necessary feature of subjectivity as such, but rather one which may vary from one subject or species of subjects to another. (Common examples of the contingent features to which truth is relativized include conceptual scheme, psychological constitution, and system of beliefs.) Thus the significance of the relativist thesis lies not so much in its assertion that truth is a function of some characteristic of subjectivity, as in the assertion that this characteristic is a variable one. This is the assertion that gives rise to the more notorious thesis of relativism, i.e., that truth itself is subject to 'contingent' variation, variation which arises merely through variation in the relevant conditioning subjective factors. Thus what is true for one subject or species may be false for another, and what is true at one time may be false at another, due solely to differences in the constitution of the subject.

1.1 *The Self-Refutation Argument*

Having set forth this preliminary characterization, Husserl presents formal arguments to demonstrate that relativism as thus characterized is self-contradictory and incoherent. Surprisingly, the most familiar of all such arguments attacking the formal coherence of relativism is given only cursory treatment by Husserl. However, because this argument is a veritably perennial one in the history of philosophy, remaining central even in contemporary debate, and because its conclusiveness and significance are far from matters of general agreement, we may suitably begin our discussion with a critical evaluation of it.

This most familiar of arguments points out that the relativist asserts that it is absolutely true that all truth is relative, thus claiming for the thesis of relativism itself a type of validity this thesis asserts to be impossible. Although Husserl begins the critique of relativism by mentioning this argument, here he does not so much employ it as note that it is one which a relativist would in no way find convincing. Husserl summarizes the familiar self-refutation argument and an equally familiar rebuttal to it in the same breath:

"[The relativist] will also not be convinced by the common objection that in advancing his theory he claims that it will convince others, and therefore he presupposes the very objectivity of truth which his thesis denies. He will of course reply, 'My theory expresses my standpoint, a standpoint which is true for me and need not be true for anyone else'."[3]

In the familiar rebuttal to the self-refutation argument, the relativist specifies that he is not asserting that it is an absolute truth that truth is relative, but rather that this too is a relative truth, a principle which is valid for him, or in general for whomever the subjective truth-conditioning features of the appropriate nature obtain. With this specification, the relativist produces a position which is at least self-consistent, and thus one which the self-refutation argument would not persuade him to abandon.

Now it is often objected, and Husserl's own presentation suggests, that in this way the relativist is able to preserve the self-consistency of his position only at the cost of relinquishing the right to urge its adoption by anyone other than himself, or at least by anyone who does not presently adhere to it.[4] For to hold that it is only relatively true that truth is relative seems to mean that relativism is true for those who believe it, and false for those who do not. Thus it would be senseless and contrary to the relativist's own position to attempt to persuade anyone to adopt relativism: according to a consistent relativism, relativism is actually false for those who are opposed to it. Thus a consistent relativist should find nothing needing alteration in the following division of opinions: relativists, on the one side, holding that relativism is true for those to whom it appears true, and false for those to whom it appears false; and absolutists, on the other, holding that relativism is false 'for everyone' (if such language will be permitted by the absolutists).

To respond to this objection, it is useful to distinguish between two importantly different forms of relativism, forms which are surreptitiously merged in Husserl's own initial characterization. According to the one form, often termed 'subjectivism', and associated with Protagorean idealism, truth is identical with appearance or opinion: whatever *seems* to be true or is believed to be true by an individual, *is* true for that individual. Clearly, according to a subjectivist position, it is in principle impossible to err regarding any matter (since whatever one believes *is* true, for oneself), and therefore a subjectivist can have no purely theoretical motive to attempt to alter the opinions of anyone else, or even his own.

However, the second, non-subjectivist form of relativism does not reduce truth to opinion. The general principle guiding this form is that an assertion is true for a subject when the principle bears a specific relation to features of the subjective constitution. Here the existence or non-existence of the relation, and hence the truth of a judgment for a given subject, is a fact not reducible to the opinion of the subject on the matter. Thus according to non-subjectivist relativism, it is also possible for an individual to have incorrect beliefs, i.e., to hold as true what is false, relative to himself.

Many types of relativism are non-subjectivist. For example, according to a coherence account of truth, it is not the opinion of the individual regarding a particular judgment that determines whether this judgment is true for that individual, but rather whether the judgment in fact coheres with the individual's background beliefs and practices, no matter what the individual thinks of the matter. Similarly, psychologism equates truth in the case of logical principles not with the opinion of the subject as to their truth, but with the consistency of these principles with the empirical laws governing the subject's cognitive constitution and conscious representations.[5] Because this consistency is a fact apart from the beliefs of the subject, psychologism allows for the possibility that an individual could have incorrect opinions regarding the truth of the principles of logic, even relative to himself.

There are grounds for the tendency to confuse subjectivist and non-subjectivist relativism. One is that in many cases 'objective' relative truth and subjective opinion formation go hand in hand. This is because the same constitution which determines the truth or falsity of a principle also shapes what appears to the subject and the way it appears. Thus, for example, if human representations are governed by the law of non-contradiction, then this will give rise to the appearance and the belief on the part of humans that this law is true.

Yet however tempting it may be to run the two forms of relativism together, such a blending is clearly a confusion of two essentially distinct positions. Although relative truth as determined by the subjective constitution on the one hand, and the subject's own opinion on the other, may often go hand in hand, this is neither necessarily nor always the case. There are persons with no opinion concerning the truth of the principle of non-contradiction (such as children), as well as those who believe that the law of non-contradiction is false (e.g., certain philosophers), even though their faculties of representation are governed by this principle to the same extent as other human beings. Thus the mere fact that the subject's constitution is governed by the principle is not always enough to *cause* the subject to affirm that the principle of non-contradiction is true. Similarly, while the coherence of a judgment with respect to an individual's other beliefs will tend to cause this judgment to appear to be true to the individual, this factor is not always the decisive one. Inconsistencies and incoherence within the total belief structure of a single individual are hardly an infrequent occurrence.

Thus relativism, understood as the thesis that truth is a function of contingent features of the subject, must be clearly distinguished from subjectivism, the view that truth is identical with opinion, or that each individual has infallible knowledge of truth, relative to himself.[6]

When relativism is understood in a non-subjectivist sense, it is clear that it is consistent for a relativist to argue that relativism is valid not only for himself, but also for those who do not presently adhere to it. The specific details of the argument would depend upon the precise variety of relativism being defended, but in general it would parallel the argument of a coherentist with a person who believes *p* and also believes *p implies q*, but does not believe *q*. Much as a consistent coherentist would not attempt to convince a person of the truth of *q* by arguing that *q* is true for everyone, or true in itself, but rather by arguing that *q* is true for this person, given the other beliefs he already has, so the consistent relativist would not argue that relativism is true in itself or true for everyone, but rather true for subjects having the appropriate cognitive constitution or background beliefs.[7] Of course, a relativist would still have to grant that the possession of the appropriate subjective constitution is only a contingent fact, and thus that there could be subjects for whom the thesis of relativism is actually false. However, the non-subjectivist relativist is not limited – as claimed by Husserl as well as others – to the position that relativism is valid only for those to whom it appears valid.

Non-subjectivist relativism, therefore, survives this initial, most familiar of critiques. However, prior to considering further objections which could be advanced against relativism even in the non-subjectivist form, we may pause here to note that the move to non-subjectivism is not the only one open to the relativist in response to the objection that it is inconsistent to argue on relativism's behalf. An alternate response grants that the arguments justifying relativism cannot be purely theoretically motivated ones, but denies that this leaves no place for motives or arguments of other kinds. For even if one abandons the claim that a thesis is *true* universally, or merely relative to one's interlocutor, one could still maintain that considerations other than those of mere truth (e.g., considerations of a practical nature) provide grounds for the adoption of this thesis. Thus a relativist could concede that the thesis of relativism is not necessarily true for others, but still maintain that it is a useful or beneficent thesis, one which promotes tolerance and understanding, and therefore which others should adopt, questions of truth notwithstanding.[8]

Yet clearly, this move does not so much overcome the initial difficulty as merely shift it to another level. For even if the position of the relativist is no more than that relativism is a morally, pragmatically, or otherwise valuable position, the question then becomes whether these *values* are claimed to be absolute or relative ones. Does the relativist hold relativism to be of value (1) 'in itself'; (2) only relative to himself and other relativists; or (3) relative to some shared background of beliefs, values, and practices? If the first, then the relativist finds himself in the paradoxical position of holding that truth is relative, but value (at least in some cases) is absolute. Not the least of the paradoxes endemic to this position is that judgments of the form 'x is of value' would then be true non-relatively, even though truth itself is held to be relative in nature. If the second alternative is chosen, then the relativist once again undermines his own right to attempt to persuade others to adopt relativism: if relativism is of value only for relativists, then this value can indeed stand as a reason for relativists to maintain their position, but not for opponents of relativism to alter theirs. Following the third alternative, the position of the relativist is a modified non-subjectivist relativism, a non-subjectivism with respect to the value of relativism itself. As in the case of non-subjectivism of truth, non-subjectivism of value permits the relativist to attempt to persuade others to adopt the relativist point of view, without damaging the position's consistency.

In the end, the renunciation by the relativist of the claim to truth alters little: a non-subjectivist position, whether regarding truth or value, is necessary to preserve the consistency of the doctrine of relativism with attempts at its propagation.[9] This does not mean, however, that non-subjectivist relativism encounters no other difficulties. In a rather elliptical formulation, Husserl suggests what is perhaps the most serious of these: relativism in the non-subjectivist form presupposes the existence of non-relative truth regarding, minimally, the subjective constitution itself, as that to which all else is asserted to be relative:

> "It is not possible to relativize truth and yet maintain the objectivity of being. Clearly the relativization of truth presupposes an objective being as a point of reference, and therein lies relativism's inconsistency."[10]

Although Husserl here presents more a hint than a full-scale argument, this critique can be reconstructed as follows. Non-subjectivist relativism asserts that truth, and correspondingly, reality, vary as functions of features of the cognizing subject. This in turn presupposes that the constitution of the subject itself is not something about which there are truths only relative to a subject, or something that exists only relative to a subject, but rather something in itself. For the thesis of relativism is not that reality is wholly indeterminate, but rather that reality and truth are indeterminate until certain features of the subject have been specified. For example, psychologism does not hold that there is *no* fact of the matter about whether the fundamental principles of logic are true, but only that there is no fact of the matter until the psychological constitution of the subject has been specified. But then this presupposes that there are truths about human psychology, its mechanisms, its functioning, the laws it obeys, etc. For if there were no such truths, the human psychological constitution would be ontologically indeterminate, and consequently it would be absurd to say that the laws of logic are true relative to it. Similarly, when a coherentist asserts that a proposition is true relative to the subject's overall background of concepts and beliefs, he presupposes that there is such a thing as the subject's body of concepts and beliefs, and that these concepts and beliefs are determinate in nature, constituting a unique set of facts. A parallel presupposition is made by *Weltanschauung* relativism: the *Weltanschauungen* of various epochs are 'in themselves', there is a uniquely determined set of facts concerning the constitution of each *Weltanschauung*, and the truth of other principles (e.g., of ethics, philosophy, or religion) is relative to these. The psychologist, coherentist, and *Weltanschauung* relativist thereby merely overlook the entire problematic of the ontological and aletheic status of the conditioning subjective features themselves, of psychological constitutions, beliefs, and *Weltanschauungen*.[11]

However, relativist positions which attribute absolute being to the subjective constitution or conditioning features are highly questionable. Why, for example, should there be an absolute fact of the matter regarding the functioning of the human faculty of representation, whereas only a relative fact, a fact for this or that species of subjectivity, regarding the law of non-contradiction? Must not the very same considerations which lead to the relativization of the validity of logical principles lead also to the relativization of the validity of any alleged laws regarding the functioning of human psychology? Clearly, were the fundamental principles of logic false relative to beings of some other species, then laws describing human psychology, even if true for us, could easily be false relative to this species as well. Thus it might result that relative to this other species, with its different, relatively true description of the human psychological constitution, the law of non-contradiction would be false ... *relative to humans*. That is, this other species might be so constituted such that relative to it, it is false that the human psychological constitution is governed by the law of non-contradiction. Thus this species would (relatively validly) judge that the law of non-contradiction is false relative to humans, and there would then be no single fact of the matter concerning even the *relative* truth of the principle of non-contradiction.

This difficulty emerges even more clearly in the cases of coherentism and *Weltanschauung* relativism. For if truth is coherence, why should it be thought that there is only one set of facts concerning the nature of a given subject's body of beliefs? If two investigators carry out an inquiry into a given subject's beliefs, and these two investigators themselves have diverse background beliefs, then a different description of the object of investigation will be true relative to each investigator. There will therefore not be a single fact of the matter about this body of beliefs, but rather as many diverse sets of facts as there are possible investigators, and these sets of facts may also be incompatible. Yet if there are divergent sets of facts concerning a subject's body of beliefs, then there will also be divergent correct assessments of whether a given assertion is true relative to this particular subject. A coherentist, therefore, cannot hold that p (a proposition) is true, relative to S (a subject), but rather only that p is true relative to S, relative to I (an investigator), and possibly p is false relative to S, relative to I' (another investigator).

If relativism is to be adopted consistently, then the same arguments which lead to the relativizing of truth in general must lead to the relativizing of truth regarding subjective features such as psychological constitution, beliefs, and *Weltanschauungen*. However, if it is conceded that there is not a unique but a plurality of facts of the matter regarding the subjective features, each fact in turn obtaining relative to subjective features at a higher order, then an infinite regress results, and the original thesis of relativism disintegrates. For if every assertion is only relatively true or false, true or false relative to another only relatively true or false assertion, then it will be impossible for an assertion to be even relatively true. Whether p_1 (some arbitrary assertion) is true relative to S will depend upon whether p_2 (a description of the cognitive background constitution of S) is true, and then whether p_2 is true will depend upon whether p_3 (a description of the cognitive background constitution of an investigator) is true, and so on *ad infinitum*. Thus even in relation to S, p_1 is neither true nor false but of indeterminate truth value. The relativist must either arbitrarily assert that at some level there is a non-relative truth, or abandon the thesis that truth is relative to the cognitive constitution of the subject, in favor of the thesis that truth is indeterminate.

Is this regress inevitable? Must the assertion that truth is determinate only relative to the subjective give way to the assertion that it is wholly indeterminate? If so, why is the relativist not persuaded when this simple argument is set forth?

As noted above, the underlying motive for many forms of relativism is the conception of the subject as *constituting* if not the entirety then at least the structure of the objects it cognizes. The cognized objects exist relatively to the constituting subjectivity: were the constituting subject different, then these objects could not 'exist for' (be constituted by) a subject of this type. However, it could be held that here the distinction between *constituting* subject and *constituted* subject (the subject taken as an object of cognition) is essential; and further, that where this distinction is respected, the regress does not occur. For while the *constituted* subjective constitution does indeed have relative being, the *constituting* subject is an active power with its own determinate nature, existing 'in itself' and not merely as an object of cognition. But if this is the case, then the regress always stops with the *constituting* subjectivity. For example, when an historian studies the world-view of the ancient Greeks, the Greek world-view exists as an object of cognition and possesses only relative being, being relative to the historian's own subjective constitution. However, the subjective constitution of the historian is 'in effect' during the act of cognition, and is not relative to anything further.

Of course, some further defense must be provided for the notion that constituting subjective constitutions may legitimately be attributed a non-relative nature, whereas constituted ones (as well as any other objects of cognition) may not. One such argument could posit a distinction in the type of knowledge available in the case of this subjective constitution, and then attempt to ground a distinction in its type of being upon this. For example, it could be held that a subject has privileged access to his own cognitive constitution, e.g., through introspection, so that this constitution is knowable as it is 'in itself'. All else, however, including both ordinary objects and alternate cognitive constitutions, is knowable only as it appears, as mediated by the subject's cognitive faculties and background. Applying the principle that all posited objects must be possible objects of cognition, the subject's constitution as it is in itself is admitted to our ontology, but all other 'in themselves' are excluded.

Yet the position that one's own subjective constitution can be known as an 'in itself' is in contradiction with the relativist's general principle that the subject *constitutes* its objects of cognition. For insofar as my own constitution is cognized, it follows from the relativist's basic position that this objectified subjective constitution is itself constituted by the inquiring subjectivity, and thus is relative to it.[12]

A second possible argument could grant that there is no immediate cognition of the subjective constitution, and yet maintain that the constituting constitution has a non-relative existence, although possibly an unknowable one. This position could be justified as a best possible explanation, based on an inference from effects to their cause. The effects to be explained are given in the form of appearances, or what presents itself in experience. Certain elements of or variations in these appearances are not adequately explained by reference to what is external to the apprehending subject. Thus it must be presumed that these appearances are in part caused by the cognitive constitution of the apprehending subject. But if this constitution is acting as a cause, then it must exist and have a determinate nature. This conclusion stands firm regardless of any difficulties involved in knowing this nature.

Yet the flaw in this second argument is that if its reasoning is consistently applied, it requires the abandonment of relativism with regard to the non-subjective as well. For this argument defends the non-relative nature of the effective subjective constitution on the grounds that this constitution must be posited as a cause of what appears to consciousness. However, at least as strong an argument can be made that these appearances are caused also by what is external to the subjective, and not by the subjective constitution alone. Now if the difficulty of knowing the subjective cause in an unmediated way does not deter the relativist from attributing a non-relative character to it, the difficulty of attaining such knowledge of the objective causes cannot be taken as a ground for their relativization either. Thus to be consistent, the relativist would have to hold that not only the effective subjective constitution, but also any other posited causes of conscious presentations, have non-relative being. There is no reason to posit a possibly unknowable being behind the appearances of the effective subject, but not behind what is external to the subject. Thus this final attempt to salvage the relativist thesis fails.

The results of our analysis of the familiar self-refutation argument may be summarized as follows. In order to circumvent the objection that it is inconsistent with relativism to attempt to persuade others to adopt it, the relativist must reject subjectivism in favor of relativism in a non-subjectivist form; that is, in a form which asserts that whether a principle is true relative to a subject is itself not merely a matter of opinion, but of the factual existence of a relation between the principle and the subjective constitution. Yet non-subjectivist relativism presupposes that subjective constitutions are themselves not relative, a presupposition which is not and cannot be made compatible with the thesis of relativism itself. When this inconsistency is removed, and the subjective is also relativized, the position itself collapses: truth and being turn out to be not relatively determinate, but wholly indeterminate. Thus relativism proves to be either inconsistent with attempts at its propagation, or inconsistent with itself.

1.2 *The Argument by Way of the Meaning of 'Truth'*

Husserl presents another quite different line of argument against relativism, and it is this second line of argument which in fact plays the central role within the *Prolegomena* critique. Here Husserl maintains that relativism is incompatible with the very concept of truth. According to this position, it belongs to the very meaning of the term 'true' that what is true is true 'in itself', so that the truth of a proposition – as it were, by definition – cannot vary as a function of the subject apprehending it:

"What is true is true absolutely, true 'in itself'. Truth is identically the same, whether humans or non-humans, angels or gods apprehend it in their judgments."[13]

Husserl develops this position further by arguing that the principle of non-contradiction and the other fundamental laws of logic are not assertions which might be either true or false, depending upon other factors. Rather, the truth of these principles follows merely from what 'truth', 'assertion' and other related terms mean. In particular, that a proposition does not assert *p and not p*, constitutes part of what is meant when it is held that this proposition is true. Husserl therefore maintains, against the psychologists, that it is absurd to hold that there could be beings for whom propositions contradicting the law of non-contradiction are true. There might be beings who *believe* that such propositions are true (and, as Husserl points out, human beings not infrequently fall into this category, although generally unawares), but these propositions would nonetheless not *be* true, if 'true' is taken in its proper meaning.

"Thus the fundamental principles of logic express nothing more than certain truths which arise from the mere sense (content) of certain concepts, such as truth, falsity, judgment (proposition), and the like."[14]

According to this position, truth is not something over and above the basic principles of logic, which may or may not apply to them, but rather the concept of truth and these basic principles stand as a totality, the principles bringing to explicit expression what already lies immanently in the concepts, or alternately, the concepts being defined in part through these principles. Thus the concept of truth is clearly incompatible with the way the term 'truth' is used by relativism. Indeed, Husserl's position seems to be that in speaking of 'truth for a subject' or 'truth for a given historical context', the relativist employs language which is self-contradictory and unintelligible. The term 'truth' is not one which can be qualified by relativizing phrases, because it already belongs to the meaning of this term that truth is as it is, independently of the contingent features of subjects.

Husserl concedes that it is of course possible to attach a different meaning to the term 'truth', a meaning such that it would not be absurd or self-contradictory to say 'a principle is true for one species but false for another', or a meaning compatible with the falsity of the fundamental principles of logic. However, holds Husserl, those who attach such a meaning avoid self-contradiction at the expense of hopeless equivocation:

"If, for example, they term 'trees' what we term 'propositions', then of course the assertions in which we express the fundamental principles of logic are not valid; but then they will also have lost the sense in which we affirmed them. Thus it comes to pass that relativism totally alters the sense of the word 'truth', and yet claims to speak of truth in the sense laid down by the laws of logic, and the only sense intended by us all whenever we talk of truth."[15]

However, this position obviously raises the question of justification. How is it to be demonstrated that there is a single, sufficiently well-defined, 'proper' meaning associated with linguistic usage involving 'truth' and its cognates; and further, that this meaning *essentially* excludes any relativist interpretation of truth?[16]

Given the formal, non-phenomenological approach of the *Prolegomena* discussion, it could appear that Husserl's prospects for grounding the 'propriety' of the absolute conception of truth are only of the most un-promising kind. Here his attempts consist solely in asserting that the absolute conception of truth is the one 'we all' have and use. Since what 'we all' in fact mean when we affirm a proposition is that it is true 'in itself' and absolutely, and the relativist interpretation of truth is incompatible with this intended meaning, the relativist interpretation is illegitimate and unacceptable.

This is the argument advanced in the passage quoted above, where it is held that the absolute conception of truth is "the only one intended by us all whenever we talk of truth."[17] This sort of argument is employed again in the critique of Sigwart. According to Husserl's reconstruction, Sigwart holds that a judgment cannot be true in the absence of an intelligence which thinks this judgment.[18] Now if Sigwart's position is correct, argues Husserl, then prior to the birth of Newton, the law of gravity was not true. But this is an absurd conclusion, for if the law of gravity were not true prior to the birth of Newton, then it could not be true at all, since what it means for the law of gravity to be true is for it to be true for all time:

"[It is alleged that] the judgment expressed by the law of gravity was not true before Newton. But then, strictly speaking, it would actually be self-contradictory and **completely** false, since unconditional validity for all time plainly belongs to what is intended in its assertion."[19]

Thus here Husserl holds that the law of gravity must be true for all times or not at all, because a claim to atemporal validity belongs to the intentional horizon of the assertion itself, to what we actually (although possibly only implicitly) mean when we think, believe, or claim that this law is true. Sigwart's psychologistic reformulation of truth is thus refuted on the grounds that it is in contradiction with what we actually mean when we assert.

However, if the sole justification offered by Husserl for the absolute conception of truth is the fact of its employment, then this exhibits a willingness to collapse the *quæsito juris* to the *quæsito factis* in blatant contradiction with his own insistence on the impossibility of deriving validity from empirical fact. Furthermore, it is not even clear that this absolute conception *is* the conception of truth that 'we all' have and use in all instances of assertion or talk about truth, especially given the widespread influence of relativism within the thought and idiom of popular culture. Thus both the universality and the justification of the employment of the absolute conception of truth remain in doubt.

Now it could be held that the demand for a *justification* of a conception of truth is itself unreasonable, posing a task which could not possibly be fulfilled. Any such justification would necessarily be circular, since a specific notion of truth would already have to be employed in order to evaluate the argument's validity. Thus the most that could be reasonably required of a conception of truth is that it be internally consistent, and also possess a sufficient measure of coincidence with 'ordinary' intuitions and linguistic usage.[20]

However, Husserl's own later, properly phenomenological treatment of the problem does provide a justification of the concept of truth, at least of a sort, and this constitutes an important advance of the phenomenological approach over the formal one. Now according to the *Prolegomena* treatment, the justification of a concept consists solely in the demonstration of its actual employment, and thus ultimately depends on the specific contents of actual acts of thought. By contrast, according to Husserl's later analysis (which begins its development as early as the second volume of the *Logical Investigations*, and reaches its mature stage in *Formal and Transcendental Logic*), the accurate description of the contents of acts of thought is only an important preliminary step in the justification of a concept. This step provides an explicit elucidation of a concept as it actually exists for us and is thought by us within acts of judgment. According to Husserl, this descriptive derivation of the content of a concept is superior to one which derives the concept merely by recourse to traditional or conventional formulations, formulations whose meaning and degree of correspondence with 'the phenomena' (i.e., with the concepts as intended and fulfilled) remains unclear.

However, Husserl makes plain that an accurate descriptive or phenomenological elucidation of a concept is not yet a justification of its validity. The preliminary description provides a clarification of what the concept is. In order for the concept as thus defined to be justified, two further steps are needed. These steps constitute the subjection of the concept to critical evaluation, evaluation designed to test the 'reality' of the concept, the possibility that something real (whether concrete or abstract) could instantiate it. (The nature of these two further steps will be only very briefly indicated here, but will receive further treatment in the following chapters.) The first level of critique consists in evaluating the formal consistency of the concept. The second level of critique consists in evaluating the degree and kind of *Evidenz*, of fulfillment in intuition, which the concept attains and is in principle capable of attaining. The validity of the concept depends upon the possibility of something being evidently experienced as an instantiation of this concept.[21]

Husserl's position in the *Prolegomena* seems to be that any relativist conception of truth fails even at the preliminary stage of analysis, since this is not a conception which is actually employed within intentional acts. However, as will be discussed in Chapter Five, Husserl's own later analysis of the lifeworld reveals that this position is incorrect, and that in fact there are many intentional acts in which a relativist or quasi-relativist type of conception is at work, a conception which Husserl terms 'lifeworld' or 'situational' truth. The truth-assertions made at the level of the lifeworld are overlooked by Husserl in the *Prolegomena* because here he is concerned primarily with the domains of logic and, to a lesser extent, of natural science. The claim that the type of truth and validity we have in mind is always absolute truth and absolute validity is made more plausible when assertions from logic and natural science are taken as archetypical (which is precisely what is done by Husserl in the *Prolegomena*, where the primary examples of assertions are the principle of non-contradiction and Newton's law of gravity.) Although the lifeworld notion of truth differs in certain important respects from the relativist one opposed in the *Prolegomena*, the discovery that assertion also takes place within a conditional, non-absolute mode makes the problem of justifying the absolute conception all the more acute. The questions of the nature of lifeworld truth, and the defense of the absolute notion proposed by Husserl despite his recognition of the existence of a non-absolute notion, will be discussed in further detail in Chapter Five. Here it suffices to note that Husserl's own later analysis undermines his argument in the *Prolegomena* that relativism is untenable because incompatible with the absolute conception of truth, which is the only conception we have and the only justifiable conception.

Yet despite the weakness and incompleteness of Husserl's second line of argumentation in the *Prolegomena* (the argument by way of the concept of truth) the first line of argument nonetheless stands as a conclusive demonstration that relativism as reconstructed by Husserl in this particular text is an unsatisfactory philosophical position.

2. RELATIVISM RECONSIDERED

A refutation of relativism does not yet constitute a vindication of absolutism. The question of the nature of the positive defense mounted by Husserl in favor of a non-relative notion of truth, and a critical evaluation of its adequacy, will be taken up in subsequent chapters. However, in the context of our evaluation of the formal arguments against relativism, it is important to consider whether the very definition of relativism in the *Prolegomena* is an accurate one. This is not a trivial question for the Husserlian formal critique (and others similar to it), for if not relativism but only a false reconstruction of it has been defeated, then the critique has failed of its aim. It is true that there is nothing particularly striking or unfamiliar in Husserl's reconstruction: it is one which can be encountered in any number of contemporary discussions. Yet significantly, definitions of this kind, definitions which characteristically lead more or less immediately to the conclusion that a principle can be true for one subject yet false for another, are to be encountered only in the writings of relativism's *opponents*. From this it follows either that no one is a relativist, or that relativism has not been adequately defined. Thus it may be more instructive to seek the definition of relativism not from its detractors, but from those who are at least sympathetic to it.[22]

David Carr, for example, argues that Husserl's critique of relativism fails precisely because the reconstruction on which it is based does not apply to many of the most significant philosophical views typically characterized as relativist. While Husserl presents relativism as a thesis, Carr maintains that modern relativism takes the form of a questioning, a suggestion, a series of examples, and not an articulated position which is formulated, asserted, and then defended:

"This refutation fails, not, in my opinion, because it presupposes a conception of truth that has been surpassed, say by Heidegger or Gadamer, as some claim, but rather because it is too narrow to cover all the varieties of philosophical expression. The relativism of Heidegger, of Derrida, or of Foucault – and also that of the late Wittgenstein – is not set forth in a series of theses, not justified by arguments that appeal to logical principles, as if it laid claim to an objective, timeless truth. Rather, through aphorisms, metaphors, and – especially in Foucault's work – countless examples, a position is suggested which is never formally articulated. The only real effect of Husserl's refutation was that philosophers of this sort tend to avoid, for good reasons, traditional philosophical argumentation. Thus the *belief* in relativism has also affected the *style* of philosophical writing. The weakness of Husserl's refutation [in the *Prolegomena*] is that it is aimed not at the content of the belief itself but only at its straightforward expression in traditional language."[23]

According to Carr, a relativism that limits itself to a questioning or suggestive but non-assertoric mode avoids the objection that it is self-defeating. Much as the skeptic who merely asks the question "Is there knowledge?", the relativist who merely suggests that truth varies with variations in subjectivity, or who merely questions whether there could be such a thing as absolute truth, does not slip into self-contradiction. Thus, Carr concludes, the relativist is free to *believe* in relativism, but not to express this belief in traditional philosophical language, with its arguments, assertions, and claims to objective validity.

Where relativism is no more than a state of uncertainty, an unwillingness to affirm the validity of an absolute conception of truth, Carr is correct that the self-refutation argument is powerless against it. Relativism in this form could be overcome only by a positive defense of the absolute notion of truth. Indeed, it is very likely that this uncertainty is a common one among the philosophical, which would explain the practical ineffectiveness of the perennial self-refutation argument. However, it is not clear that a mere doubt should be termed 'relativism', or a philosophical 'position', even of a post-modern kind. This is particularly the case because the *belief* in a relativism of this sort, or a belief that its doubt is a justified one, cannot be consistently maintained. For the claim by Carr that the *belief* in relativism is equally immune to the self-refutation argument – so long as this belief is not expressed in assertoric language – is based on an invalid distinction between belief and assertion. A relativist who silently believes in relativism asserts this position to be true just as much as one who asserts this belief expressly to others, and thus the two are equally susceptible to the argument that it is self-contradictory to maintain (or to believe) that it is true that all truth is relative. And if it is rebutted that the silent relativist believes not that relativism is true, but only that relativism is true for himself (or for others who believe in it), then the argument will take precisely the same course outlined above. Indeed, the very notion that relativism is something in which one believes is incompatible with Carr's earlier suggestion that relativism does not take the form of a thesis but of a doubt, suspicion, or questioning. If relativism is a state of doubt, then it cannot be properly said that one believes it, but rather that one *has* it or lives in it.

Thus Carr begins with an alternate construal of relativism and shows that relativism so construed is not subject to the standard objection. However, he concludes by attempting to slide back to the usual construal of relativism, and to declare it as well to be immune to the self-refutation argument. If relativism is not a thesis, it is not self-refuting; but then it is also not an object of belief, which certainly lessens its interest and force as a properly philosophical position. If, on the other hand, it is a belief, then it is also a thesis, and hence self-refuting.

Within the contemporary analytic literature, the thetic nature of relativism is generally unquestioned, by opponents and proponents alike. The same is not the case, however, for the specific form this thesis takes. According to the foremost defenders of the strong sociology of knowledge, Barnes and Bloor, relativism in its desirable and tenable form is not (at least in the first instance) a thesis about the nature of truth, but rather one about the causes of belief. Whereas rationalists have held that in some cases a proposition is believed merely because it is true, or because of evidencing reasons and demonstrations, this relativism asserts that in all cases an individual is caused to believe what he does by sociological conditioning and the incumbent blind acceptance of standards and norms indigenous to his community. Thus, Barnes and Bloor argue, it is as appropriate to seek and provide a sociological explanation of belief in, for example, the principles of geometry, as in the magical powers of certain rites:

"All beliefs are on a par with one another with respect to the causes of their credibility. It is not that all beliefs are equally true or equally false, but that regardless of truth and falsity the fact of their credibility is to be seen as equally problematic. The position that we shall defend is that the incidence of all beliefs without exception calls for empirical investigation and must be accounted for by finding the specific, local causes of this credibility."[24]

Clearly, the position of Barnes and Bloor is meant as a critique of the view of Mannheim that sociological explanations of knowledge should not be undertaken in certain domains, such as mathematics and natural science. However, their central claim can be interpreted in two different ways, one weaker and one stronger. According to the first, weaker interpretation, they hold only that no matter what the field of discourse, the question of the sociological reasons why something is believed remains a valid and distinctive one, over and above the question of what evidence exists to the effect that the principle is true. Yet developed in this way, the critique of rationalism is not relativist. For the view that beliefs are brought about in part or even largely by factors other than their truth, or by factors other than ones which could be admitted as rational grounds in a demonstration, is entirely compatible with the view that beliefs themselves are either true or false *tout court*.

However, according to the second, stronger interpretation, and the one clearly adopted by Barnes and Bloor, the very distinction between 'sociological' explanation of belief on the one side, and 'scientific' or 'rational' justification on the other, and thus between what they term 'credibility' and 'validity', is of only limited applicability. For at some point in any 'rational' demonstration, argue Barnes and Bloor, it will be necessary to introduce principles or to employ modes of reasoning which themselves have no other ground than their local acceptability, their conformity with norms and standards prevailing solely within a particular social context. With respect to *these* principles and modes of reasoning, the distinction between rational and sociological causes of belief, between validity and credibility, is empty: the only grounds that can be adduced for these principles are either the principle themselves (which would be circular), or the fact that they are accepted locally, i.e., that they are credible. Validity can be distinguished from mere credibility only where a set of locally accepted norms and standards is already presumed. Given such a background, that a proposition is valid means that it coheres with or can be demonstrated on the basis of the locally accepted methods and norms; whereas that a proposition is credible means only that it is in fact believed, whether a demonstration is possible or not, or even if it is possible to give a refutation.

Barnes and Bloor assert, then, that the distinction between validity and credibility is applicable only when a background of knowledge is taken for granted. Yet from this it would follow that the word 'valid' on the lips of the sociological relativist should mean no more than 'justifiable given the background of knowledge I take for granted'. Although Barnes and Bloor do not formulate their position in precisely these terms, they do hold that when the relativist employs words such as 'true' and 'false', these words only express the preferences of the relativist as to which beliefs to adopt and which to reject, preferences which are in turn conditioned by the taken-for-granted background:

"The relativist, like everyone else, is under the necessity to sort out beliefs, accepting some and rejecting others. He will naturally have some preferences and these will typically coincide with those of others in his locality. The words 'true' and 'false' provide the idiom in which those evaluations are expressed, and the words 'rational' and 'irrational' have a similar function."[25]

Now if the relativist holds that the word 'true' simply expresses a conditioned preference, then what he should *mean* when he says 'true' should be simply 'what I prefer, given the taken-for-granted background'. A relativist who, when he says 'p is true', thinks to himself, 'p is true, *tout court*', has failed to assimilate his own thesis that the word 'true' simply expresses his conditioned preference. Reflective self-consistency would require the relativist to alter what he *means* in actual employment of the word 'truth' so that it would comply with his philosophical thesis about what the word 'truth' expresses.[26]

Yet if the term 'true' on the lips of a relativist means no more than 'what I prefer, given my background', then all the difficulties which Barnes and Bloor hold essential to avoid re-emerge triumphant. For when truth is understood in this way, what is true for one subject or community will be false for another, and the entire line of argumentation presented in part one of this chapter can be brought to bear against the relativism of Barnes and Bloor as well.

Other defenders of relativism present positions quite similar to that of Barnes and Bloor, but which more consistently divorce relativism from the truth problematic. Characteristically, in such attempts *justification* is held to be relative, but truth (and validity) to be absolute. According to these positions, there is no independent way to decide which among the divergent historico-cultural backgrounds of conventions, conceptions and criteria generates beliefs which are true. Here justification consists in coherence with the conventions, beliefs and standards of rationality generally accepted within one's own context, and is therefore relative. Truth, by contrast, is truth in the traditional correspondence sense. Thus although a belief may be justified relative to one historical context but unjustified relative to another, the same belief is either true or false, *tout court*.[27]

However, this hybrid position avoids the paradoxes of relativizing truth at the cost of rendering all beliefs wholly irrational. If there is no valid way to determine which set of conventions and standards is more likely to lead to beliefs that are – over and above being concordant with contingently prevailing criteria – also true in the traditional correspondence sense, then the affirmation that one's beliefs are true is of a rationality precisely equal to the affirmation that one's beliefs are false. For on this account, only the *coherence* of a belief with a particular historical background can be justified, and not that this coherence leads to truth in the posited correspondence sense. To be consistent with its basic tenets, one would therefore have to eschew all claims about truth and falsity, and limit one's judgments to evaluations of relative coherence with prevailing conventions and norms.[28]

Further, once assertions regarding truth have been explicitly acknowledged to be unwarranted, it becomes apparent that assertions about justification are equally so. For to hold that a belief is justified, at least when 'justification' is taken in the ordinary sense, means to hold that there are grounds for taking the belief to be true. By contrast, because coherence given the standards of one's culture does not provide grounds for claims to truth in the traditional correspondence sense, such coherence does not constitute justification according to the ordinary meaning. Thus the relativist is left with the view that we simply have the beliefs and standards for selecting beliefs that we have inherited from our culture, and the best we can do is attempt to bring our beliefs and standards into a coherent, unified whole, even though such coherence does nothing to justify our beliefs, nor to improve the likelihood that they correspond with reality. Yet if this is the case, one wonders why we should even bother to strive for coherence, supposing we have a choice.

All of the alternate conceptions examined thus far have proved unsatisfactory, either falling prey once again to the formal arguments presented earlier, or eluding these only by exposing themselves to other difficulties. Here I will conclude by briefly sketching one further version of relativism proposed within the contemporary literature, a version of interest both because it does not fall prey to the *Prolegomena* argumentation, and because it has certain elements in common with the later position of Husserl himself.

This version of relativism is proposed by Joseph Margolis, who prefaces his definition with the remark that the usual version of relativism, claimed to be the 'central' doctrine, is generally "trotted out in order to be exposed as hopelessly incoherent," the results of attempts at patching and revision being "uninteresting if viable ... and even at times incoherent in ways not unlike that of the 'central' doctrine."[29] According to Margolis, relativism in its interesting, coherent, and defensible form is neither the view that truth itself is relative, nor the view that justification is so, but rather the view that in *some* domains of knowledge or discourse the categories of truth and falsehood as conceived by formal logic do not apply. In these domains, assertions are characterized not by bipolar truth-values but by logically weaker truth-like values, values (to cite Margolis' examples) such as 'plausibility', 'reasonableness', 'aptness', etc. A central characteristic of a truth-like value of this kind is that it may apply to a multiplicity of assertions which, were the categories of truth and falsity to be imposed, would have to be deemed mutually incompatible. Thus, again following Margolis' example, a relativist might hold that in the realm of interpretations of works of art, a variety of interpretations are reasonable or worthwhile, and also that some are more reasonable and more worthwhile than others, but that there is no such thing as a 'true' interpretation in the bipolar sense, an interpretation such that any second interpretation logically inconsistent with this one would be false.

The central point of this relativism, then, is not to propose an alternate, relativized conception of truth, but to argue that truth as understood by formal logic is not an appropriate category for assertions in all domains of human inquiry. Margolis' conception of relativism further distinguishes itself from the one attacked in the *Prolegomena* in its emphasis on relativism as a regional thesis, and not a universal one. Indeed, the main questions which relativism in this form must face are precisely to which domains truth as understood by formal logic fails to apply, and which truth-like values are to replace it. Margolis indicates that grounds for judging the category of truth inapplicable in a particular domain could be provided by either an epistemological or ontological theory regarding this domain: either a theory which asserts that the in-principle limitations of our cognitive capacities rule out the possibility of knowledge of truth, in the strict sense, in this domain; or one which holds that there is simply no unique fact of the matter, either in general or in answer to specific questions, in this particular domain.

Similarly to the relativism of Margolis, Husserl's own later position emphasizes the need to distinguish among different domains of discourse, and the types of validity-claims and fulfillment of validity-claims proper to each of these. Here Husserl no longer maintains that truth as understood by formal logic is always and everywhere the applicable or even the intended sense of validity. The willingness to admit that in some cases only 'weaker' notions of validity are both appropriate and at work emerges most clearly in Husserl's analysis of the lifeworld, and of the contrast between it and the world posited by scientific theory, the world 'in itself'. However, as will be discussed in Chapter Five, even the weaker, 'relativist' notion of truth developed by Husserl continues to obey the law of non-contradiction. Further, unlike what appears to be the case for Margolis, Husserl draws the line demarcating the domains where each notion of truth is to apply between 'natural' or pre-scientific life on the one side, and theoretical activity on the other. Indeed, as early as "Philosophy as Rigorous Science," it becomes clear that the main concern of Husserl in relation to the relativism problematic is the vindication of the strong notion of truth for theory in the form of *philosophy*, to defend it against the perceived threat first of the *Weltanschauung* philosophy of Dilthey, and later of the existentialism of Heidegger. The focus of the discussion of the next chapter will accordingly be upon Husserl's arguments in "Philosophy as Rigorous Science" against a historicist view of philosophy itself, and in favor of a non-relative conception of truth as the correct guiding ideal within this domain.

The type of formal arguments presented in the *Prolegomena* successfully refute a certain variety of relativism. However, such arguments remain inconclusive because they do not address relativism in its more tenable forms. Further, a refutation of relativism does not yet constitute a positive defense of absolutism. Because a formal approach lacks the resources for a positive justification of a non-relative conception of truth, such an approach cannot yield a satisfactory response to the question of relativism.

NOTES

1. *Hua XVIII* 122 (*P A/B* 114). ("Aller Wahrheit Maß ist der individuelle Mensch. Wahr ist für einen jeden, was ihm als wahr erscheint, für den einen dieses, für den anderen das Entgegengesetzte, falls es ihm ebenso erscheint.")
   The notation "*Hua XVIII* 122 (*P A/B* 114)" indicates that the original German version of the passage is located on page 122 of the *Husserliana* edition, Volume XVIII, and page 114 of both the first (*A*) and second (*B*) editions of the *Prolegomena*. Here as elsewhere, the German is given in parenthesis in the note.
2. *Ibid.*, 122 (*P A/B* 114). ("Alle Wahrheit [und Erkenntnis] ist relativ – relativ zu dem zufällig urteilenden S u b j e k t.")
3. *Ibid.*, 123; (*P A/B* 115). ("Man wird ihn auch nicht durch den gewöhnlichen Einwand überzeugen, daß er durch die Aufstellung seiner Theorie den Anspruch erhebe, andere zu überzeugen, daß er also die Objektivität der Wahrheit voraussetze, die er *in thesi* leugne. Er wird natürlich antworten: Mit meiner Theorie spreche ich meinen Standpunkt aus, der für mich wahr ist und für niemand sonst wahr zu sein braucht.") This passage reveals the inaccuracy of the Carr reconstruction of the *Prolegomena* critique of relativism. Carr reduces the entirety of the critique to this single self-refutation argument, and then dismisses it on the grounds that it would be unconvincing to a relativist. However, Carr thereby overlooks both that this argument is only a small part of a larger critique, and that Husserl himself does not pretend that a relativist would find this argument persuasive. (See "World, World-View, Life-World: Husserl and the Conceptual Relativists," reprinted in *Interpreting Husserl*, Phaenomenologica, vol. 106, [Dordrecht: Martinus Nijhoff Publishers, 1987], especially 221.)

4. A typical argument to this effect can be found in William Vallicella, "Relativism, Truth, and the Symmetry Thesis," in *The Monist* 67:3 (July, 1984), 452–66. The Vallicella argument consists largely in objecting to the relativist: "How can a proposition be true *for* me if I reject that proposition?" (Vallicella, 463.)

5. See Benno Erdmann, *Logik. Logische Elementarlehre*, third revised edition, edited by Erich Becher (Berlin and Leipzig: Walter de Gruyter, 1923), especially 226ff., and 472. (It should be noted that Husserl's critique addresses the position outlined by Erdmann in the first edition, which Erdmann apparently modified in subsequent editions, although he claims not to have changed anything essential. See 477, n. 1.)

6. Discussions of the distinction between subjectivism and non-subjectivist relativism occur frequently in the contemporary literature, especially in the writings of those who wish to defend relativism in a non-subjectivist form. C. Behan McCullagh, for example, sets forth this distinction and then attacks Putnam's critique of relativism, claiming that Putnam's account falsely equates relativism with subjectivism, whereas subjectivism is a position no real relativist holds: "If, as Putnam suggests, the relativist means by 'this doctrine is right', nothing more than 'I think this doctrine is right', and has no objective reference for the word 'right', then his claim would indeed be not just trivial but meaningless. However Putnam has not represented the relativist's claim correctly. When the relativist says 'this doctrine is right' he does not mean merely 'I think this doctrine is right' but also 'this doctrine is justified by the beliefs and standards of rationality generally accepted in my culture'." (See C. Behan McCullagh, "The Intelligibility of Cognitive Relativism," *The Monist* 67:3 [July, 1984], 320–1.)

   Mark Okrent develops the distinction between subjectivist and non-subjectivist relativism in terms of the contrast between Protagorean and Kantian idealism. According to Okrent, Protagorean idealism is the thesis that *esse* is *percipi*; whereas Kantian idealism holds that the subjective constitution determines only the formal structure of objects of experience, and not their entire being. On the Kantian view, the object as it is 'objectively' or in truth is therefore not necessarily identical with the object as it appears, and illusion and deception are possible.

   Okrent maintains that most modern versions of relativism are variations of the position which results when one begins with a Kantian conception of objects of knowledge as 'formed' (although not wholly created) by the subjective cognitive constitution, but then rejects the Kantian view that the relevant subjective structures are universal and invariant features of humanity. In contrast to Kant, modern relativists hold that the form given by the subject to the object of knowledge is an historically and culturally variable one. Thus while Kant is a 'species' relativist regarding the truths of mathematics and the natural world, maintaining that judgments in these domains are true for all finite subjects with spatio-temporal forms of intuition, modern relativists tend to be cultural relativists, holding that judgments regarding a certain domain are true only for subjects sharing a common cultural and historical background. (See Mark Okrent, "Relativism, Context, Truth," in *The Monist* 67:3 [July, 1984], especially 342–353.)

7. Thus the non-subjectivist relativist McCullagh, for example, maintains that relativism is justified given the beliefs and standards of rationality generally accepted within our society, and that whoever shares these ought to become a relativist. In this way, McCullagh presents an argument on behalf of relativism aimed to persuade others to adopt a position they may at present not hold. (It should be pointed out that McCullagh

combines epistemic relativism with metaphysical realism, or truth absolutism, and therefore his thesis is that *justification* is relative to one's standards and beliefs, and not that *truth* is so. However, this does not affect the present argument, the aim of which is only to establish whether it is inconsistent for a relativist to attempt to persuade others to adopt relativism.)

8. A position of this sort is sketched by Goodman in regard to his general theory of the multiplicity of worlds. Without prejudging the question of whether this theory is a relativist one, the theory can be seen to encounter a difficulty similar to that of relativism in the area of self-justification. How can a theory that worlds are multiple be shown to be true? Will it not – as all other theories – be true in some worlds but false in others? Goodman's response is that the merit of the theory lies not in its truth (indeed, he holds it has no truth-value, and is not even a theory, but a way of conceptualizing), but rather in its practical value, its 'efficiency in world-making': "I am not so much stating a belief or advancing a thesis or doctrine as proposing a categorization or scheme or organization, calling attention to a way of setting our nets to capture what may be significant likenesses and differences. Argument for the categorization, the scheme suggested, could not be for its truth, since it has no truth-value, but for its efficiency in world-making and understanding .... Put crassly, what is called for in such cases is less like arguing than selling" (Nelson Goodman, *Ways of World-making*, [Indianapolis: Hackett, 1978], 129).

9. The arguments set forth in this passage have a straightforward application to the form of relativism or 'categorization' presented by Goodman. For when Goodman denies that the 'way of thinking' proposed by him possesses a truth-value, holding instead merely that it commends itself on the basis of its 'efficacy in world-making and understanding,' it is not clear whether Goodman claims this efficacy itself to be something which obtains in all worlds, according to all correct descriptions, or only for some and not for others, with no reason for preferring the descriptions which hold the categorization to be inefficient to those which hold it to be efficient. If Goodman's position is the latter, then even the justification for 'selling' is undermined. If his position is the former, then the efficiency of the way of conceptualizing is attributed an absolute ontological status which the conceptualization itself declares does not and cannot obtain.

10. *Hua XVIII* 137 (*P A/B* 132). ("Man kann nicht Wahrheit relativieren und an der Objektivität des Seins festhalten. Freilich setzt die Relativierung der Wahrheit doch wieder ein objektives Sein als Beziehungspunkt voraus – darin liegt ja der relativistische Widerspruch.")

11. A related objection against relativism is raised by Putnam. Whereas Husserl points to the surreptitious supposition of non-relative truths about the subjective constitution, Putnam notes that many relativists assume that *whether* a given judgment is true relative to a given constitution is itself non-relative: "[The relativist] just takes it for granted, of course, that whether X is true (or justified) relative to these [views, standards, presuppositions] is *itself* something 'absolute'" (Hilary Putnam, *Reason, Truth and History* [Cambridge: Cambridge University Press, 1981], 121). But it seems to me that a conception of the non-relative subject as constituting the objective is more basic to relativism than the presupposition criticized by Putnam, and in fact gives rise to it.

12. This is of course the type of position advanced by Kant in the Transcendental Deduction, where he asserts that I can know myself only as I appear to myself (i.e., as an

object-consciousness constituted in time, the 'contingent' subjective form of intuition) and not as I am in myself. (Immanuel Kant, *Kritik der reinen Vernunft*, in Gesammelte Schriften, vol. III, Royal Prussian Academy of Science Edition [Berlin: G. Reimer, 1911], *B* 155.)

13. *Hua XVIII* 125 (*P A/B* 117). ("Was wahr ist, ist absolut, ist 'an sich' wahr; die Wahrheit ist identisch eine, ob sie Menschen oder Unmenschen, Engel oder Götter urteilend erfassen.")

14. *Ibid.*, 144 (*P A/B* 139). ("So drücken die logischen Grundsätze nichts weiter aus, als gewisse Wahrheiten, die im bloßen Sinn [Inhalt] gewisser Begriffe, wie Wahrheit, Falschheit, Urteil [Satz] u. dgl. gründen.")

15. *Ibid.*, 126, *P A/B* 118. ("Nennen sie z.B. Bäume, was wir Sätze nennen, dann gelten die Aussagen, in die wir Grundsätze fassen, natürlich nicht; aber sie verlieren dann ja auch den Sinn, in dem wir sie behaupten. Somit kommt der Relativismus darauf hinaus, daß er den Sinn des Wortes Wahrheit total ändert, aber doch Anspruch erhebt, von Wahrheit in dem Sinne zu sprechen, der durch die logischen Grundsätze festgelegt ist, und den wir alle, wo von Wahrheit die Rede ist, ausschließlich meinen.")

16. Despite the *ad hominem* and unconvincing character of an argument which simply presupposes as 'proper' or 'valid' the very concept of truth which relativism puts into question (thus 'refuting' relativism by denying that the absolute character of truth is open to intelligible debate), similar appeals to the 'traditional' or 'original' or 'our' conception of truth are not uncommon within contemporary critiques of relativism, such as that of Putnam. Indeed, many self-styled relativists appear to find compelling the claim that some form of the traditional conception of truth has priority, adapting their positions accordingly. For example, Barnes and Bloor proclaim themselves relativists, but reject as unacceptable any form of relativism which leads to the conclusion that a proposition could be true for one society but false for another, and hence both true and false. Nor do they trouble themselves to make out a defense for the absurdity of relativism in this form, but simply take the validity of the non-relative conception of truth and of the law of non-contradiction to be self-evident. (See Barry Barnes and David Bloor, "Relativism, Rationalism, and the Sociology of Knowledge," in *Rationality and Relativism*, edited by Martin Hollis and Steven Lukes [Cambridge: MIT Press] 1984, especially 22–3.)

17. *Hua XVIII* 126 (*P A/B* 118).

18. See *ibid.*, 134 (*P A/B* 127); and Christoph Sigwart, *Logik I*, second revised edition (Freiburg: J.C.B. Mohr, 1889), 248.

19. *Hua XVIII* 134 (*P A/B* 128). ("Das Urteil, das die Gravitationsformel ausdrückt, wäre vor Newton nicht wahr gewesen. Und so wäre es, genau besehen, eigentlich widerspruchsvoll und überhaupt falsch: Offenbar gehört ja die unbedingte Geltung für alle Zeit mit zur Intention seiner Behauptung.")

20. Indeed, the impossibility of an actual demonstration of the validity of a conception of truth, and the adequacy of self-consistency and adherence to 'intuitions' and previous tradition, is the unexpressed but consensus view within contemporary discussions of relativism. For within such discussions, definitions and characterizations of truth are generally either merely asserted, or at most shown not to be self-contradictory, and positive justifications are neither provided nor even attempted.

21. Thus the phenomenological justification of the concept of truth is indeed circular, in that what is demonstrated is only the coherence of a given concept, although this

coherence is of a particular sort. The concept is to be derived from actual intentional acts, and not simply posited by an abstract theory. Further, the concept must be consistent with the formal and intuitive character of actual experience (fulfillment), and not merely with some arbitrary system of principles or beliefs.

22. Even in the absence of strong preconceptions about the 'true' definition of relativism, finding self-proclaimed relativists is not an easy task. Certainly none of those Husserl charged with relativism (whether psychologists, historicists, or neo-Kantians) would have acknowledged that label. Thus in this section I take the δευτερος πλους of considering contemporary proponents.

23. Carr, 221.

24. Barnes and Bloor, 23.

25. *Ibid.*, 27.

26. In this argument, I have simply applied the Husserlian phenomenological requirement that our philosophical elucidation of truth should correspond to the concept employed in actual intentional acts.

27. A position of this sort is elaborated by C. Behan McCullagh, who maintains "not that truth is determined by convention but that what we mean by 'true' and what we judge to be true is determined by convention" (McCullagh, 334). This also seems to be the view of Charles Larmore in "Tradition, Objectivity and Hermeneutics", in *Hermeneutics and Modern Philosophy*, edited by Brice Wachterhauser (Albany: State University of New York Press) 1986, 147–167. Although Larmore too argues for the combination of a contextualist theory of justification with a metaphysical realist interpretation of truth, unlike McCullagh Larmore considers such a position to be *anti*-relativist.

28. For a more detailed development of this argument, see Chapter Three, pp. 62 ff. below.

29. Joseph Margolis, "Historicism, Universalism, and the Threat of Relativism," *The Monist* 67:3 (July, 1984), 320.

CHAPTER TWO

The Critique of Historicism and *Weltanschauung* Philosophy in "Philosophy as Rigorous Science"

Husserl's next major confrontation with the relativism problematic takes place in the 1911 *Logos* article, "Philosophy as Rigorous Science." Despite the rather polemical and popular character of this text, it reflects a number of important developments in Husserl's position, both on the systematic and the historical levels. Whereas in the *Prolegomena* the main concern is to defend the non-relativity of logic, in the *Logos* essay the focus has shifted to philosophy. Further, although here too Husserl presents a number of formal arguments reminiscent of the *Prolegomena* treatment, these are now supplemented by ethical arguments and at least references to phenomenological ones. These two developments are by no means unrelated. For in the time between the largely pre-phenomenological *Prolegomena* and the *Logos* essay, Husserl more clearly realizes the impossibility of grounding logic through logic alone, and hence the inadequacy of purely formal arguments when taken in isolation. Rather, the drive to found logic leads Husserl from logic to phenomenology. This latter is employed by him as a method but not explicitly thematized in the main text of the *Logical Investigations* (1901), and then first presented systematically as a discipline in *Ideas I* (1913). According to this more mature view, only philosophy – and indeed, only philosophy in the form of phenomenology – has the resources to combat the relativism and skepticism against which even logic, that most rigorous of sciences, has proven no match.

The emergence in Husserl's thinking of philosophy as the primordial locus of non-relative truth is accompanied by a corresponding shift in opponent: the psychologists of the *Prolegomena* are succeeded by the prevalent philosophical relativists of the time, the historicists, personified for Husserl by Dilthey. Accordingly, the first part of this chapter will contain a reconstruction and evaluation of the *Logos* critique of historicism. The second part will address the *Logos* essay's first beginnings of a positive defense of non-relative truth. In this context Husserl's defense is mounted in terms of 'philosophy as rigorous science', which means considerably more than 'non-relative philosophy'. As we will see, ultimately Husserl's efforts to overcome relativism cannot be detached from his opposition to skepticism and his entire foundationalist enterprise. Thus in this second part, after an elucidation of the notions of 'science' and 'scientific philosophy', and an evaluation of the positive *Logos* arguments in their behalf, I discuss the relation between Husserl's approach to relativism and his epistemic project as a whole. This will lay the groundwork for an understanding of Husserl's full defense of a non-relative philosophy, a defense which depends crucially upon the more specific details of his pheno-menology and which will be addressed in the subsequent chapters.

1. THE CRITIQUE OF HISTORICISM

The *Logos* critique contains a brief account of the origins and motives of historicism. Although Husserl does not make much use of this account, appropriately amplified and interpreted it can be seen to make an important contribution to the critique itself. According to this amplified account, the roots of historicism are to be found in the romanticism of the 19th century, with its tendency to view philosophy as a form of expression, similar to art, and its intensification of the study of history. The philosophy of Hegel marks a turning-point. Hegel himself was able to avoid relativism in virtue of his metaphysics, which permitted him to reconcile an intensive study of the multiplicity and diversity of historical philosophies with a firm belief in the absolute character of philosophy itself. In Hegel's system, the seemingly incompatible historical philosophical systems are interpreted as expressions of various stages in the knowledge of a single, universal Spirit, stages through which Spirit gradually progresses towards knowledge which is absolute. Thus although Hegel stresses the historical conditionedness and merely relative validity (validity as the expression of a given stage in the self-understanding of Spirit) of the philosophical systems of the past, his speculative positing of a Spirit uniting all individual periods and schools, progressing from the partial and perspectival to the total and unconditioned, still permits him to claim absolute validity for philosophy, and for his own philosophy in particular.

However, Hegel's historicist successors remained more deeply impressed by his doctrine of the relative validity of historical philosophies than by his teleological conception of a universal Spirit. In their attempts to purge the

Hegelian conception of its metaphysics, they abandoned the universality and teleology of Spirit, and with it, the claim that over the course of history, philosophy eventually attains validity which is absolute. The resulting position is committed instead to a basic principle of equivalence: all major philosophical systems are of equal validity, each valid for the age and culture to which it belongs. Later philosophical systems are no more absolutely valid than are earlier ones, for no philosophy ever has nor ever will attain the objective, trans-historical validity traditionally sought by the philosophers, and which Hegel claimed for his own system.[1]

Thus the essential relativist characteristic of historicism as here understood is its assertion that validity in philosophy is always validity relative to a historical context. The validity of a philosophical system is said to lie in its ability to express in theoretical constructs the spiritual life of a culture or an age, or to provide a coherent overall *Weltanschauung* enabling a human community better to understand its world and to carry out its basic life practices. Clearly, because the spiritual life and practices of human communities change over the course of history, and vary from one culture to another, there will be no single philosophical system valid for all cultures and all times. Historicism therefore rejects the traditional notion of universal, objective validity which guided historical philosophies. The very notion of a universally valid, 'scientific' philosophy is held to be no more than a chimera.[2]

Husserl follows this general characterization of historicism with an extended critical attack. Whereas the *Prolegomena* proceeds by examining the coherence of the thesis of relativism, the *Logos* essay maintains that the usual arguments in favor of historicism are inadequate and inconclusive. In order to see the unity of Husserl's various and apparently scattered criticisms, it is useful to keep the earlier account of the historical genesis of historicism in mind. The central idea underlying the manifold *Logos* critique is that the historicists combined a Hegelian affirmation of the historical relativity of philosophies of the past with a rejection of the Hegelian Absolute, thereby producing a position which undermines its own ground, and which cannot be rationally motivated. That is, the historicists took over certain basic premises from Hegel (premises which made good sense and could be justified within the Hegelian system as a whole) but then drew very different conclusions from them, conclusions incompatible with the premises themselves. Thus the true motivation for the historicist position is itself only an historical and not a rational one.

The first common historicist argument addressed by Husserl takes as premises: (1) the diversity and even incompatibility of philosophical systems over the course of history; and (2) their relative coherence and consistency with respect to the historical contexts to which they belong. On the basis of these two – allegedly evident – premises it is concluded that philosophy itself is an historically conditioned achievement, one which will always vary depending upon its historical context of origin, and therefore one which is not able to attain universal validity.

Husserl's first response to this argument is to grant that philosophy is a human cultural product, and as such will reflect the historical context from which it arises. However, he points out that if this alone demonstrates the impossibility of attaining trans-historical validity, then not only philosophy but also the 'positive' sciences (including mathematics and logic) have been pursuing a chimera. For these too are human cultural products, bearing the clearest traces of their historical contexts of origin in their specific concepts, principles, and motivations, as well as overall 'style':

"Certainly a *Weltanschauung* and a *Weltanschauung* philosophy are cultural products which arise and pass away in the flow of human development, whereby their spiritual content is definitely motivated by given historical conditions. But the same holds good for the rigorous sciences. Do they for **that** reason lack objective validity?"[3]

According to this line of critique, the historicist attributes trans-historical validity to disciplines such as mathematics and logic, but denies it to philosophy. However, a good sociologist of knowledge could very likely recognize the period and even the nationality of the author of classic texts in any of the 'positive' sciences, including mathematics, without this undermining the trans-historical validity of their claims. The telltale sociological marks may in some instances be largely incidental to the substance of the work, e.g., affecting the style of the presentation, or the particular direction of interest, rather than bearing essentially on the truth or falsity of what is asserted. Further, in many cases one thing that 'locates' a work is the possession and employment of results which would not have been available in earlier times. Now although such results constitute part of the thinker's received historical heritage, it can hardly be held that their employment necessarily damages the work's validity. If this were the case, then progress and trans-historical validity would necessarily be mutually exclusive. Thus the general tendency of this first argument is to press the historicist with a question: what is the *proof* that historical conditioning obviates the possibility of universal validity? This question is especially pointed given the apparent compatibility of the two in the domains of mathematics and logic.[4]

A second line of attack is brought by Husserl against the inductive argument advanced in favor of historicism. Here the historicist begins with the premise that there has never been an objectively valid philosophical system in the past, and concludes from this that in principle none is possible. Husserl criticizes this justification by way of the common critique of inductive arguments: the mere empirical fact of the failure of past philosophies cannot demonstrate an *in principle* impossibility. For such a demonstration would require a *theoretical* analysis, and not merely an historical, empirical account:

> "Historical grounds can give rise only to historical consequences. The attempt either to prove or to refute ideas on the basis of facts is nonsense – *ex pumice aquam*, as quoted by Kant."[5]

Husserl strengthens this criticism by pointing out that even the basic premise, according to which all previous philosophies have failed to attain trans-historical validity, is inadmissable. Although Husserl himself fully embraces this highly critical evaluation of the validity of all philosophical systems of the past, he holds that the historicist is prevented by his own position from asserting such an evaluation. This is because the historicist asserts that trans-historical validity is unattainable in philosophy. But since the evaluation of the validity of a philosophy falls within the province of philosophy itself, it follows that the historicist's evaluation cannot itself be a trans-historically valid one. Thus the most that can be claimed is that it is an empirical fact that the philosophies of the past have varied, and that, relative to the point of view of a specific *Weltanschauung* (i.e., the historicist's own), none of these philosophies is trans-historically valid:

> "To justify the **unconditional** assertion that any scientific philosophy is a chimera with the argument that the failed attempts of the millennia make it probable that such a philosophy is intrinsically impossible, is wrong-headed not only because to draw a conclusion about an unlimited future from a couple of millennia of higher culture would be bad induction, but wrong-headed in the way of an absolute absurdity, such as $2 \times 2 = 5$. And this is for the indicated reason: [if] philosophical criticism finds something it can objectively refute, then there is also a field in which something can be objectively proven ..."[6]

Thus it is not merely that the inductive argument is a weak one, one which successfully demonstrates the unlikelihood of a trans-historically valid philosophy even if not its certain impossibility. Rather, the argument fails altogether, since if the conclusion is true, then the premise cannot be granted.[7]

Husserl is clearly correct that an adequate demonstration of historicism can be provided only on philosophical or theoretical, and not merely historical grounds. That is, historicism must be based on a theory which explains why it is impossible *in principle* for philosophy to attain trans-historical validity. Such a theory could take one of two possible forms, one epistemic, the other ontological. An epistemic defense would show why trans-historical validity in philosophy is rendered impossible by the limitations of our cognitive powers. An ontological one would hold that there is simply no objective reality or unique fact of the matter in the spheres which philosophy addresses. However – and this is crucial – whichever form the theoretical justification of historicism might take, in order to surmount the sort of reflexivity critique presented by Husserl both here and in the *Prolegomena*, the historicist would have to hold that the justifying theory itself lies *outside* the domain of philosophy, having an epistemic or ontological status such that this meta-theory (unlike first-order philosophy itself) is or can be trans-historically valid.

Yet a major difficulty confronts such a project of theoretically grounding historicism. This difficulty consists in establishing a sufficiently firm separation between the domain of first-order, relativist philosophy, and the second-order, non-relativist theory of the nature of philosophical validity, such that the analysis which demonstrates the relativity of philosophy will not apply to the second-order theory. For supposing some theory holds that there is no objective fact of the matter regarding the issues addressed by philosophy, it is difficult to see why this theory should apply to the domain of 'the issues addressed by philosophy' but not reflexively to itself.

One attempt to overcome this difficulty is made by Dilthey. Although in "Philosophy as Rigorous Science" Husserl accuses Dilthey of mounting a hopelessly flawed inductive defense of historicism of the kind reconstructed above, Dilthey makes clear in his correspondence with Husserl that he understands himself to have relied upon not an inductive but a theoretical justification of 'historicism'. Further, historicism in the sense advanced by Dilthey does not assert the impossibility of objective or trans-historical validity in philosophy in general, but rather the impossibility of such validity in metaphysics. Thus Dilthey writes:

"I derive the proof of the impossibility of a universally valid metaphysics on 'the arguments developed since Voltaire, Hume and Kant.' I do not draw my conclusions from the previous failures of metaphysics, but rather from the general relation between the tasks it sets and our means for carrying them out .... Here the conflict between systems, the previous failures of metaphysics, appear only as the historical facts which led philosophical thinking to the dissolution of metaphysics, and not as the proof of its impossibility. This latter is sought in the essence of the same."[8]

According to Dilthey's account, the justification of the form of historicism he embraces falls into the epistemic category: the impossibility of metaphysics is held to follow from the nature and limitations of the cognitive subject. Of course, Dilthey conceives of metaphysics in a Kantian rather than a Husserlian sense, thus his position is that human beings are incapable of attaining knowledge of Platonic forms or Kantian things-in-themselves, entities wholly beyond the concrete world of historical reality. Insofar as historical philosophies or *Weltanschauungen* are embodiments of speculative metaphysics, they have no trans-historical validity but only validity as expressions of the spirit and life of various epochs. However, this does not lead Dilthey to the self-refuting conclusion that no trans-historically valid philosophy is possible at all. Rather, Dilthey's analysis requires a distinction between metaphysical and non-metaphysical philosophy, with the latter being at least capable of attaining trans-historical validity. According to Dilthey, the arguments against the possibility of metaphysics, his own general theory of the types of *Weltanschauungen*, and the theory of human psychology which accounts for the production of specific types of *Weltanschauungen*, all fall into this latter category.[9]

The final line of argument advanced by Husserl in his criticism of historicism concerns the historicist conception of validity. Here Husserl's general position is that the historicists have lost sight of the character of validity as a distinct category, confusing it with or reducing it to categories which are essentially different. In the first instance, Husserl accuses historicism of reducing validity to subjective belief (in the manner of subjectivism, as defined in Chapter One), so that for historicism the validity of a philosophical thesis consists in nothing more than its being *held* valid in a given historical context. Thus Husserl writes, according to the historicist:

> "That an idea is valid [supposedly] means that it is a factual spiritual formation held to be valid, and that, through its factually being held valid, it determines thought."[10]

Now it could be argued that a historicist, even one fitting the general characterization presented by Husserl, need not reduce validity to historical acceptance and effectiveness, much as a relativist need not be a subjectivist. Indeed, if, as was said above, the historicist holds the validity of a philosophical system to lie in its ability to give expression to the spirit of the age, thereby providing an overall world-view consistent with the background conceptions and beliefs of a historical community, and facilitating the carrying out of its life practices, then it is clear that the relativism of the historicist is *non*-subjectivist. For according to this conception, validity is determined by criteria such as consistency, coherence, and a variety of spiritual and practical values relative to a context, criteria which are clearly distinguishable from factual acceptance and belief. Of course, there might be a general tendency for the two sets of criteria to be satisfied in tandem (just as there is a tendency for an individual to hold as valid those principles which are consistent with his background conceptions and beliefs), but this will not always or necessarily be the case. Thus the historicist does not confuse validity and opinion, and therefore retains the right to criticize accepted philosophical systems and ideas, and to declare them invalid, even relative to the historical context from which they arose.

Husserl provides a possible response to this objection only indirectly, in his later discussion of the motives of historicism. Here he argues that the historicists may have been led to their doctrine of the relative *validity* of philosophical systems through their vivid perception of the relative *value* of these systems:

> "What may still mislead the historicist is the circumstance that when we enter into a historically reconstructed spiritual formation – into its guiding thought and intention, as well as into the motivational contexts belonging to it – then we are able not only to understand its inner meaning, but also to judge its relative worth."[11]

What Husserl here terms the 'relative worth' of a philosophy consists not only in what usually goes under the heading of value (i.e., the spiritual or practical value of the philosophy for a community) but also the internal consistency of the system, its coherence relative to the background conceptual and motivational context, as well as its success in providing solutions given the means and results available at the time. He emphasizes his agreement with the historicists that historical philosophies do indeed possess such value in tremendous measure, and that this value is relative in nature. However, his criticism is that the historicists have erred by simply equating possession of this relative value with validity itself, thereby losing sight both of validity as a separate category, and of its *non*-relative character. According to Husserl, after the internal consistency and coherence of a philosophy has been acknowledged, as well as its value relative to a historical context, the question of its objective validity still remains.

Thus the more genuine and fundamental conceptual confusion of historicism identified by Husserl's analysis is not of validity and historical acceptance, but rather of validity and value. It might seem that a historicist position could accommodate this Husserlian critique simply by limiting itself to claims about the relative value of historical philosophies (where 'value' is understood to include consistency and coherence, in addition to intellectual, spiritual, or practical merits), and neglecting the question of trans-historical validity altogether. That is, the historicist (whether the historicist philosopher or the historian of philosophy) could analyze and evaluate the relative value of historical philosophies, while holding that a determination of their trans-historical validity exceeds our powers, or that there is no fact of the matter regarding such validity, or simply that the question of validity is not the concern of the historicist. In this way, historicism could still assert the historical relativity of philosophical systems (i.e., as their relative value), while avoiding the objection that it reduces validity to value.

However, Husserl's position leads to the conclusion that even this more limited form of historicism is problematic. For even the limited assertion of the relative value of a philosophical system or idea already presupposes that trans-historically valid philosophical principles obtain:

"Contrary to [the historicist], we of course maintain that the principles even of such relative evaluations lie in the ideal sphere. The **evaluating** historian, one who does not merely wish to understand developments, can only presuppose these principles, but cannot – qua historian – ground them."[12]

Husserl's point here is again similar to the one made in the *Prolegomena* critique of non-subjectivist relativism: the assertion of relativities, whether of relative truth or of relative value, presupposes non-relative principles as their ground. Thus the assertion of the historicist that, for example, a philosophical system is of value for a community with a specific historical and cultural heritage, presupposes that there is a principle specifying the characteristics a philosophy must possess in order to be of value relative to this community. Further, this latter principle must be an objectively, trans-historically valid one. For even if the value of the philosophy is only a relative value, still, the historicist asserts that it is *objectively* the case that the philosophy is of value relative to a given historical context, and not merely that it is his personal opinion that the philosophy is of relative value. But in order for the philosophy to be objectively of relative value there must be objective principles specifying what constitutes relative value, i.e., what criteria a philosophy must fulfill in order to be of value relative to a community. Further, if, by contrast, the historicist chooses to abandon the claim to the objective validity of his judgment, asserting instead that this judgment too has only relative validity (or relative value), then his position will encounter the problems of the infinite regress discussed in Chapter One. Thus the historicist cannot consistently limit his position to the relative coherence and value of philosophy, remaining neutral as to the existence or non-existence of non-relative philosophical truths. The historicist may choose not to devote himself to the specification of these principles, but their existence must be presupposed.

Husserl expands upon this argument in his correspondence with Dilthey, extending it from philosophy to religion and art as well. Here Husserl argues once again that the relative and the non-relative are not mutually exclusive but complementary. He holds, for example, that the 'validity' (or value) of a religion could be thought to be relative to the character of the human community which is to follow it. But if this is the case, then there must be a sphere of objective, 'ideal' principles specifying what constitutes a valid religion for a community with a given constitution:

"All objective validity, hence even that of religion, art, etc., refers to ideal and thus to absolute ('absolute' in a specific sense) principles .... However, this in no way excludes relativities .... Analogously, a religion may be 'true religion' and its truth a 'merely relative' one – namely, truth in relation to a 'humanity' that lives in the context of a 'nature', is in a certain stage of development, etc. In this case, truth depends upon the content of the presuppositions, a content which is to be grasped ideally – the *idea* of a generically thus and thus determined 'humanity', the *idea* of a thus and thus formed 'nature', the idea of thus and thus to be characterized individual or social motivations, etc. Were we to think of the presuppositions as varying in their essential content, then another religion, or no religion at all, would be the 'true' one. Thus the truth of a religion would be something relative and yet, as all truth, something ideal, i.e., referring to relations which, by means of their essential content, determine principles a priori as conditions of the possibility of *such* truth at all."[13]

Thus here Husserl applies the very same argument previously employed against relativism of truth to a relativism of religion: the assertion that a religion is of value relative to a particular community presupposes non-relative principles grounding the relative ones. This argument will obviously apply similarly to ethics, art, or any other primarily value-oriented domain. According to Husserl, a position which couples science- or truth-absolutism with value-relativism is incoherent, because the problems facing truth- and value-relativism are similar ones.

However, this extension of the argument to the realm of values makes its questionableness clear. For although the reasoning is formally correct, insofar as the assertion of the relative validity of religion does indeed presuppose non-relative principles of the type Husserl describes, still, this in no way shows that we do or even can attain knowledge of these principles. This objection can be raised quite generally regarding the Husserlian/formal challenge to the historicist or relativist. That is, granted they do indeed (inconsistently) presuppose that universally or trans-historically valid principles exist; it remains for Husserl to show that this presupposition is itself justified, and that knowledge of these principles is possible. Only this latter demonstration would constitute a positive and definitive victory against the relativists, rather than a mere stalemate. Clearly, doubts about the possibility of such a demonstration are particularly inevitable in the case of religion. For it is highly implausible to think that we could secure knowledge of absolute laws of religion similar to laws of physics, so that if the 'input' is a description of a specific human community, the 'output' would be a specification of the correct religion for this community. Yet considered formally, the two domains are in precisely the same position. Thus to grant the conclusiveness of the formal argument is to commit oneself to non-relative principles even in the realms of values, art and religion.

The critique of historicism in "Philosophy as Rigorous Science" once again highlights the difficulty of providing a rational, self-consistent motivation for relativism. It clearly demonstrates how this difficulty becomes an impossibility in the case of a 'totalizing' theory of relativity, such as an historicism which asserts that *all* validity in philosophy is of a relative character. Further, Husserl forcefully argues that the same obstacles confront a totalizing theory of the relativity of value. However, the most that can be accomplished by the formal arguments of the sort presented above is a stand-off, an undermining of the rational motives for relativism, but not a positive and definite justification of relativism's opposite, whatever form that might take.

2. THE DEFENSE OF PHILOSOPHY AS A SCIENCE

Husserl opposes the historicist conception of philosophy with a defense of the ideal of philosophy as 'rigorous science'.[14] There is no question that the rhetorical power of this conjunction of 'science' and 'philosophy' has since been diminished, if not lost. Yet despite the untimeliness of Husserl's terminology, a considered evaluation of this defense depends significantly upon clarity regarding what, according to Husserl, constitutes 'the scientific' in general, and the scientific in philosophy in particular. Thus in the first part of this section, I begin by reconstructing Husserl's conception of the scientific, arguing that it contains an ambiguity which is crucial to

Husserl's overall effort to overcome relativism. I then consider a preliminary objection that the requirements set out for science could not be
satisfied by any discipline at all. In the second part, I turn to the *Logos*
arguments in favor of a scientific philosophy as thus defined, arguments
which reveal the true ethical (rather than purely formal) motivations
underlying Husserl's opposition to relativism. The chapter concludes with
some remarks on the inseparability of the establishment of philosophy as a
'rigorous science' (and hence the entire foundationalist project) and the
more specific problematic of the overcoming of relativism.

2.1 *The Idea of Science*

Husserl presents two importantly different general characterizations of
science, although he does not draw attention to this duality, and is perhaps
largely unaware of it. Further, while in "Philosophy as Rigorous Science"
more emphasis is placed upon the first than the second, I believe that the
second is the more essential one within the general context of Husserl's
thought, above all insofar as concerns philosophy. According to the first
notion, science is characterized by its possession of a generally accepted,
intersubjectively verifiable body of concepts, principles, and results (here
termed the *Lehrgehalt* or *Lehrsystem* of a discipline: the teachable content
or system), passed down from generation to generation of scientific researchers and gradually increasing in scope over the course of history.
Husserl acknowledges that this basic body of knowledge is subject not only
to expansion but also to revision, and that it may contain certain unresolved
problems and points lacking in clarity. However, he holds that this is not a
sign of *Unwissenschaftlichkeit* (an unscientific character), but rather of
Unvollkommenheit (an incomplete character) in a science. For the decisive
point here is that at any given time there is *some* sphere of secure results,
providing a fairly well-defined basis for further research. Thus Husserl
writes, in the case of a science:

> "A basic body of knowledge is at hand, constantly growing and branch-
> ing out in new directions .... Here, by and large, there is no room for
> private 'opinions', 'views', or 'standpoints'."[15]

According to Husserl's conception, science is characterized by intersubjective demonstrability and general consensus, at least with respect to its
epistemic base. Further, not only are intersubjective demonstrability and
general consensus factual attainments of the sciences, but they function as
criteria and guiding ideals as well. In order for a principle or result to be
admitted as valid even by an individual researcher, it must be possible for

general consensus regarding its validity to be attained. That is, there must exist a demonstration of the result which can be carried out by all members of the community of investigators concerned. Thus intersubjectivity and consensus function both *descriptively* and *prescriptively*: a common body of concepts, principles, and results exists in fact, and the possession and development of this body is something science aims to achieve.[16]

Husserl places great emphasis on intersubjectivity, consensus, and the possession of a *Lehrsystem* as criteria of science in the *Logos* essay.[17] However, a rather different characterization of what is essential to the establishment of philosophy as a science emerges from Husserl's discussion contrasting scientific and *Weltanschauung* philosophy. In this discussion Husserl holds that the primary concern of *Weltanschauung* philosophy is wisdom, understood as the ability to realize the various human virtues in the best way, and so to live the best possible human life. *Weltanschauung* philosophy achieves this by providing a general outlook or world-view which answers the significant questions facing members of a community. Further, maintains Husserl, this task is carried out in the great historical philosophical systems in a way superior to conventional wisdom or everyday good sense. However, because the central aim of *Weltanschauung* philosophy is to address the immediate life questions and needs of a specific society, philosophy in this form retains a certain speculative, unscientific character: rather than providing universally valid demonstrations and conclusive proofs, *Weltanschauung* philosophy offers practical solutions and 'working' answers suitable to a given historical context.

For this reason, Husserl characterizes *Weltanschauung* philosophy as providing a kind of *Kunstlehre* for human life: a practical doctrine or technique for realizing the highest ideal of humanity possessed by a given historical community.[18] By contrast, a scientific philosophy would produce not wisdom or practical know-how, but knowledge in the sense of insight and theoretical justification, providing a secure demonstration for the concepts and principles it employs. This insight and justification, as Husserl elaborates throughout his specifically phenomenological writings, is obtained in the form of *Evidenz* (self-evidence, or fulfilling intuition). A thorough discussion of *Evidenz* will be taken up beginning in Chapter Three, but in this context we may note that in the case of a science, the *Evidenz* regarding concepts and principles must be of an especially 'rigorous' and perfect kind. Scientific *Evidenz* must be criticized and founded, its degree of adequacy and apodicticity evaluated, and a demonstration given of its basis in more primitive, immediately self-evident principles, and ultimately in perfectly self-evident ones. Thus the contrast of scientific philosophy to philosophy as a *Kunstlehre* emphasizes that to be scientific, a discipline must everywhere be guided by the demand for perfect or maximal *Evidenz*.

Husserl's two notions of science in the *Logos* essay can therefore be summarized as follows. According to the first notion, science is characterized by its possession of a generally accepted and continually expanding body of concepts, methods, principles and results. According to the second notion, science fulfills the demand for *Evidenz* to the highest degree, and therefore provides not merely wisdom or practical know-how, but knowledge founded on intuition and insight.

Now it should be noted that at least in "Philosophy as Rigorous Science," Husserl views these two notions as two parts of a single, unified whole. According to the *Logos* essay, the satisfaction of *both* criteria is necessary for genuine science, and further, it is the satisfaction of the second that is supposed to lead to satisfaction of the first. That is, the requirement that the concepts and principles be either immediately or mediately self-evident insures that the epistemic base will contain only what is ultimately verifiable in intuition. It is this intuitive and thoroughly grounded demonstrability that in turn insures general consensus regarding the epistemic base, and its relative stability over time. In short, the criterion of self-evidence is at the same time a criterion of verifiability of the most stringent sort, and this verifiability produces intersubjective consensus among those in a position to effect the demonstration, i.e., the community of researchers concerned.

Yet contrary to what is suggested by the *Logos* treatment, it is not necessary for the two sets of criteria (intersubjective consensus and a *Lehrsystem* on the one hand, and maximal *Evidenz* on the other) to be satisfied together. In particular, there is no requirement for a discipline to satisfy the latter in order to satisfy the former. Disciplines which are largely practical or mechanical may well possess a body of accepted methods and principles, and attain a high degree of intersubjective consensus regarding these, without having satisfied any especially stringent requirements for *Evidenz*. Indeed, in later writings (especially the *Crisis*) Husserl accuses the existing sciences, above all physics, of having degenerated into just such mere technologies, producing principles with only an instrumental justification and lacking any thoroughgoing analysis of the foundations of these principles in *Evidenz*. This lack of clarity regarding *Evidenz*, and the neglect of questions concerning foundations and insight in favor of practical and technological successes, leads Husserl near to charging these sciences with not being genuine sciences at all.

Thus, as is eventually granted even by Husserl himself, fulfillment of the requirement of intersubjective consensus and an epistemic base does not necessarily depend upon fulfillment of the requirements of rigorous and founded *Evidenz*. However, one of Husserl's interpreters has gone even further, arguing that these two requirements for science are actually opposed. In his essay "*Lebenswelt und Technisierung unter Aspekten der Phänomenologie*," Hans Blumenberg maintains that the degree of success and achievement attained by the modern sciences was made possible in part by their *rejection* of the traditional philosophical ideals of perfect comprehension and ultimate justification, ideals Husserl continues to defend.[19] This is because, according to Blumenberg, pursuit of the goal of *Evidenz* impedes fulfillment of *Leistung* (achievement). As Husserl later emphasizes in *Formal and Transcendental Logic*, the idea of science as based upon ultimate insight and foundations is closely associated with that of unremitting criticism of pre-given results, whether these are results inherited from the tradition, or results one has previously attained oneself. Science as thus conceived is fundamentally opposed to a division of labor or an acknowledgment of authority, where one individual or group simply takes over and applies the conclusions produced by another. Rather, each individual must work in quasi-Cartesian fashion, examining the chains of demonstrations or verifying phenomena for himself, from the ground up. Blumenberg, however, argues that this sort of procedure would have the effect of slowing the accumulation of shared knowledge, if not of halting it altogether. Blumenberg grants that Husserl's linking of the concept of science with ultimate *Evidenz* and final foundations is one deeply rooted in the philosophical tradition. Yet the opposition between the requirements of *Evidenz* and those of productivity and achievement leads Blumenberg to conclude that the tradition itself is a paradoxical one, containing a paradox Husserl fails to resolve:

"Technologization arises out of the tension between the tasks of theory, which reveal themselves to be infinite, and the available existential capacity of man, given as constant. The antinomy of technology is that between *achievement* and *insight*. Phenomenology ... has not resolved this antinomy but sharpened it, rendering it evident and influential for our spiritual situation."[20]

However, although Blumenberg accuses Husserl of failing to acknowledge the necessity and the legitimacy of the separation of the sciences from philosophy and its demands,[21] in later writings Husserl shows a growing tendency to distinguish between the sense in which the positive sciences are or can be scientific, and the sense of science or rigor appropriate to philosophy. In particular, Husserl later explicitly holds that while demonstration and justification of some sort are necessary to every science, the task of providing ultimate or maximal insight and justification is one which rightfully belongs to philosophy alone. Given this distinction, the imposition of the criteria of science as advocated by Husserl would not, as Blumenberg holds, hamper their 'productivity'. At the same time, Husserl's analysis implies that the positive sciences are not themselves capable of fulfilling the most stringent requirements of science, but rather must depend upon philosophy to investigate questions of their own ultimate foundations and justification. Even as early as the *Logos* essay, Husserl indicates this limitation of the sciences, and their dependence upon philosophy to carry out this task, thereby 'perfecting' them. Thus in a note, Husserl writes:

> "Perhaps the word 'philosophy', in connection with the titles of all the sciences, signifies a kind of investigation that in a certain sense gives them all a new dimension and a final perfection."[22]

The distinction between the task of philosophy and the task of the sciences qua science undercuts Blumenberg's claim that the demands Husserl places on the positive sciences would eradicate them altogether. It also emphasizes that Husserl's conception of scientific philosophy is in the end patterned not so much after the existing sciences, their practices and achievements, as after a traditional ideal of perfect knowledge. The resulting notion of scientific philosophy is a critical one, one which brings out the limitations of the positive sciences, rather than merely taking them as model and ideal. The roles of philosophy and the sciences are thereby reversed: philosophy is not merely to mimic the positive sciences, but rather, philosophy is to be *more* scientific than they, in the sense of fulfilling more radically and rigorously the ideal of knowledge based on ultimate insight.

However, while Husserl thereby resolves the conflict between achievement and insight for the positive sciences, this resolution renders the conflict all the more acute for philosophy itself, the discipline which, even according to Husserl's most mature conception, must satisfy both of these ideals.

Ernst Tugendhat has attempted to address this dilemma by distinguishing between two senses in which Husserl's principle of ultimate *Evidenz* and final justification may be understood. According to the first way, termed by Tugendhat the 'critical' conception, ultimate *Evidenz* is only a regulative idea and not a concrete attainment. Taken in this way, the main function of the notion of ultimate *Evidenz* is to give rise to constant criticism and readiness to overthrow pre-given results, as well as to the attempt to provide ever more certain and fundamental demonstrations for principles posited. By contrast, according to the second conception, which Tugendhat terms the 'dogmatic' one, it is not sufficient merely for philosophy to be led by the ideal of perfectly founded knowledge. Rather, philosophy must also realize this ideal in concrete results, results which would then form the basis of the desired *Lehrsystem* to be handed down from generation to generation. This basic set of perfectly founded results, holds Tugendhat, would not be subject to any further doubt, criticism, or revision. Further, according to Tugendhat, while Husserl tends to shift between the critical and dogmatic conceptions, never wholly abandoning the dogmatic component, the critical conception remains the only valid one, and the more decisive one for Husserl's overall position.[23]

If Tugendhat's abandonment of the dogmatic conception of ultimate insight is accepted, it might seem to resolve the conflict between insight and achievement by simply removing the demand for 'achievement' in the form of a *Lehrsystem*. For it could be held that the dogmatic tendency in Husserl's thought on the one side, and his demand for a philosophical *Lehrsystem* on the other, must stand or fall together. This is because this latter demand presupposes that philosophy is capable of concretely realizing the ideal of perfect *Evidenz*, at least with respect to this limited body of principles. Thus once the dogmatic interpretation of perfect *Evidenz* has been rejected, the requirement of a *Lehrsystem* must fall away as well. The scientific character of philosophy would then lie solely in its *pursuit* of ultimate *Evidenz* and justification as a guiding ideal. Indeed, it could even be argued that, given the tendency of the demand for *Evidenz* and the demand for fixed results to conflict, the failure of philosophy to develop a *Lehrsystem* is actually a sign of its *higher* degree of scientific rigor, at least in the only sense of 'scientific rigor' which is appropriate to philosophy itself.

However, the flaw in the Tugendhat interpretation is that it equates philosophically *established* and self-evident knowledge with *indubitable*, *incorrigible* knowledge, thereby assuming that ultimate *Evidenz* as a principle of criticism and ultimate *Evidenz* as a concrete attainment are fundamentally opposed. Tugendhat is led to this error by his non-phenomenological understanding of ultimate *Evidenz* and the sense of its ultimacy. As will be shown in Chapter Four,[24] this ultimacy is a phenomenological one, so that when Husserl asserts that a principle is absolutely founded or self-evident, what this means (expressed non-phenomenologically) is that the principle appears indubitable and incorrigible (where this appearance is of a specific character). However, this does not mean that there is an absolute guarantee that the principle will always appear so, that it will never take on a doubtful character, or even the character of being false (although again, these possibilities appear excluded). Thus even principles possessing ultimate *Evidenz* may at some point be overturned, and for this reason cannot be exempt from further criticism.

Thus it is not the case, as suggested above, that rejection of the dogmatic conception of ultimate *Evidenz* must bring with it rejection of the demand for a *Lehrsystem* as a valid requirement for a scientific philosophy. For it is possible to hold that all knowledge is subject to criticism, and yet to require a shared body of philosophical knowledge, founded upon (phenomenologically) ultimate *Evidenz*. But more fundamentally, the dogmatic notion of *Evidenz* as characterized by Tugendhat is not one Husserl espouses. Tugendhat is certainly correct to note that Husserl considers ultimate *Evidenz both* as a guiding ideal *and* as a concrete attainment (at least in regard to a limited number of principles). Tugendhat is also correct to emphasize that the conception of ultimate *Evidenz* as a regulative idea is the more significant one for Husserl's thought, especially in its mature stages. However, he is incorrect in his depiction of these two conceptions as mutually exclusive, and in his characterization of the notion of concrete attainment as dogmatic. The claim that ultimate *Evidenz* can be attained concretely is based on a phenomenological characterization of experience, and does not dogmatically exclude further criticism or revision. (Indeed, the assertion that such *Evidenz* is wholly *impossible* would be the more dogmatic one, inaccurately representing the actual character of experience.) Similarly, the demand for constant criticism does not rule out the possibility that a philosophical *Lehrsystem* based on such principles could be developed. Simply because every posited principle is subject to further criticism, and may possibly be refuted, does not mean that every principle will in fact be overturned. Thus Husserl's two requirements for a scientific philosophy are at least minimally compatible, even if, as Blumenberg argues, its degree of 'achievement' will necessarily be more limited than that of the positive sciences, with their greater pragmatism.

2.2 *Philosophy as **Weltanschauung** and Philosophy as Science*

Before giving positive arguments in favor of a philosophy satisfying this notion of science, Husserl first stresses that in his view, *Weltanschauung* philosophy and scientific philosophy are complementary and not mutually exclusive. *Weltanschauung* philosophy is of particular value to humanity, according to Husserl, because human life demands that decisions be made at the moment, without time for reflection upon foundations or for scientific treatment of all questions of immediate significance. The answers provided by *Weltanschauung* philosophy are speculative and non-scientific, but often best-possible and practically suitable answers to pressing questions facing a human community. Here Husserl gives an ambivalent compliment by comparing the role of *Weltanschauung* philosophy in providing practical solutions to immediate needs in the absence of a developed science to that of engineering and applied science in general:

"Technical tasks are pressing, the house, the machine needs to be built; it is not possible to wait until natural science can give exact information about everything pertinent."[25]

Further, he urges that the contemporary situation is one of especially extreme need for assistance from philosophy in addressing the problems and riddles life poses. The urgency of this need renders *Weltanschauung* philosophy all the more valuable:

"It is certain that we cannot wait. We must take a position, we must make an effort to resolve the disharmonies in our attitude towards reality ... [creating] a rational, even if unscientific 'world- and life-view'. And if the *Weltanschauung* philosopher helps us in this, should we not thank him for it?"[26]

With these qualifications, Husserl presents a number of arguments in favor of a scientific philosophy. In contrast to the formal approach of the *Prolegomena* and earlier *Logos* treatments, these arguments are largely ethical/pragmatic ones, urging the desirability of a scientific philosophy. Firstly, Husserl points out, a scientific philosophy, as science in general, would have the virtue of providing more conclusive and certain results than those of a *Weltanschauung* philosophy, which, due to its speculative character, will always remain controversial. Were concrete approaches and solutions available from both to address a single problem, argues Husserl, there would be no question as to which to prefer.[27]

A second strand touches upon Husserl's concern with the problem of skepticism. Here he argues that only scientific philosophy, and not *Weltanschauung* philosophy, is in a position to rescue contemporary culture from this opponent. Now it could be thought that skepticism always has and always will survive the attempts of philosophy to be rid of it, for insofar as skepticism is a manifestation of a rigorously critical attitude, it is an intrinsic part of philosophy itself. However, here it is important to emphasize that the *Logos* essay is concerned not so much with some perennial form of skepticism, nor with a skepticism limited largely to the philosophers, but rather with skepticism in a form specific to the age, and one which has spread throughout the general culture. Skepticism in this form, according to Husserl, is a positivistic outgrowth of empiricism, and the empiricist prejudice in favor of 'facts' (*Tatsachen*). Through this prejudice, he maintains, the belief arises that only empirical facts – particulars as opposed to universals, matters-of-fact as opposed to values and norms – are knowable and real. Thus it comes to be thought that universal principles and value-based norms must be reducible to statements about facts, and that to the extent that they are not, they are meaningless, or 'metaphysical'. However, argues Husserl, the reduction of such principles to statements about facts wholly alters their sense, so that when these principles are taken according to their original meaning, they are declared empty, or at best of a validity which is undecidable. If, for example, it is asserted that a given sort of life constitutes a good human life, the empiricist reduces this statement to the assertion that, e.g., it is *believed* that this sort of life is good, or it is *felt* that this is a good life. Insofar as the initial assertion is taken in its original and usual sense, i.e., that this life is ('objectively') a good one, it is held that there is no fact of the matter regarding its truth or falsity; or if there is, it is unknowable. Thus the prejudice in favor of empirical facts leads to skepticism regarding the objective validity of all universal principles and norms, a skepticism which, according to Husserl, will therefore affect all of human practice. Further, Husserl emphasizes that this empiricist prejudice and the skepticism to which it gives rise is characteristic not only of naturalism, but of historicism as well:

> "All life is position-taking, and all position-taking stands under an ought: that of doing justice to validity and invalidity in accordance with purportedly absolutely valid norms. When these norms were not attacked, threatened or ridiculed by any skepticism, there was only **one** life question: how these could best be satisfied practically. Yet how now, when each and every norm is disputed or empirically falsified, and robbed of its ideal validity? The naturalists and the historicists are battling over the *Weltanschauung*, and yet both are at work from different sides misinterpreting ideas as facts and transforming all reality, all of life, into an incomprehensible hotchpotch of 'facts' free of ideas. The mythical faith in the fact is common to them all."[28]

Weltanschauung philosophy, as a *Kunstlehre*, is able only to determine the practically best means of fulfilling given ideals and norms, where these are set by the historical context itself, and not to justify or found them. Thus *Weltanschauung* philosophy is helpless in the face of a skepticism which challenges all existing norms and ideals, and the objective validity of all norms and ideals as such.

The claim that philosophy in a scientific (i.e., phenomenological) form can successfully combat skepticism therefore is not to be understood only in the general Cartesian sense, i.e., as the claim that philosophy can establish absolutely and indubitably self-evident principles, and thereby prove that knowledge is indeed possible. Rather, the point here is that a philosophy guided by the principle of *Evidenz* (and not by the prejudices and presuppositions of empiricism) can rescue the realm of the ideal in general (including universal principles and norms), demonstrating it to be as meaningful and knowable as that of the empirically real. Husserl attempts this concretely by means of his analysis of categorial intuition, an analysis which does not metaphysically posit ideal entities outside of all experience, but rather attempts to show that categorial entities such as universals, norms, and ideas have their own kind of phenomenality, and are as much a part of experience as empirical particulars. Husserl argues that the ideal is also given in perception of a sort, even if this perception is not precisely the same as in the case of real particulars. Thus while empiricism makes an appeal to experience as its justifying base, in the end the empiricists distort and misrepresent the character of experience, insofar as they hold that experience yields testimony only to facts and particulars. By contrast, the phenomenological, *Evidenz*-directed analysis of the realm of the ideal is supposed to vindicate this realm, and thereby undercut the specific form of skepticism that extreme empiricism has produced.[29]

In a final line of argument, Husserl appeals to the notion that philosophy constitutes an embodiment of an ethical ideal to guide human life. Different forms of philosophy, he holds, represent different ethical ideals, and infuse these ideals into the culture as a whole. Scientific philosophy embodies the ideal of pure theory, with its demands for comprehension and justification, unmitigated by practical compromises and concessions. By contrast, *Weltanschauung* philosophy is both more speculative and more pragmatic. Here Husserl argues that the life directed by the ideals of theory – at least to the greatest extent possible – is the more responsible life, the one in which the demand for reasons and justification is in principle always valid (even if these demands can be addressed only at certain moments and not at others). In such a life, the individual is committed to a thorough and relatively constant criticism of the principles by which he lives and acts, rather than to an unquestioning faith in prevailing or pragmatically convenient ideas. Therefore, concludes Husserl, philosophy as rigorous science is needed to infuse the ideal of responsibility through rational comprehension and justification into human life and throughout the general culture.[30]

The *Logos* arguments in favor of a scientific philosophy clearly reflect the ethical motivations underlying Husserl's attempts to overcome relativism. However, the employment of arguments of this character poses a peculiar problem for Husserl's overall analysis. For these arguments seem themselves to belong much more to what Husserl characterizes as *Weltanschauung* philosophy than to a rigorously scientific philosophy, one everywhere guided by the principle of complete *Evidenz*. Here Husserl argues that a scientific philosophy is necessary and valid because such a philosophy would undermine skepticism, promote responsibility, improve human life, etc., in short, by way of the *pragmatic* value of scientific philosophy for the fulfillment of ethical ideals arising from a specific culture. Further, as in all *Weltanschauung* philosophy arguments, Husserl does not actually provide a justification of the ideals whose fulfillment scientific philosophy would promote (e.g., immunity to empiricist skepticism, final responsibility) but simply takes these ideals over from existing background opinions and beliefs. Thus, it could be maintained, his arguments would not hold good for anyone not already sharing these ideals.

Perhaps the use of *Weltanschauung* philosophy to establish the validity and necessity of scientific philosophy (and so in a sense, to 'found' it) should not be seen as especially problematic. As Husserl himself points out, *Weltanschauung* philosophy too is necessary and proper, especially in cases of moral urgency, where no scientific method is at hand. This, it could be argued, is precisely such a case. However, such a position would indeed be problematic for Husserl, since it admits a higher degree of unity and mutual dependence between *Weltanschauung* and scientific philosophy than he seems prepared to grant. The *Logos* essay maintains insistently that although throughout the history of philosophy, philosophers engaged in a mixture of *Weltanschauung* and scientific philosophy, this tendency towards mixture must come to an end.[31] Thus according to Husserl's own analysis, *either* the arguments presented in the *Logos* essay constitute 'rigorous science'; *or* they fall into the category of *Weltanschauung* philosophy, in which case no matter how valuable and suitable they may be given a specific historical context, they will always remain provisional and controversial. Therefore the demand that *Weltanschauung* and scientific philosophy be kept wholly separate seriously weakens any ethical defense of scientific philosophy itself, unless this ethical defense can itself take on a scientific form.[32]

Indeed, the difficulty facing arguments for a particular conception of philosophy (much as for a particular conception of truth) by way of its *desirability* reflects a general difficulty facing the entire Husserlian project: the problem of the beginning. As is well known, Husserl demands that an authentic philosophical beginning be 'presuppositionless'. However, the substantive content of this often criticized and poorly understood requirement is that the first principles of a scientific philosophy (including the idea of this philosophy as such) must be established by maximal intuitive self-evidence. Thus any justification of the idea of scientific philosophy must be carried out wholly *within* this philosophy itself, and not with some other, less rigorous theoretical means, such as those of historicism or *Weltanschauung* philosophy).

But how is the very *idea* of philosophy to be derived, if not from a particular (if influential) historical tradition? This is a problem with which Husserl is still grappling as late as the *Cartesian Meditations*. Here he seems more to defer than to resolve the issue by holding that it is legitimate for us simply to provisionally take over this idea from actual practice, so long as we do not assume at the outset that this idea can actually be realized in the concrete.[33] This implies that the idea itself must be presupposed as a contingent historical product, and the justification limited to the possibility of its fulfillment. The demonstration of the possibility of fulfilling this idea, and not an ethical/pragmatic justification by way of desirability, would then be the only one consistent with the Husserlian requirement of a presuppositionless first beginning. While even this approach is not absolutely presuppositionless – since a specific historical conception of knowledge is presupposed – at least the *validity* of determinate conceptions and values is not simply asserted but taken as to be demonstrated through insight.[34]

We may suitably conclude this chapter by noting the broader scope which our analysis of the relativism problematic has taken on. For in the *Logos* essay, much as in all the properly phenomenological works, Husserl is concerned to defend the idea of a 'scientific' philosophy, and not that of a non-relative, universally intersubjective one. The resulting project is considerably more involved than a mere overcoming of relativism – itself no simple task. This is because, as discussed above, science as understood by Husserl is not only intersubjective, but also founded on maximal *Evidenz*. Thus the final aim is not solely the overcoming of relativism, but of skepticism as well, and indeed to accomplish both of these through a single grand intuitionist and foundationalist enterprise.

It could seem that from the more narrow perspective of the question of relativism, this detour through the larger foundationalist project involves needless and possibly even detrimental complexities. As was discussed earlier in this chapter, not only are intersubjectivity and intuition two distinct desiderata, they also could seem to conflict. The attempt to found all knowledge on ultimate *Evidenz* could therefore seriously hinder the production of intersubjective agreement. This will seem even more inevitable if one also takes into account the apparently private nature of intuition.

However, for Husserl the approach to relativism through ultimate *Evidenz* is neither a detour nor a dead-end, but the only possible path to a true resolution of even the more limited question of intersubjectivity. The reasoning behind this approach is that intersubjectivity cannot be detached from the larger issues of truth and knowledge in general. For whenever it is claimed that intersubjective truths exist, there remains the question of how we are to *know* and to *justify* that a particular principle is indeed intersubjective. This question can be addressed only in terms of an overall account of truth and knowledge, as well as of intersubjectivity. According to Husserl's phenomenological analysis of truth, the intersubjectivity of a principle is established in the same way as all other truths: through insight, i.e. through *Evidenz*. Therefore not only is *Evidenz* as understood by Husserl not essentially private, but there is even an *Evidenz of* intersubjectivity.

Thus against the above reservations, I would argue that a longer path of this sort is the only correct one not only in terms of the specifically Husserlian project, but for any thoroughgoing analysis of relativism. As we have seen, one of the major defects of the formal approaches prevalent in the contemporary relativism literature is that although they successfully show that relativism is incoherent, they fail to demonstrate in a positive and conclusive manner that non-relative, intersubjective truths can be known. But to accomplish this latter, a general theory of truth, intersubjectivity, and also of the *cognizability* of intersubjectivity is required.[35] Thus there is no promising short-cut which can circumvent the broader issues that Husserl's phenomenology addresses. It is to this more circuitous route that we will now turn.

NOTES

1. *Hua XXV* 6–7.
2. Husserl explicitly attributes historicism in this relativist form to Dilthey. However, Dilthey was rather taken aback to learn that the then little-known thinker whose *Logical Investigations* Dilthey had hailed as 'epoch-making', had repaid the favor by branding Dilthey a relativist and a skeptic. In a letter to Husserl, Dilthey protested: "Frankly, it was difficult for me to express an opinion [on the *Logos* essay] while under the effect of its initial impression, for your characterization of my standpoint as historicism, having skepticism as its legitimate consequence, could not but cause me to wonder. A large part of my life's work has been dedicated to formulating a universally valid science which would provide the human sciences with a firm foundation and an inner related-

ness to a whole." ("Offen gestanden war mir unter dem ersten Eindruck eine solche Äußerung schwer, denn Ihre Charakteristik meines Standpunktes als Historizismus, dessen legitime Consequenz Skeptizismus sei, mußte mich billig wundern. Ein großer Teil meiner Lebensarbeit ist einer allgemeingiltigen Wissenschaft gewidmet, die den Geisteswissenschaften eine feste Grundlage und inneren Zusammenhang zu einem Ganzen schaffen sollte"), "Der Briefwechsel Dilthey-Husserl," edited by Walter Biemel, *Revista de Filosofia de la Universidad de Costa Rica* (San José), 1 (1957), 109. (Subsequent references to this correspondence will be abbreviated '*BDH*'.)

Clearly, Dilthey shared with Husserl the goal of overcoming the relativism and skepticism characteristic of the age. However, their respective conceptions of the requisite foundations and the proper method for attaining them differed.

3. *Hua XXV* 43. ("Gewiß, Weltanschauung und Weltanschauungsphilosophie sind Kulturgestaltungen, die im Strom der Menschheitsentwicklung werden und verschwinden, wobei ihr Geistesgehalt ein unter den gegebenen historischen Verhältnissen bestimmt motivierter ist. Dasselbe gilt auch von den strengen Wissenschaften. Entbehren sie d a r u m der objektiven Gültigkeit?")

4. The historicist defense here criticized by Husserl is similar to the one advanced by Gadamer in his debate with Emilio Betti regarding the objectivity of hermeneutical understanding. Against the claims of Betti that such objectivity is possible, Gadamer argues that no product of the *Geisteswissenschaften* can escape being thoroughly conditioned by the historical heritage (the concepts, motives, interests, presuppositions, 'prejudices') of its author. Thus Gadamer writes: "For example, when you are reading a classic investigation by Mommsen, you too immediately know the only time it could have been written. Even a master of the historical method is unable to keep himself entirely free from the prejudices of his time, his social surrounding world, his national situation, etc." ("Auch Sie z.B. wissen sofort, wenn Sie eine klassische Untersuchung Mommsens lesen, wenn das allein geschrieben sein kann. Selbst ein Meister der historischen Methode vermag sich nicht von den Vorurteilen seiner Zeit, seiner gesellschaftlichen Umwelt, seiner nationalen Position usw. ganz freizuhalten"), Hans-Georg Gadamer, "Hermeneutik und Historismus," *Philosophische Rundschau* 9 (1961); reprint, Gesammelte Werke (Tübingen: J.C.B. Mohr, 1986), 2:394 (page references are to the reprint edition). Against this, Husserl's claim is that even if one can immediately recognize the historical period of a work, and even if one grants that the author's thought is guided by a particular conceptual framework and set of interests, this does not in itself demonstrate that none of the work's conclusions possesses trans-historical validity.

5. *Hua XXV* 45. ("Historische Gründe können nur historische Folgen aus sich hergeben. Aus Tatsachen Ideen sei es begründen oder widerlegen wollen ist Widersinn – *ex pumice aquam*, wie Kant zitierte.")

6. *Ibid.*, 45. ("Die u n b e d i n g t e Behauptung, jede wissenschaftliche Philosophie sei eine Chimäre, mit der Begründung, daß die angeblichen Versuche der Jahrtausende die innere Unmöglichkeit solcher Philosophie wahrscheinlich machen, ist nicht nur darum verkehrt, weil ein Schluß von den paar Jahrtausenden höherer Kultur auf eine unbegrenzte Zukunft keine gute Induktion wäre, sondern verkehrt als ein absoluter Widersinn, wie $2 \times 2 = 5$. Und das aus dem angedeuteten Grunde: Entweder philosophische Kritik findet etwas vor, es objektiv gültig zu widerlegen, dann ist auch ein Feld da, etwas objektiv gültig zu begründen ...")

7. It should be noted that this argument is equally effective against the historicist who bases the claim that historical philosophies failed to attain trans-historical validity not on an appeal to some external standard of validity but only on an immanent critique, i.e., by showing that historical philosophies contain internal contradictions and so fail to meet their own internal standards. This is because even the historicist who advances only the (admittedly weaker) claim that historical philosophies contain internal contradictions still asserts that *this* claim is a trans-historically valid one. This in turn implies that the historicist claims to possess at least *some* objectively valid standards and beliefs, including, for example, his standards of consistency and coherence, his beliefs about the content of the philosophical systems in question and whether or not these satisfy the posited standards, etc. Nor would this amount to a very limited, trivial claim on the part of the historicist as to what admits of trans-historical validity, given the hermeneutical difficulties in univocally determining the actual content of the philosophical systems of the past.

8. *BDH* 110. ("Ich berufe mich dort für den Nachweis der Unmöglichkeit einer allgemein-giltigen Metaphysik auf 'die seit Voltaire, Hume und Kant entwickelten Gründe.' Ich schließe nicht etwa aus dem bisherigen Mißlingen der Metaphysik, sondern aus dem allgemeinen Verhältnis zwischen ihren Aufgaben und unseren Mitteln der Lösung. . . . Der Widerstreit der Systeme, das bisherige Mißlingen der Metaphysik, treten hier nur als die historischen Tatsachen auf, welche das philosophische Denken zur Auflösung der Metaphysik geführt haben, nicht als die Begründung ihrer Unmöglichkeit. Diese wird im Wesen derselben aufgesucht.")

9. This discussion brings out the inaccuracy of Gadamer's critique of Dilthey, which accuses Dilthey of "fundamentally nothing other than the epic self-forgetfulness of Ranke" (Gadamer, *Gesammelte Werke*, 1: 236). According to Gadamer, Dilthey, much as Ranke, inconsistently neglects to apply the principle of the knower's being historically conditioned to himself, and only for this reason is able to believe in the trans-historical validity of his own philosophical reflections. However, as I have argued above, the principle of universal historical conditioning – which both Dilthey and Husserl would surely grant – does not provide a conclusive demonstration of the principle of universal historical relativity – which both would reject. Further, although Dilthey affirms the relativity of validity, it is only for a limited domain of philosophy, and thus his continued pursuit of the ideal of objectivity is self-consistent.

10. *Hua XXV* 43. ("Eine Idee habe Gültigkeit, bedeutete, sie sei ein faktisches Geistesgebilde, das für geltend gehalten wird und in dieser Faktizität des Geltens das Denken bestimmt.")

11. *Ibid.*, 46. ("Was den Historizisten noch irreführen mag, ist der Umstand, daß wir durch Einleben in eine historisch rekonstruierte Geistesgestaltung, in das in ihr waltende Meinen, bzw. Bedeuten, sowie in die zugehörigen Zusammenhänge der Motivation, nicht nur ihren inneren Sinn verstehen, sondern auch ihren relativen Wert beurteilen können.")

12. *Ibid.* ("Demgegenüber bleiben wir selbstverständlich dabei, daß die Prinzipien auch solcher relativen Wertungen in den idealen Sphären liegen, die der wertende Historiker, der nicht bloße Entwicklungen verstehen will, nur voraussetzen, nicht aber – als Historiker – begründen kann.")

13. *BDH* 115–6. ("Alle objektive Giltigkeit, also auch die der Religion, Kunst usw. weist auf ideale und damit auf absolute [in einem gewißen Sinn 'absolute'] Prinzipien hin....

Das schließt aber keineswegs Relativitäten aus.... Analog mag eine Religion 'wahre Religion' sein und ihre 'Wahrheit' eine 'bloß relative' – nämlich mit Bezug auf eine 'Menschheit', die im Zusammenhang mit einer 'Natur' lebt, sich in einem gewißen Entwicklungsstadium befindet usw. Die Wahrheit hängt hierbei <ab> von ideal zu fassendem Inhalt Ihrer Voraussetzungen – [*Idee* der spezifisch so und so bestimmten 'Menschheit', *Idee* einer so und so gearteten 'Natur', Idee so und so zu charakterisierender individueller oder socialer Motivationen usw.] Dächten wir die Voraussetzungen geändert, ihrem Wesensgehalt nach, so wäre eine andere oder gar keine Religion die 'wahre'. Also Wahrheit einer Religion wäre etwas Relatives und doch wie alle Wahrheit ein Ideales, nämlich bezogen auf Relationen, die durch ihren Wesensgehalt Prinzipien a priori bestimmen als Bedingungen der Möglichkeit *solcher* Wahrheit überhaupt.")

14. Of course, here Husserl has his own phenomenology in view. However, the *Logos* essay attempts the more ambitious (and polemical) project of defending the idea of a scientific philosophy in general, leaving it to the reader's imagination to fill in the concrete form that the realization of this highly abstract concept is to take. I follow the *Logos* treatment in this regard, although the resulting discussion may have a certain air of anachronism and implausibility (especially for contemporary readers, weaned on anti-foundationalism), an air which could be lessened by substituting 'phenomenology' for 'scientific philosophy' in this discussion. Hopefully this defect will be made good by the more concrete analyses of phenomenology in the subsequent chapters.

15. *Hua XXV* 4–5. ("Ein Lehrgehalt ist vorhanden, immerfort wachsend und sich neu verzweigend .... Hier ist – im großen und ganzen – kein Raum für private 'Meinungen', 'Anschauungen', 'Standpunkte'.")

16. Husserl rather mournfully contrasts this state of affairs with the contemporary situation in philosophy, where, he claims, everything is subject to controversy, and there is not the smallest bit of generally accepted doctrine. (See *ibid.*, 5.) Implicit in Husserl's criticism is the charge that not merely is there *de facto* no general consensus in contemporary philosophy, but very often general consensus is not even recognized as a valid criterion or guiding ideal. Rather, philosophers are content to work out their individual standpoints, perspectives, and world-views, without pretending that others should adopt them as their own.

17. Indeed, in one passage, he seems prepared to equate science with the possession of an established and generally accepted *Lehrsystem*, holding that philosophy has not realized the idea of science to the slightest degree because no such common epistemic base exists. See *ibid.*, 53.

18. Although Husserl only mentions the term here (*ibid.*, 50–1), extensive use is made of the concept of a *Kunstlehre* throughout Husserl's writings on logic and psychologism, including the *Prolegomena*. In these writings, Husserl notes that in his own time it is common to think of logic itself as a *Kunstlehre*, i.e., as a technology or set of practical rules and procedures for correct reasoning. However, he criticizes this conception, arguing that logic must have two parts: not only a technological part specifying practical rules, but also a theoretical part providing the justification for these rules, and for the norms which these rules seek to embody. Thus while in the *Prolegomena* treatment of logic, much as in the *Logos* discussion of *Weltanschauung* philosophy, Husserl stresses the validity and the necessity of a technical discipline concerned with practical methods and results, the term '*Kunstlehre*' in Husserl's usage retains a certain

pejorative sense. For what is characteristic of a *Kunstlehre* is its inability to provide insight into the validity of the practical rules that it propounds.

19. Hans Blumenberg, "Lebenswelt und Technisierung unter Aspekten der Phänomenologie," in *Wirklichkeiten in denen wir leben* (Stuttgart: Reclam, 1981).
20. *Ibid.*, 51 and passim. ("Technisierung entspringt aus der Spannung zwischen der sich als unendlich enthüllenden theoretischen Aufgabe und der als konstant gegeben vorgefundenen Daseinskapazität des Menschen. Die Antinomie der Technik besteht zwischen *Leistung* und *Einsicht*. Die Phänomenologie ... hat diese Antinomie nicht aufgelöst, sondern verschärft, für unsere geistige Situation spürbar und wirksam gemacht.")
21. *Ibid.*, 42.
22. *Hua XXV* 5, n. 1. ("Vielleicht bedeutet das Wort Philosophie in Verbindung mit den Titeln aller Wissenschaften eine Gattung von Untersuchungen, die ihnen allen gewissenmaßen eine neue Dimension und damit eine letzte Vollendung geben.")
23. Ernst Tugendhat, *Der Wahrheitsbegriff bei Husserl und Heidegger* (Berlin: de Gruyter, 1967), 195–6 passim.
24. See Chapter Four, section two below, pp. 122 ff.
25. *Hua XXV* 55. ("Die technischen Aufgaben wollen erledigt, das Haus, die Maschine soll gebaut sein; es kann nicht gewartet werden, bis die Naturwissenschaft über alles Einschlägige exakte Auskunft geben kann.")
26. *Ibid.*, 56. ("Es ist sicher, daß wir nicht warten können. Wir müssen Stellung nehmen, wir müssen uns mühen, die Disharmonien in unserer Stellungnahme zur Wirklichkeit ... auszugleichen in einer vernünftigen, wenn auch unwissenschaftlichen 'Welt- und Lebensanschauung.' Und wenn uns der Weltanschauungsphilosoph darin hilfreich ist, sollten wir es ihm nicht danken?")
27. *Ibid.*, 53.
28. *Ibid.*, 56. ("Alles Leben ist Stellungnehmen, alles Stellungnehmen steht unter einem Sollen, einer Rechtsprechung über Gültigkeit oder Ungültigkeit, nach prätendierten Normen von absoluter Geltung. Solange diese Normen unangefochten, durch keine Skepsis bedroht und verspottet waren, gab es nur e i n e Lebensfrage, wie ihnen praktisch am besten zu genügen sei. Wie aber jetzt, wo alle und jede Normen bestritten oder empirisch verfälscht und ihrer idealen Geltung beraubt werden? Naturalisten und Historizisten kämpfen um die Weltanschauung, und doch sind beide von verschiedenen Seiten am Werk, Ideen in Tatsachen umzudeuten und alle Wirklichkeit, alles Leben in ein unverständliches ideenloses Gemenge von 'Tatsachen' zu verwandeln. Der Aberglaube der Tatsache ist ihnen allen gemein.")
29. As will be discussed in Chapter Three, in other writings Husserl is concerned to overcome the skepticism engendered not by naturalism and empiricism but by Cartesian objectivism.
30. Indeed, Tugendhat holds that it is Husserl's ideal of final responsibility and his belief in the necessity of this ideal for an ethical life that provides the key to Husserl's conception of philosophy as perfectly founded knowledge: "Husserl's initial concept of philosophy peaks in the idea of absolute self-responsibility ... and takes its sensible motivation from it." ("Husserls Vorbegriff von Philosophie gipfelt also in der Idee der absoluten Selbstverantwortung ... und bezieht aus ihr seine einsichtige Motivation"), Tugendhat, 191.
31. *Hua XXV* 51–2.

32. Clearly, as is reflected in his many lectures on ethics, Husserl believed that phenomenology would make possible a scientific grounding not only of logic and the sciences, but of values as well. Thus, at least in Husserl's own view, ethical arguments need not necessarily be *Weltanschauung* ones. However, insofar as this grounding remained for Husserl merely an idea and not an actual accomplishment (as is clearly the case in the *Logos* essay), the scientific character of his ethical arguments is subject to doubt.

33. *Hua I* 48–9 (*CM* § 3).

34. As will be discussed in Chapter Five, in writings around the time of the *Crisis* Husserl bolsters the ethical defense of the idea of philosophy with a teleological-phenomenological argument for its universality. That is, he claims that although this idea is to be found only in specific historical contexts, the roots of this idea and the teleological tendency towards it are universal to all human lifeworlds. If this claim can be supported phenomenologically, then this would provide a phenomenologically presuppositionless justification even of the idea of philosophy itself, rather than the historically contingent, *Weltanschauung* beginning proposed here. See Chapter Five, pp. 188 ff. below.

35. Even the usual consensus accounts of truth (in the style of Habermas) are deficient in this regard as compared to Husserl's. For while here a general theory of intersubjective truth is indeed presented (i.e., as what would be agreed upon as a result of ideally rational discourse), the entire epistemic problematic of consensus is treated in a most unsatisfactory way. How do we *know* whether another person with whom we are conversing agrees or disagrees with us (not to mention whether any other 'rational' person whatsoever would do so)? A full-fledged justification of intersubjective truth cannot simply assume that the existence or non-existence of consensus is obvious, but rather must, as does Husserl, take consensus itself to be a phenomenon with its own specific *Evidenz*, and hence with its own mode of justification.

CHAPTER THREE

The Phenomenological Elucidation of Truth: Between Skepticism and Relativism

Husserl's most comprehensive efforts to overcome relativism are in the end inseparable from the larger project of establishing phenomenology as a foundational discipline. The starting-point of this project is the conviction, in the tradition of Descartes and Brentano, that intuition is the ultimate source of all knowledge and certainty.[1] Initially Husserl's aim is to make clear the basis in intuition of knowledge in the specific fields of arithmetic (*Philosophy of Arithmetic*) and logic (*Logical Investigations*). This more limited project leads to the elaboration of a general intuitionist epistemology and *Evidenz*-theory of truth; that is, to a systematization of the initial guiding conviction that intuition is the ground of all knowledge. At this early stage (i.e., through the first edition of the *Logical Investigations*), Husserl uncritically combines his intuitionism with a realist, Cartesian-style ontology inherited from Brentano. However, as the inconsistencies of this combination become clear, the definitive outlines of the project take shape. The guiding aim becomes twofold: to establish a discipline which will found the sciences while itself fulfilling the demand for *Evidenz* (truth) to the highest degree; and in so doing to perfect the overcoming of the Cartesian conception of truth and reality.

In this chapter, I reconstruct Husserl's phenomenological elucidation of truth and discuss its implications for the question of relativism. The contributions of Husserl's theory to the issue of relativism can usefully be seen in terms of the tradition of critical epistemology initiated by Berkeley and Kant and opposed to the objectivism of Descartes and Locke. Accordingly, in the first part of the chapter I sketch the historical problematic which motivates the Husserlian position. Here I argue that Cartesian objectivism falls prey to the epistemic critique and so degenerates into skepticism. Thus despite its absolutism, this conception of truth cannot successfully overcome relativism. On the other hand, a view in the style of

Descartes' successor Kant successfully addresses the epistemic critique and so avoids skepticism, but only at the cost of affirming or at least engendering relativism. The problem, then, for the Husserlian position is to pass between the Scylla of skepticism (an outgrowth of Cartesian objectivism) and the Charybdis of relativism (engendered by Kantianism and coherence theories of truth).

In the subsequent sections of this chapter, I trace the development of Husserl's *Evidenz*-theory of truth in the *Prolegomena*, the Sixth Logical Investigation, and *Ideas I*. In addition to bringing out the high degree of consistency in Husserl's thought, I show how his position is responsive to the concerns of critical epistemology while preserving the non-relativity of truth.

1. CARTESIAN OBJECTIVISM AND THE EPISTEMIC CRITIQUE

According to Cartesian epistemology, the mind is in immediate relation only to its ideas (*cogitata*), and not to external things. In the case of physical reality, the relation between thing and idea is a causal one. There is a long chain of causal interactions in which the (mechanistically conceived) physical object acts upon the sense organs, producing mechanical changes. Other mechanical changes are produced in the nerves, then in the brain, finally creating the idea or perceptual sensation in the soul. An idea is correct (and correspondingly, the judgment based on it is true) when it is an accurate representation of the object at the beginning of the causal sequence.

Thus Descartes affirms a version of the correspondence theory of truth: a judgment is true when it corresponds with reality. However, he combines this with an objectivist understanding of reality: reality is never given immediately in experience. Because of the way in which human perception takes place, the mind perceives only its ideas, and is in principle incapable of a direct relation with the real.[2]

Yet the crucial question to which this general conception gives rise is the epistemic one raised by Berkeley and Kant: if all that is ever given in experience is ideas, and reality is not an idea or a relation among ideas, how can we ever know whether our ideas correspond with reality? Perhaps, as argued by Berkeley, there is no reality apart from ourselves and our ideas except God, who imprints these ideas directly upon our minds. Or perhaps, as maintained by Kant, we cannot know anything at all about the reality underlying the realm of appearances, it remaining a mere X, a mere concept, possibly not even existent.[3] Descartes thought he could bridge this abyss between subjective representation and objective reality via the *veracitas dei*: when an idea is clear and distinct, it must be true, because God would not deceive us about our clear and distinct ideas. But if this theological underpinning of the Cartesian position is rejected, the logical consequence is skepticism: knowledge is impossible for human beings.

It could be objected against Berkeley and Kant that Cartesianism can be saved from this skeptical conclusion without recourse to a beneficent divinity. For even lacking the a priori, rationalist resources of clear and distinct perception, Descartes still has the empiricist means of the hypothetico-deductive method for attaining knowledge of the real. According to this latter method, when our theories about reality adequately explain or predict our phenomenal experiences, then we have evidence that these theories are true. Through this indirect means, the gap between subject and object can be bridged, and knowledge of a reality never immediately given is still possible.[4]

However, the impossibility of an *empiricist* foundation for knowledge of a reality as conceived by Descartes was already clearly seen by Berkeley and Kant, not to mention Descartes himself. For an empirical justification shows only that a theory successfully explains or predicts experienced phenomena (ideas). Yet Berkeley argues that the ability of a theory to order and predict the sequences of our ideas provides not the slightest evidence that the theory gives a true account of reality apart from these ideas. Rather, according to Berkeley, the sole extra-subjective cause of the entire phenomenal world is God, although this does not alter the phenomenal character of experience in the least.[5] Further, Berkeley argues against Locke (and hence against an empiricist justification of Cartesian objectivism) that the alleged 'explanation' of the phenomenal realm provided by the Cartesian ontology and the distinction between primary and secondary qualities is, even by Locke's own admission, really no explanation at all. For Locke himself points out that the mechanism of perception posited to explain the phenomenal world is entirely incomprehensible to us: we cannot in the least comprehend how motions and extensions can give rise to, e.g., phenomenal color and sound, nor in general how the material can causally interact with the spiritual. Thus the justification by way of the 'best possible explanation' fails as well.[6]

Similarly to Berkeley, Kant maintains that natural causal laws only specify rules to order the phenomena, and do not provide any knowledge of a thing in itself behind the phenomenal realm. Thus even if a reality as conceived by Descartes and Locke exists, and even if this reality is causally related to the phenomenal world, it remains a mere X, wholly beyond the bounds of knowledge.[7]

Indeed, although Descartes himself couples his rationalist grounding of first principles with an empiricist justification for lower-level scientific theories, he is in no way tempted to justify the possibility of knowledge of reality as such on the basis of the hypothetico-deductive method. This emerges especially clearly in Part Four of the *Principles* where Descartes asks, how can we know that our theories about the imperceptible, underlying structure of nature accurately depict this structure? His answer is that in most cases we cannot, because the hypothesized causes could be false, and yet nonetheless successfully explain and account for the phenomena. However, he continues, even Aristotle did not achieve or even attempt more than a successful explanation of the phenomena, and such explanations, even if false, are in any case sufficient for all practical purposes. Rather, holds Descartes, we can attain absolute certainty, and so knowledge which is not merely instrumentalist, only by way of the *veracitas dei*: we are certain that principles are not just pragmatically valuable but also accurate depictions of physical reality only when we perceive them clearly and distinctly, and only because God would not deceive us in cases of clear and distinct perception.[8]

It should be emphasized that the force of the Berkeleyan/Kantian epistemic critique is not simply that truth as conceived by Descartes and Locke cannot be known with *certainty*. Rather, the claim is that the belief that a judgment is true in the Cartesian sense cannot be given the slightest degree of rational justification, and thus that on this view there can be no knowledge at all, no matter how imperfect, indirect, or uncertain. For any empiricist attempt to show that rational justification is possible on the Cartesian view, must involve the Cartesian in a crucial slide. That is, the Cartesian must simply slide from the claim that a belief or perception possesses a certain kind of coherence in relation to other beliefs and perceptions, to the quite different claim that this coherence provides rational grounds for the truth of the belief in the Cartesian sense. For example, the empiricist Cartesian such as Locke might hold that predictive power, explanatory power, simplicity, or other practical and cognitive values constitute rational grounds for belief. But what is missing here is any reason why the possession of predictive power, coherence, etc., provides rational grounds not merely for the belief in the predictive power and so forth of a principle (and hence its truth in a wholly non-Cartesian sense), but also for belief in its correspondence to a reality which is not and cannot be given in experience.

As a final defense, the Cartesian could assert, the above critique notwithstanding, that it still *might* be the case that some of our judgments are true in the Cartesian sense. For the epistemic critique does not prove that all of our judgments are *false* in this sense, nor that reality as conceived by Descartes simply does not exist. Therefore it is not demonstrated that the Cartesian notion of truth should be abandoned, or replaced with another.[9]

The Cartesian is correct that the epistemic critique does not demonstrate the falsity of our judgments in the Cartesian sense. However, the force of the critique is that we do not and cannot have any epistemically valid justification *either* for the claim that a judgment is true in this sense, *or* for the claim that it is false in this sense. Thus the consistent consequence of a Cartesian conception of truth is skepticism, and a complete suspension of judgment regarding all truth and falsity.

In the end the difficulty facing a de-theologized Cartesianism is the same one confronting the combination of a coherence theory of justification with a metaphysical realist conception of truth:[10] reality and truth are conceived so differently from justification that there is no way to bridge the gulf from one to the other. Descartes himself does not conceive of justification as coherence, and so consistently avoids skepticism. However, coherence is one of the few resources left for those who reject the *veracitas dei*.

Thus the epistemic critique of Cartesianism focuses attention squarely upon the problems which arise when too sharp a distinction is maintained between truth on the one hand, and criteria for belief on the other. Where to be true means something over and above the possession of all forms of rational justification, truth becomes a further fact, and therefore the claim that a judgment is true (and not merely justified) cannot itself be a rationally justified one. The most obvious solution to this difficulty is to modify the conception of truth so as to bring it closer to that of justification; that is, to conceive of truth as some (possibly quite complex) form of coherence. A strategy of just this sort is adopted both by Berkeley and Kant. For both of these thinkers, a physical object is real (as opposed to illusory) when it exhibits a certain rule-governed behavior within the overall context of experience. Thus at least in the realm of sensible judgments, to be true is not to correspond with the extra-phenomenal cause of our perceptions, but to cohere with these perceptions taken as a systematic unity.

Husserl's own theory of truth stands squarely in the tradition of Berkeley and Kant, and is designed to remedy the same defects of the Cartesian view that they oppose. However, Husserl takes objection to certain aspects of the positions of Berkeley and Kant as well. A thorough comparison of their views to Husserl's will have to await our reconstruction of the Husserlian position. However, to set this position into clearer relief, here we can briefly indicate some of the more important difficulties of these earlier solutions.

While Berkeley opposes Descartes in many respects, in the end he retains the Cartesian conception of reality at least in relation to God, and similarly to Descartes, grounds his entire position theologically. For Berkeley holds that God himself exists not merely as a rule-governed sequence of ideas but as a non-phenomenal cause of ideas, and thus in the way attributed by Descartes to the material. Yet the very same arguments employed so convincingly by Berkeley to demonstrate the impossibility of knowledge of a non-phenomenal *material* reality apply equally well to a non-phenomenal *spiritual* reality. If this latter is neither an idea nor a relation among ideas, how can we ever know anything about it? Berkeley himself justifies the claim that God is indeed the cause of all our sensible perceptions by asserting that God would not employ superfluous intermediaries to accomplish what he could bring about directly.[11] Thus as in Descartes' system, the movement from the phenomenal realm of ideas to the non-phenomenal underlying causal reality is made by way of a dogmatic preconception of the nature of God's goodness. For Descartes, this goodness entails God's truthfulness, at least in the case of clear and distinct perception; for Berkeley, God's disdain for intermediaries and a profusion of entities.

While Husserl's mature position is certainly closer to Kant than to Berkeley, here too there are important points of disagreement. In the *Prolegomena*, Husserl goes so far as to class Kant or at least the neo-Kantians among the psychologists and anthropologists, i.e., those who relativize truth to the human species. Clearly, Husserl has in view the Kantian position that the spatio-temporal realm of nature exists only for beings with our forms of intuition and categorial concepts, and not for all beings whatsoever. This position is further relativized by the anthropomorphizing neo-Kantian equation of 'beings with finite intuition' with 'human beings'. Although both the Kantian and even the neo-Kantian positions might seem to be weak, rather innocuous versions of relativism, they are still opposed by Husserl, who maintains that truth must be truth for all beings whatsoever, without qualification. According to Husserl, all truths, including truths regarding the spatio-temporal realm, must be truths for God and angels as well as finite beings, which is not the case for Kant.[12]

A later objection to Kant addresses the Kantian theory of the subjective faculties, raising the epistemic question in relation to the faculties themselves. How does Kant know that the faculties are of just the number and kind he specifies, and with precisely the designated categorial concepts?

Husserl alternately terms the Kantian method for determining the nature of the faculties 'regressive', 'hypothetical', and 'mythical', thereby indicating that this method lacks the direct, intuitive and exhibiting quality Husserl requires.[13] Rather, Husserl suggests that Kant (at least in some places) attempts to deduce the nature of the faculties by reasoning from given effects (the contents of consciousness, with structures 'built in'), to the hypothetical, non-phenomenal causes of this structuring (the subjective faculties of cognition, conceived as agents). Yet such an attempt falls victim to the same critique advanced by Berkeley and Kant against the Cartesian realist ontology: the hidden causes of the structuring could be quite different from what Kant proposes, while the phenomenal character would remain the same. And although Kant also provides a general 'deduction' of categories, as well as extended individual arguments for some principles, this does not remove all of the mystery surrounding the determination of the specific twelve categories and principles.

Thus Husserl's more general criticism of Kant concerns his lack of clarity about the correct *method* for establishing the a priori structures of experience, which Kant roots in the (at least somewhat contingent) subjective faculties. This second objection is importantly related to the first: the charge that Kant's position is or easily degenerates into a form of relativism. Because Kant roots the a priori structures of objectivity in the subjective faculties, truth is relativized to subjects having faculties of the designated sort. This relativization is the least restrictive in Kant himself, who holds that the relevant faculties are the same in all human beings, and possibly in all beings with finite powers of intuition. However, given the weakness of the Kantian arguments justifying the specific concepts and principles he asserts, and his lack of a clear method for determining these, it is a small step to reject the particular Kantian Table of the Categories, and to hold that the subjective structuring principles vary from one species, cultural group, or individual to another. With such a step, one produces the neo-Kantian anthropologists, psychologists, and cultural relativists familiar to us in contemporary times.[14]

Yet the threat of relativism is by no means limited to a specifically Kantian solution of the skeptical dilemma. Any position which forsakes the clear absolutism of the Cartesian conception of the real in favor of a theory of truth based on coherence will have to confront this difficulty. Indeed, it could be thought that a turn to a coherence theory, and hence to relativism, is a natural consequence of sensitivity to the demands of critical epistemology. If this is the case, then one could say that there is a clear path leading from Cartesianism itself to relativism, via a rejection of dogmatic theology, an acceptance of the epistemic critique, and an aversion to out-and-out skepticism.

The task addressed by Husserl's account of truth is that of providing a conception which overcomes Cartesianism and its skeptical consequences, in the style of Berkeley and Kant, while at the same time avoiding the theological dogmatism and relativism to which Berkeley and Kant themselves were susceptible. This task is carried out by Husserl through his elaboration of an *Evidenz*-theory of truth, and his establishment of phenomenology as a method for uncovering the a priori structures of reality. The remainder of this chapter is devoted to an historical/textual exegesis of the theory of truth, and its implications for the relativism problematic. (The foundational discipline of phenomenology as such will be taken up in Chapter Four.)

2. TRUTH AND *EVIDENZ* IN THE *PROLEGOMENA*

Husserl does not present a full account of an *Evidenz*-theory of truth in this text, but only some fairly opaque remarks attacking the conception of the psychologists. However, once the meaning of these remarks has been penetrated, they reveal the inner logic of the development of Husserl's thought. For they allow us to see how the same notion of intuition which Husserl uses in the *Prolegomena* to ground logical and mathematical truths is later extended to all truths whatsoever.

Husserl agrees with the psychologists that we know the fundamental principles of logic because they are intuitively self-evident to us. However, the psychologists conceive of *Evidenz* as a subjective feeling (*Gefühl*) of conviction experienced in the presence of certain judgments. Because this feeling is produced by the psychological constitution, it is subject to variation, and thus what feels self-evidently true to one species may feel self-evidently false to another.[15]

Against this, Husserl maintains that *Evidenz* is not a feeling of conviction; further, that it is not an extrinsic accompaniment of an act of judgment, such that the very same judgment could be self-evidently true to some individuals and self-evidently false to others. He then supports these criticisms of the psychologists with his own characterization of *Evidenz*: it is the experience of the agreement between what is meant in an assertion, on the one hand, and what is 'present' (i.e., given in intuition) on the other. As formulated in the central statement of the *Prolegomena*:

"*Evidenz* is the **experience of the agreement** between the intention and the present experienced object which it [the intention] intends; between the experienced **meaning of the assertion** and the experienced **state of affairs**; and truth is the idea of this agreement."[16]

This basic account clarifies the grounds for Husserl's assertion, against the psychologists, that *Evidenz* is not a feeling of conviction. An intense subjective conviction can be produced in many different ways. For example, something may be firmly believed based on the reports of others, without any first-person experience of the matter. However, the feeling of conviction accompanying the relevant judgment would in no way constitute *Evidenz* in Husserl's sense. Of course, *Evidenz* in this sense would also bring with it a sense of conviction, but only for the specific reason that in a self-evident act of judging, what is judged and what is given agree.

In his second criticism of the psychologists, Husserl emphasizes that *Evidenz* is not like a feeling because emotions are extrinsic to the meaning-content of a judgment. Thus the very same judgment (e.g., 'Tomorrow it will rain') could be accompanied with feelings of joy, anger, fear, hope, and so on, while its meaning remains the same. By contrast, he holds, *Evidenz* is so bound up with the intentional content of an act of judgment that the very same judgment with the very same meaning could not be accompanied sometimes by positive and sometimes by negative *Evidenz*.

The key to clarifying this puzzling assertion lies in recalling that the *Prolegomena* is addressed primarily to 'eidetic' judgments such as those of mathematics and logic. Thus the ground for the claim that the same judgment could not sometimes be self-evidently true and sometimes self-evidently false is that in the case of an *eidetic* judgment, *Evidenz* is a direct consequence of the meanings involved. At first this could seem to make matters even more perplexing, since it is not obvious what *Evidenz*, as defined above, would be in the domains of mathematics and logic. What, for example, would it be for a judgment such as $2 \times 2 = 4$ to be 'self-evident' in the sense of 'given in intuition'?

Yet as has been noted by Farber, Ströker, and Willard, the distinction between empty and fulfilled intentions fundamental to Husserl's conception of *Evidenz* is an extension of Brentano's distinction between purely symbolic and authentic representations, and this distinction is applied by Husserl in the realm of mathematics as early as the *Philosophy of Arithmetic*. In symbolic arithmetical thinking, numbers and operations are represented only by means of signs (e.g., numerals, a cross or dot for multiplication, etc.). By contrast, in non-symbolic representation, numbers and signs are 'given' in intuition by way of intuitive illustrations. The number 2, for example, is brought to intuition by viewing or imagining two objects (e.g., two dots), and then regarding these not as two concrete individuals with their identifying features, but as any two 'somethings' in general, thereby perceiving them as a general instantiation of what is meant in the intention of the number 2. Similarly, a symbolic representation such as 2×2 can be given intuitively by transforming it symbolically into $2 + 2$, then $1 + 1 + 1 + 1$, and then generating and 'collecting' the appropriate numbers of intuitive instantiations of the number 1. If the same is then done for the number 4, and the two are compared, the judgment $2 \times 2 = 4$ will have been executed in intuition. This intuitive enactment of the judgment gives rise to what Husserl terms *Evidenz*, the experience of truth: the truth of the judgment is not merely thought or represented symbolically, but rather it is perceived in the correspondence of the judgment and the intuitive illustration. Thus the grounds for Husserl's claim that there is mathematical *Evidenz* or intuition are brought out most clearly by comparing the experience of an imaginative fulfillment of a mathematical judgment to a purely symbolic judgment; and *not* by comparing this fulfillment to ordinary sense perception.[17]

The assertion, then, that *Evidenz* (at least for eidetic judgments) is independent of psychological constitution and intrinsic to the act of judgment is based on the fact that eidetic truths are a consequence of the very *meanings* involved in the judgments. No one could self-evidently judge that $2 \times 2 = 3$, if the judging person understands the same things we do by '2', '3', multiplication, and so forth, since the truth of $2 \times 2 = 4$ follows self-evidently from the relevant meanings.[18]

However, it should not be thought that all eidetic judgments are *analytic*, nor, correspondingly, that *Evidenz* escapes psychological relativism simply because it applies solely to tautologies. Many eidetic judgments, according to Husserl, (including those mentioned above) are *synthetic*, even though their truth follows directly from the meanings (essences) involved. This finer distinction can be elucidated by way of the example of a synthetic eidetic judgment discussed in the Third Investigation: 'no color without extension'. According to Husserl, this principle is made self-evident first by producing an intuition of color in general (i.e., imagining an intuitive illustration of color, and considering only what is essential to color in this illustration), and then attempting to vary the extension of this illustration to zero. When such an attempt is made, it is seen that as the extension reaches the limit of nothingness, the color vanishes as well. This provides an intuitive demonstration, Husserl maintains, that color cannot be perceived without extension, regardless of the psychological constitution of the subject. This is because it is implicit in what is meant by 'color' that for anything to count as a 'colored something', it must be extended. The process of eidetic analysis then serves to bring to intuitive clarity the conditions for the possibility of a fulfillment of color, given what is meant in the intention of color.[19]

Thus Husserl's point is that an intention implicitly contains a specification of the conditions for the fulfillment in intuition of an intention of this type. The truth or falsity of eidetic principles is then independent of the psychological constitution of the subject much in the same way as in the case of analytic principles. However, the principle 'no color without extension' is not analytic, for it belongs not to the mere *concept* of color that color is always accompanied by extension, but rather to its *essence*. Although a Husserlian essence, much as a concept, is no more than a particular kind of meaning formation, an essence has a direct relation to perception which a concept lacks. In general, the essence 'A' contains the rule or rules specifying the manifold of perceptual presentations which can count as instantiations of the intention of 'A'. By contrast, the concept of 'A' concerns only the realm of intentions, including only what is contained in the 'empty' thought of 'A'. Thus, 'no red without color' is an analytic truth. However, it does not belong to the mere concept of color that color is extended: the thought of non-extended color is logically consistent, unlike the thought of colorless red or a square circle. Rather, to say it belongs to the *essence* of color that color is extended is to say that extension belongs to what it is to be (able to be recognized as) a perceptual presentation of (what is meant in the intention of) color.[20]

The sense in which *Evidenz* is not dependent upon contingent psychological features can now be made plain. Clearly, this independence does not exclude what might be termed psychological 'pre-conditions' for *Evidenz*: the possession of the relevant meaning formations, faculties of intuition, and so forth, necessary for understanding and executing the judgment in question. In this way, the psychological constitution of a subject will determine whether a particular judgment can even be a candidate for either positive or negative *Evidenz*.[21] However, once these conditions are met, it is impossible for the psychological constitution to determine whether the judgment presents itself as self-evidently true or self-evidently false. Rather, this is determined by what is meant in the judgment itself. Therefore conflicting *Evidenz* regarding a single judgment is impossible.

For example, in the case of 'no color without extension', even if there were beings with faculties of perception very different from our own, regardless of what they might perceive, they could not perceive non-extended colors. This is because nothing unextended could count as an instantiation of what is meant by 'color' in the self-evident judgment, 'no color without extension'. Further, neither can it be granted that other beings might have a different conception of color, such that it would be compatible with this conception for color to be given without extension. For extension is an *essential* feature of what is meant by 'color' in this usage. Thus any meaning which is compatible with unextended instantiations would be a meaning essentially different from the meaning intended when it is held that 'no extension without color' is self-evident. It would therefore be only equivocation to hold that 'no color without extension' is self-evidently false to beings who employ this alternate meaning.

If this account is correct, then at least in the case of eidetic principles *Evidenz* is not only psychologically but also historically and culturally non-relative. However, Husserl's analysis of the *Evidenz* of eidetic principles has been criticized on the grounds that meanings themselves are not fixed and atemporal entities. For example, David Levin argues that it is not sufficient to assert (as was done above) that any apparent disagreement over eidetic principles must be due to the employment of *essentially* different meanings. Rather, he maintains, a single meaning can vary in *content* while preserving its identity as the same *meaning*.[22]

Levin focuses his critique around the specific Husserlian example of an eidetic truth, 'color and sound are distinct in kind, and not merely in degree'. Levin points out that conceptions of color and sound vary over history, and are in part products of the current state of scientific theory. In particular, modern science reveals that both color and sound are waves, and that "an amplifier constructed to accept light waves picked up by a photocell and sound waves picked up by a microphone, will register the difference between colors and sounds only in terms of wave-length differentiation. In such a system, however, it makes no sense to speak of an absolute eidetic distinction between colors and sounds." If we then imagine beings with vision and hearing similar to the microphone/photocell amplifier system, for such beings the difference between color and sound will be a difference not of kind but of degree.[23]

The meanings attached by such a being to the terms 'color' and 'sound' would clearly be different in content (Frege: *Sinn*) from those of the everyday language of sense perception. However, although Levin does not explicitly state this, the force of his argument seems to be that these are not *essentially* different meanings, because the terms maintain the same reference (Frege: *Bedeutung*). Thus the eidetic judgments of the laboratory-equipment being and our own do not address two mutually exclusive sets of objects, but disagree about a single set. And more generally, all 'self-evident' eidetic judgments will be similarly disputable due to variations over history in the concepts they employ.

But I do not think the theory of meaning implicitly sustaining the Levin argument can be accepted. Of course meaning (*Sinn*) can vary while reference (*Bedeutung*) remains the same, as even Husserl recognizes.[24] However, the reference of a term cannot be completely detached from its meaning, as though this reference could remain fixed despite *arbitrary* variations of meaning. A reasonable view and one which is compatible with Husserl's own analysis of meaning is that in the case of universals such as color and sound, reference is fixed by those aspects of the meaning which are taken to be essential to an instance of this type. If this view is accepted, then for the Levin critique to hold good, it must be possible to show that the meanings of 'color' and 'sound' remain essentially the same in the new usage, so that their reference does as well.

Clearly, supporting Levin's argument is a hidden appeal to the view that these terms refer rigidly to color and sound as they exist in the object, and not as they are given in our senses, or as they are described by current scientific theories. It is only for this reason that meaning (as determined by a contingent form of sense perception or theory) can vary while reference remains the same, so that disagreements about eidetic truths will be possible. However, as noted above, this rigid reference cannot simply be posited apart from meanings but must itself be built into them, and indeed into that part of the meanings which does not change. To satisfy this requirement Levin might hold, for example, that when we use the term 'color', the meaning-content is 'that in the object which causes a particular phenomenal experience in us, and could produce a different phenomenal experience in a being of a different sort'. It would then follow that the terms as used by us and as used by the imaginary being would have the same reference, although the meaning-content would be different. That is, the fleshed-out version of what is meant as the phenomenal experience 'for us' would vary from one being to another.

Yet three points should be noted against this position. Firstly, this is not the meaning-content of 'color' and 'sound' in everyday usage. In such usage, these terms mean and refer to the phenomenal properties of everyday things, the color we see, the sound we hear, and not the non-phenomenal causes of these. Hence this theory is accurate only as an account of atypical or scientific usage. Second, this latter type of usage cannot possibly replace the everyday, phenomenal usage, because it *presupposes* it. In order to establish a reference to an objective, non-phenomenal cause of the phenomenal, the phenomenal itself must be included in the meaning. Thus, for example, the proposed scientific meaning of 'color' was 'that in the object which causes a certain phenomenal experience in us', which itself includes the everyday meaning, phenomenal color. Similarly, if a scientist says, 'sound is a wave motion of air', this can only mean 'sound, the phenomenal property, is really a wave motion of air'. Finally, if both we and the imaginary being were using the terms 'color' and 'sound' according to their scientific usage, then for neither of us would it be an eidetic truth that color and sound are different in kind. For that in the object which causes a certain experience of color need not be different in kind from that which causes an experience which is different in kind. Further, any judgment concerning the nature of objective causes would not be eidetic but empirical, so that where the scientific usage is at work, the judgment would not be eidetic. If, on the other hand, these terms are employed by us according to their primary, phenomenal meaning (which is clearly what Husserl intends in this example), then an eidetic difference in kind between color and sound still obtains: the imaginary being is simply unable to verify it because this being is blind to color as we intend it. In the end, it is impossible to detach (admittedly historically evolving) claims about reality from the phenomenal realm, and at the level of the phenomenal, the meanings of terms such as 'color' and 'sound' remain essentially constant.

Thus *Evidenz*, at least in the case of eidetic judgments, is neither psychologically nor historically relative.

The next stage in the *Prolegomena* account is the correlation of *Evidenz* with truth. Here Husserl's position, consistently maintained in later writings, is that truth is the correlate of the possibility of *Evidenz*:

> "It is evident that there is a general equivalence between the statements, 'A is true' and 'it is possible for anyone to judge self-evidently, A is the case'."[25]

The equivalence between truth and the possibility of *Evidenz* is associated with the idealism of Kant, who holds that to be an object is to be a possible object of experience. Yet the adoption of idealism in even this relatively weak form might seem to commit Husserl to a type of relativism he attacks and rejects. This is because for Kant the possibility of experience is a possibility only for beings with specific forms of intuition and categorial concepts. Thus truth, at least in domains depending upon these particular forms of intuition and concepts (which would include not only the physical world, but also mathematics and logic), would be truth only for a certain type of being, and in general, truth would be made a function of the subjective faculties. Of course, as shown above, even on the Kantian view the same judgment could not be true for us but false for some other being.

However, if a being lacked the appropriate concepts or faculties of perception, this judgment would be neither true nor false relative to it.

Yet an even more serious difficulty for this account of the relation between truth and *Evidenz* is that it seems to imply that the vast majority of the principles of mathematics would not be true or false, even relative to *humans*. A significant part of the *Philosophy of Arithmetic* is devoted to arguing that virtually all arithmetical principles are cognizable by humans only symbolically, and not by way of intuition. Hence according to Husserl, *Evidenz* regarding these principles is *not* possible for human beings. Here he notes that human beings are capable of producing intuitive illustrations of only the smallest numbers, and as soon as the numbers increase slightly we must immediately have recourse to symbolic representations and mechanical rules for calculation.[26]

However, although Husserl equates truth with the possibility of *Evidenz*, this does not constitute the adoption of a strictly Kantian idealism, nor the incumbent (if limited) relativism. Further, he does not believe that arithmetical judgments lack truth value relative to humans. These conclusions are avoided by an essential qualification of the correlation between truth and possible *Evidenz*: this possibility is an *ideal* possibility, and not an empirical one:

> "What is psychologically impossible may well be ideally possible. The solution of the general '3-body problem', or, let us say, the '*n*-body problem', may exceed all human cognitive capacities. However, the problem **has** a solution, and therefore *Evidenz* regarding it is possible. There are decimal numbers with trillions of places, and there are truths about them. Yet no one can actually imagine such numbers, nor actually carry out the additions, multiplications, etc. involving them. *Evidenz* is here psychologically impossible, and yet it is, **ideally** speaking, certainly a possible psychical experience."[27]

This passage provides a purely negative characterization of ideal possibility: ideal possibility is *not* psychological possibility, which is possibility for a real subject with a particular psychological constitution. It is difficult to locate a positive analysis of the crucial notion of ideal possibility in Husserl's writings. One way around this difficulty is to elucidate ideal possibility in terms of a related notion frequently employed by Husserl: an *ideal consciousness*. The concept of an ideal consciousness is clearly at work as early as the *Philosophy of Arithmetic*, where Husserl often speaks of a consciousness capable of carrying out even the most complex arithmetical calculations in the same fully intuitive manner which is possible for human beings only in the case of very small numbers.[28] A similar notion of a consciousness with unlimited powers of intuition is suggested in the *Prolegomena* in the passage immediately following the one quoted above. Here Husserl asserts that a perception is possible in which the entire world would be given in a single glance, although this would be possible only for an ideal consciousness, and not a real one.[29] In *Ideas I* as well as several of Husserl's unpublished manuscripts, discussion of the ideal consciousness is formulated in terms of God and what God would or could perceive. Husserl emphasizes, however, that here the notion of God is not to be understood theologically but only as a conceptual construction necessary for epistemology. Thus in a note to *Ideas I*, Husserl writes:

> "The idea of God is a necessary limit concept in epistemological analyses, that is, it is an unavoidable guiding notion for the construction of certain limit concepts which even the philosophizing atheist could not do without."[30]

Employing this notion of an ideal consciousness, the basic correlation of truth with the ideal possibility of *Evidenz* can then be rendered: the judgment 'A is true' is logically equivalent to 'it is possible for a cognitively perfect consciousness to judge with *Evidenz* that A is the case'. Thus although truth is correlated with what is possible for consciousness, it is not made a function of a plurality of diverse subjective constitutions, with the consequent plurality of diverse and possibly incompatible truths. Rather, truth is correlated with what is possible for a *single* subjective and ideal consciousness, one which need not even exist. Thus in the end, truth is everywhere the same, unaffected by the contingencies of the actual judging subject.

It could be objected against this account, however, that it preserves the non-relativity of truth only by setting truth itself beyond the bounds of our knowledge. For here whether a judgment is true will depend upon the meaning formations and perceptual faculties of an ideal consciousness, meanings and faculties which cannot simply be assumed to be similar to our own. In the absence of a theory of these faculties, we cannot know whether even judgments evident to us are in fact true.

Yet the above objection misconstrues Husserl's notion of an ideal consciousness and its function within the analysis of truth. Behind this objection is the thought that an ideal consciousness might possess concepts and cognitive faculties wholly different from our own, and further, that it is in any case unclear how we are to determine the nature of ideal cognitive capacities. Against this, it should be noted that the way in which the ideal consciousness is conceived by Husserl immediately entails a certain relation between it and our own consciousness. In constructing this ideal concept,

Husserl begins by examining what he takes to be cases in which the most rigorous knowledge is actually possible and actually attained. Husserl asks of such cases: what is it in the way we apprehend *these* judgments that yields especially rigorous and perhaps even perfect knowledge? The answer he proposes is their *Evidenz*, the demonstration these judgments can attain in a corresponding intuition. An ideal consciousness is then conceived as a consciousness capable of attaining the same perfection of knowledge (i.e., positive or negative *Evidenz*) regarding all judgments that is possible for us only in a few cases. It therefore belongs to the very notion of an ideal consciousness that the domain of judgments with regard to which *Evidenz* is a real possibility will be a *subset* of the domain of judgments regarding which an ideal consciousness can attain *Evidenz*. Any meaning formations available to us or any other real subject would also be available to an ideal consciousness, since totality would be part of its ideality. The limit concept of an ideal consciousness serves to elucidate what truth *means*, especially in the case of principles for which *Evidenz* is in practice impossible. That these principles are true means that the type of intuitive verification possible for us in more simple cases is possible in these cases as well for an ideal consciousness.[31]

Further, according to Husserl, even where knowledge via immediate *Evidenz* is impossible for us, it may be possible through mediate *Evidenz*. Whereas *Evidenz* is the experience of the direct intuitive fulfillment of a judgment, mediate *Evidenz* is the experience of motivating grounds for the judgment that direct *Evidenz* is possible. In the case of a complex arithmetical calculation, for example, mediate *Evidenz* regarding the accuracy of the result is attained with the aid of symbolic manipulations. As this case makes clear, mediate *Evidenz* is *not* attained by speculating about the cognitive faculties of an ideal consciousness, but by considering such justification of the judgment as is available *to us*.[32]

Thus the *Prolegomena* correlation of truth with the possibility of *Evidenz* for an ideal consciousness preserves the non-relativity of the truth of eidetic principles, in that the same judgment could not be self-evidently true to some subjects but self-evidently false to others. At the same time, the *Evidenz*-theory of truth clearly indicates the way in which knowledge is genuinely attainable.

3. TRUTH AND *EVIDENZ* IN THE SIXTH INVESTIGATION

In the preface to the second edition of the *Logical Investigations*, Husserl urges that the analysis of truth and *Evidenz* presented in the *Prolegomena* must be taken together with the elaborations of the Sixth Investigation. He notes that the *Prolegomena* discussion is overly one-sided, oriented almost exclusively towards the *Evidenz* of eidetic principles, here termed "*vérités de raison*".[33] By contrast, in the Sixth Investigation the mathematical/logical conception of *Evidenz* is universalized, and worked out in detail for physical reality in particular. The central addition is an extensive treatment of the notions of intuitive 'fullness' (*Fülle*) and 'fulfillment' (*Erfüllung*), and with this, the development of a conception of *Evidenz* as having many different forms and degrees of perfection. Truth is then established as the correlate of the ideal of perfect, or adequate *Evidenz*.

The Sixth Investigation opens with a discussion of signitive and intuitive acts (meaning-intention and meaning-fulfillment), the Husserlian successors of the authentic and unauthentic representations of Brentano. According to this discussion, in a signitive act an object is thought in an 'empty' way, without any picture, image, or other intuitive presentation of the object. Here the object is represented (or, more properly, referred to) by way of signs, typically words or symbols. In an intuitive act, by contrast, the meant object is present in some form of intuition, such as perception, memory, or imagination. The decisive point here is that although they are significantly different kinds of acts, a signitive and an intuitive act may yet have the same 'meaning', in the sense of intending the same object or state of affairs. This point is illustrated by the example of 'There goes a blackbird!' first as pronounced by a person seeing the blackbird, then as repeated by someone who listens to this report and believes it. In the one case, the sentence expresses a perceptual experience in which the blackbird is present; in the other, a judgment which may well not be accompanied by any image at all. However, in both cases the meaning-intention of the judgment is the same.

Husserl's notion of fulfillment follows directly from this analysis: fulfillment is what we experience when first we entertain a judgment merely signitively, then subsequently experience the same meaning-content as given in intuition, and further, recognize the two contents to be the same:

"We experience how **the same** objective entity which was 'merely thought' in a symbolic act is brought to presence in intuition, and that it becomes intuitable as precisely the same thus-and-thus determined entity that at first was merely thought (merely intended)."[34]

Thus the characterization of fulfillment in the Sixth Investigation is extremely similar to that of *Evidenz* in the *Prolegomena*: it is the experience of the agreement between what is meant in an intention and what is given in intuition. However, whereas in the *Prolegomena Evidenz* occurs typically in relation to eidetic principles, and hence is of an 'all-or-nothing' character, fulfillment takes place in many realms and forms, and exhibits degrees of perfection. The precise nature of fulfillment in specific cases depends upon the intention that is to be fulfilled. Fulfillment can therefore occur for acts of varying modality (what Husserl terms "quality"): a wish, a hope, a fear, can all be fulfilled in intuition, as well as an assertoric judgment. Further, different types of intuitive presentations can fulfill a given judgment. The general feature shared by all fulfillments is that the object is in some way shown, and not simply denoted by a sign. Thus even pictures, images, and memories offer some measure of fulfillment, as compared to a purely symbolically executed judgment. The degree of perfection of fulfillments varies not only from one type of intuition to another, but also within a single type. A presentation may be more or less vivid, and correspond more or less completely to what is thought in a judgment. Husserl gives the following illustration of a sequence of increasingly 'fuller' presentations within the category of likenesses: a rough sketch, a drawing, and a finished painting.

The most perfect type of fulfillment is perception, for in perception the intended object itself is present, and not a mere image or likeness. However, Husserl emphasizes that in sensible perception there is still a certain lack of agreement between the object as intuited and the object as intended. For in sensible perception what is given is an *Abschattung* (a partial, perspectival view) or a series of *Abschattungen*, whereas the object as intended is a three-dimensional, persisting non-perspectival whole. A given perception can be more or less *abgeschattet*, presenting the object or a certain part or property of the object in a more or less partial and perspectivally distorted way; a sequence of *Abschattungen* can be more or less complete. For example, when a tall building is viewed from the ground near its base, the top appears much smaller than it 'really' is (i.e., than it is intended to be and would appear from another position). Other perceptions show the relative size of the top of the building more accurately, as when the building is viewed head-on from some distance. The more exact the correspondence between the properties attributed to the object in the intention, and the properties of the object as given in perception, the more the fulfillment will be experienced as presenting the object 'itself':

"In fulfillment we experience, as it were, a *that is the **thing itself***. Of course, this *itself* is not to be taken in the strict sense.... . The relative talk about 'more or less direct' and 'itself' indicates in a way the main point: that the synthesis of fulfillment reveals an inequality in the value of its synthesized members. The fulfilling act has a **superiority** which the

mere intention lacks, i.e., it **imparts to the intention the fullness of the
'*itself*', it leads at least** *more directly* **to the thing itself.**"[35]
Expressions such as the object 'itself' play such an important role in
Husserl's analysis that it is worthwhile to emphasize the non-Cartesian
sense of this phenomenological 'itself'. Other related expressions include
'the object just as it is in itself', 'a self-giving presentation', and of course,
the motto of Husserlian phenomenology, 'To the things themselves'.
Certainly for Husserl, as for the Cartesian, the object 'itself' is the object as
it is in reality, the object as it truly is. For the Cartesian realist, however, the
object itself is the object existing independently and outside of the subject
and its phenomenal presentations (ideas), and causally interacting with the
subject so as to produce these ideas. By contrast, for Husserl the object
itself is the object as it appears or could appear in a presentation with a
certain descriptive character: the character of showing the object completely
and directly. According to Husserl's analysis, this descriptive character
results from the more or less exact correspondence between the properties
attributed to the object in the intention, and the properties of the object as it
is given in perception. Thus the object 'itself' is the object as given in a
perfect fulfillment of the corresponding intention. Of course, it is not that
the specification of reality 'in itself' is simply written on the face of our
intentions. Rather, an intention contains implicitly a specification of further
perceptions which would have to be realized to make the fulfillment of this
intention complete. Thus additional analysis is required to make these
posited further perceptions (and so the notion of the 'object itself') explicit.
Further, even once this has been done, we can confirm that such an object
in fact exists only by actually having the specified perceptions, or at least
showing that they are possible.

Husserl argues that for any object given only imperfectly in perception, a
notion of the object itself can gradually be formed by removing the
deficiencies of the imperfect fulfillment. A presentation is experienced as
an imperfect fulfillment when a partial divergence between the object as
thought and the object as given comes to attention. For example, in the case
of the tall building viewed from the base, the presentation is experienced as
imperfect if it is noticed that the proportions of the building as given and
the proportions of the building as intended are not identical. This highlights
one element of the intention and indicates that to present the building more
perfectly the proportions would have to be given, e.g., as symmetrical.
Similarly, a head-on view of the building would still be an imperfect
presentation, insofar as some of the sides of the building are not given in
perception. Thus we can form the idea of a series of more perfect presenta-

tions, gradually approaching a limit presentation in which every element of the object as thought in an intention is given, and this precisely as it is thought. In this limit case the presentation would be adequate: the object as given would be the object itself in the 'absolute' sense:

"Thus consideration of possible fulfillment relations points to a **final limit of the series of increasing fulfillments** in which **the complete and entire intention is fulfilled...** . The representing and the represented content are here identically the same. And where an intention has attained its final fulfillment in an ideally perfect perception, there an authentic *adæquatio rei et intellectus* has been produced: **the object is actually 'present' or 'given' precisely as intended**; no partial intention remains implicit, lacking its fulfillment."[36]

The object itself, then, is the object as it would be given in this ideal limit of fulfillment. Having elaborated the conception of *Evidenz* in terms of fulfillment, the Sixth Investigation then presents a refined version of the basic *Evidenz*-theory of truth vaguely indicated in the *Prolegomena*. Here Husserl actually distinguishes between four related senses of truth: truth as correspondence, the *adæquatio* between meaning-intention and meaning-fulfillment (sense 1); truth as the idea of this correspondence (sense 2); truth as true being (sense 3); and truth as a true judgment (sense 4).[37]

The primary sense of truth in the Husserlian analysis, and the one from which the others derive, is the first one: truth as the agreement between intention and fulfillment. The second sense is no more than a generalized conception of the first, the universal of which truth in sense 1 is the particular. According to the third sense, a being is a 'true' being when it can be given adequately in intuition; that is, a being for which adequate *Evidenz* or truth in sense 1 is ideally possible. Finally, a judgment is true when it is correct (*richtig*) in the sense that it conforms to (*richtet sich nach*) true being, to an object which is or can be given adequately. Thus as in the *Prolegomena*, a true judgment is one which can be carried out with (adequate) *Evidenz*.

Because of the primacy of the first sense of truth, Husserl's conception may be conceived as a modified correspondence theory. According to the traditional correspondence formula, truth consists in an adequation of mind to thing; according to Husserl, the essential correspondence is of meaning-intention to meaning-fulfillment. However, Husserl's account also has many features of a coherence theory of truth. This is already suggested by the fact that both members of the correspondence relation as conceived by him are *internal* to experience: intention-content on the one side, and perception-content on the other. The coherence aspects of this account can be brought out further by considering the third sense of truth, according to which truth is true being. This rather unusual use of language reflects that for Husserl the qualifier 'true' applies not only to judgments, but also to things (phenomena), and even more primarily to these latter. Among all the phenomena which occur in experience, some are merely fictions, illusions, or dreams, whereas others are realities. The distinction between illusion and reality, or between true and false phenomena, is drawn on the basis of the coherence exhibited by a phenomenon within an overall context of experience. In the case of physical reality in particular, an isolated perception provides only a limited degree of fulfillment, a limited demonstration that what presents itself as real is indeed real and not illusory. By contrast, a greater degree of fulfillment can be attained by a series of perceptions, what Husserl terms a 'synthesis of fulfillment'. In a synthesis of fulfillment, the initial intention fixes a limited range of further perceptions which would count as harmonious continuations of the experience of the same object. At the same time, other further perceptions would be wholly incompatible with the initial intention, and if they were to occur, they would cause the initial object to 'break up' (*zerschellen*), to be judged an illusion, and to be replaced by a different object. For example, if an initial perception presents the front of a house, then a harmonious synthesis of perceptions could include walking around to look at the back and seeing the exterior painted in the same color, a deck, several windows, etc. However, if the back of the 'house' is missing, and there is only the back of a large piece of cardboard, then the initial object will 'break up' and be replaced by another (e.g., a façade). In general, an object is a true one when the complete set of syntheses of fulfillment harmonious with the initial intention could (ideally) be carried out, while none of those in conflict with it could be – or, in other terms, when experience is coherent with itself.[38]

Husserl draws the distinction between illusion and reality phenomenally, on the basis of a certain internal coherence of experience. In so doing he is very close to Berkeley. According to Berkeley, even though there are only ideas and no material things, realities (ideas of sense) can be distinguished from chimeras and ideas of the imagination because they have "a steadiness, order, and coherence, and are not excited at random ... but in a regular train or series,"[39] and again, because they are "more affecting, orderly, and distinct" than fictions.[40] However, Husserl gives a much more detailed and descriptively accurate account of the particular kind of coherence a phenomenon (or 'idea') must exhibit to be real. As discussed above, the intention must be capable of fulfillment; or alternately, the full aspect of experience must be consistent with the expectations, positings, and requirements of the intentional, signitive aspect. This analysis of experience into two aspects (wholly absent in Berkeley) also makes it possible to grasp the *coherence* that constitutes truth as a kind of *correspondence*, and hence to understand the motives for a correspondence theory of truth. Indeed, Husserl claims that it is the experience of the agreement between intention and perception – a ubiquitous feature of intentional life – that itself gives rise to the traditional philosophical notion that truth is a correspondence, an *adæquatio* between mind and thing.[41]

Of course another crucial point of difference with Berkeley is that according to Husserl, real physical phenomena are not ideas but things. This is a consequence of his more complete overcoming of the Cartesian tripartite ontology of mind, idea, and matter. Berkeley is convinced, I think correctly, that phenomenal realities cannot be things in the Cartesian sense of matter, for the latter is unknowable. However, this leads Berkeley to the incorrect conclusion that phenomenal realities must be ideas. For if, as Berkeley seems to presuppose, the only possible ontological categories are mind, idea, and material thing as conceived by Descartes, what else could they be? It is true that ideas as understood by Berkeley have much in common with things as understood by common sense: we can touch them, eat them, drink them, etc. However, they have this important difference: they exist only in some mind, only as accidents of a spiritual substance, and only when some mind actually perceives them. That is, *esse* is *percipi*.[42] However, Berkeley does not really have a good argument to show why the phenomenal realities themselves, and not just our experiences of them, should be thought of as depending upon present perception. For the idea that phenomenal realities such as physical objects exist only in present perception is contrary to the way we intend them, and experience itself does not (and indeed, cannot) provide evidence that this is the case.[43] By contrast, Husserl, here closer to Kant and Mill,[44] frees reality from its dependence upon empirically existing minds by correlating truth with possible rather than actual perception. Husserl does not hesitate to term a certain kind of phenomenon a 'thing', since he is not troubled by the question (as the still Cartesian Berkeley was) of whether the non-phenomenal cause behind this phenomenon is material or mental. Questions concerning the non-phenomenal are, for Husserl, meaningless, or at best completely unanswerable, as Berkeley himself concluded in other cases.

Most of the decisive elements of Husserl's theory of truth are contained in the *Logical Investigations*. However, there remain certain difficulties which lead to the theory's further development, especially in *Ideas I*. I will therefore conclude the discussion of the *Logical Investigations* by considering two of these difficulties, and then turn to Husserl's efforts to resolve them in the later work.

One such difficulty is the status of the physical world. Husserl often stresses in the *Logical Investigations* that adequate fulfillment is impossible for any physical object because such objects are always given via *Abschattungen*. Further, he holds that even the most extensive synthesis of fulfillment can only approach but not reach the ideal of adequacy:

"For in a synthetic manifold of this kind the all-sided presentation is not achieved in the way required by the ideal of adequation – i.e., at a single blow, as a pure self-presentation and without the addition of analogizing or symbolization. To the contrary, it is always achieved piecemeal and hindered by such additions."[45]

The denial that a synthesis of perception could constitute adequate *Evidenz* is based on the lack of identity between an object as perceived over time and the object as it is thought in the corresponding intention. According to the intention, all the sides and parts exist simultaneously and without perspectival distortion; what is given in perception is a developing continuum of partial views. Because of this divergence, any perception or series of perceptions will necessarily be inadequate. Yet from this it would seem to follow that the physical world is not real. For Husserl's account correlates truth (and reality) with the possibility of adequate *Evidenz*, a possibility he denies for the sensible realm.

This objection could be overcome by holding that adequate perception of physical objects is empirically impossible, impossible for humans, but nonetheless ideally possible. The physical world would then be real even on a phenomenological account. However, in the *Logical Investigations,* Husserl's position on the ideal possibility of adequate physical perception remains ambiguous. In the *Prolegomena*, he clearly believes that such adequate perception is ideally possible. In the Sixth Investigation, although he repeatedly asserts the impossibility of adequacy in the physical realm, he makes no explicit statement as to whether this is to be understood as real or ideal impossibility. (This neutrality is in keeping with his overall neutrality on the nature of the subject, and hence on the nature of the subject to which the constraints of the *Abschattungslehre* apply). Moreover, when this question is taken up in *Ideas I*, he univocally maintains that adequate perception of physical objects is *impossible* for all beings whatsoever, including God.[46]

This definitive conclusion poses some problems for the general Husserlian correlation of truth and adequate *Evidenz*, which, as we will see, has to be refined in *Ideas I*. However, it also raises what is perhaps an even more pressing question for Husserl's ultimate project. If adequate *Evidenz* is *not* possible in the physical realm, where, if anywhere, *is* it possible? This question is crucial not only for the specific theory of truth (with its claim that truth obtains if and only if this possibility does), but also for the entire project of establishing phenomenology as a foundational discipline. For phenomenology, unlike the other domains of knowledge it is to found, is itself to consist solely of *Evidenz* of the highest sort. It is the superior and even ultimate nature of the *Evidenz* of its conclusions that, according to Husserl, justifies the claim of phenomenology to be the most rigorous of all the sciences. But how is this ultimate *Evidenz* to be attained in phenomenology, if indeed it can be attained at all?

4. TRUTH AND *EVIDENZ* IN *IDEAS I*

The relation of the Husserl of the first edition of the *Logical Investigations* (the descriptive psychologist), to the Husserl of *Ideas I* (the transcendental phenomenologist), continues to be a matter of little agreement. However, I believe that *Ideas I* is the natural consequence of the basic conception attained by the end of the earlier work, so that recourse to biographical or other extra-textual explanations is unnecessary to explain the transition. As Husserl often emphasizes, the *Logical Investigations* is a 'breakthrough' work, in that a phenomenological perspective is only gradually attained over its course. This gives rise to numerous ambiguities and inconsistencies, especially between the earlier and later parts of the work. By contrast, *Ideas I* contains a more unified, consistently phenomenological approach from the outset. It is this lack of ambiguity and inconsistency on central issues (e.g., realism versus idealism, the nature of the ego) that gives the appearance of a radical change, where in fact all that has occurred is a clearer and more fundamental thinking-through. The question concerning the possibility of adequate perception of physical objects provides a pertinent case in point. In the first edition of the *Prolegomena*, Husserl makes a strong statement in favor of the ideal possibility of such perception. Indeed, he claims that it is ideally possible for God to attain an adequate perception not only of a single object but of the entire physical world, with all its atomic structures:

"The equivalence [between] the concepts [of individual being and possible perception] is indisputable, insofar as perception is understood only as adequate perception. Accordingly, a perception is **possible** which takes in the whole world in a **single** glance, its boundless infinity of bodies, with all their parts, molecules and atoms, and according to all their relations and determinations. Of course, this ideal possibility is in no way a real one which might be attributed to some empirical subject."[47]

The mixed perspective of this passage is evident. On the one hand, it affirms the strictly phenomenological correlation of being and the possibility of perception. On the other, it contains the notably unphenomenological claim that even molecules and atoms can be perceived, and this adequately. How does Husserl arrive at this latter assertion? Clearly, here phenomenology is not employed at all. Instead, an empiricist ontology of the sort posited by natural science is simply taken for granted. Coupling an ontology which has not been grounded phenomenologically with a general phenomenological conception of being, Husserl arrives at the conclusion that adequate perception of physical nature is ideally possible. The entire *Abschattungen* problematic goes unnoticed.

By contrast, in the section of *Ideas I* entitled "Clarification of a Fundamental Error", Husserl reconstructs what was in fact his own position in the *Prolegomena*, and then declares it to be absurd. According to this reconstructed position, God perceives the physical world in a manner radically different from our own. For while human beings perceive only representations or images of things, God views the things themselves, which is to say that he views physical objects without the mediation of appearances, images, or *Abschattungen*:

"Of course God, the subject possessing absolutely perfect knowledge and therefore all possible adequate perception, [allegedly] possesses the perception of the thing in itself denied to us finite beings."[48]

However, argues Husserl, this position is absurd. This is because the inability to perceive a physical object in a non-*abgeschattet* manner is not the result of the imperfection of our perceptual faculties, a limitation which the divine cognitive faculties might overcome. Rather, this limitation arises from the *essence* of a physical object as such. As discussed in section two of this chapter, an essence is a meaning formation outlining the manifold of perceptual presentations which can count as harmonious fulfillments of specific intention. Thus the claim that it is *essential* to a physical object to be given inadequately amounts to the claim that it follows from the intention of a physical object that the corresponding fulfillment must take place by way of *Abschattungen*. Anything which is not *abgeschattet* could not count as a fulfillment of the intention of a physical object, and hence could not *be* (in the phenomenological sense of existence) a physical object. Adequate perception in this domain is therefore not merely empirically impossible but a contradiction in terms; it contradicts the very meaning (essence) of 'physical object':

"A certain **inadequacy** also belongs to the perception of physical things, and this is also an essential necessity. A thing can in principle be given only 'one-sidedly', and that means not only incompletely, not only imperfectly in any arbitrary sense, but rather precisely in the way entailed by presentation through *Abschattungen* .... No God can change any of this, no more than that $1 + 2 = 3$, or any other essential truth."[49]

Husserl arrives at precisely the opposite position of the *Prolegomena* because here he employs a properly phenomenological method for establishing ontology. What it is to be a physical object is derived from an elucidation of meaning-intention and meaning-fulfillment, and their correlations; and not, as in the *Prolegomena*, by simply taking over the hypotheses of contemporary physics (hypotheses which themselves are frequently infiltrated by an anti-phenomenological Cartesianism). In *Ideas I*, Husserl presents an elaborate analysis of the phenomenological method for elucidating essences, and hence for ontology: the theory of eidetic intuition through free variation. This provides the methodological underpinning for his provocative assertion that even God could not perceive an object otherwise than via *Abschattungen*. According to this theory, essences are brought to intuition and elucidated by imagining a particular instantiation of a given intention, varying this instantiation freely in imagination, and judging whether what is imagined retains its identity as an image of the same sort of thing. This serves to make thematic the fulfillment conditions implicit in the intention, and so to set out possibilities and impossibilities of perception arising from the essence alone, and not from the faculties of the subject. Indeed, although the method of eidetic variation is neither named nor thematized in the *Logical Investigations*, much the same procedure is employed there by Husserl to establish the eidetic principle, 'no color without extension'. As we saw in section two, here an instance of color is varied in imagination, and it is found that when its extension is diminished to zero, there is no longer an instance of color. Similarly, the justification for the claim in *Ideas I* that adequate perception is ideally *impossible* is the impossibility of producing a non-*abgeschattet* physical object in free variation.

Certainly it could be and in fact it has been objected against this method of proof that it shows only that certain images are impossible *for us*, and not that they are impossible as such. Thus Tugendhat argues that the results of any imagination-experiment are always empirical, yielding proof of either empirical possibility or empirical impossibility. Further, he points out while empirical possibility logically entails ideal possibility, empirical impossibility does not logically entail ideal impossibility. Therefore, Tugendhat concludes, Husserl's theory of eidetic intuition cannot accomplish the task of demonstrating a priori truths set for it.[50]

However, to see the fallacy of the Tugendhat objection, it should be noticed that the difference between an eidetic and an empirical impossibility of imagination can itself be established phenomenologically. Something is an eidetic impossibility when it is ruled out by the fulfillment conditions implicit in the meanings themselves. By contrast, for an image to be a merely empirical impossibility it must be compatible with what is meant, although we ourselves cannot bring it about. A physical object without *Abschattungen* is a clear case of the former. For if we remove all *Abschattungen* from the image of a physical object, interpreting all parts and aspects of the image not as a perspectival view of an object, but as the very thing itself, then the resulting image is no longer (recognizable as) an object at all. Rather, it is (intentionally constituted as) a pure experience, an *Erlebnis*, and not a physical thing.

This last point can be developed as follows. In our own experience, immanent experiences (*Erlebnisse*) are given directly and (relatively) adequately. Here there are no *Abschattungen* or other forms of mediation coming between the perception and the object: in the perception of an *Erlebnis*, the fulfilled portion of the intentional content just is the *Erlebnis*, and this completely and entirely, without perspectival distortion. Now when it is proposed that God might perceive physical objects adequately, this implies that God might perceive physical objects in the same non-*abgeschattet* manner as we perceive *Erlebnisse*. However, this is impossible, for if anything were to be given in the divine consciousness in the way an *Erlebnis* is given in our own, we could not recognize (intentionally constitute) the given as a physical thing. Because of its appearance, it would necessarily be constituted as an *Erlebnis*. Thus while we can form an empty, non-contradictory concept of a physical object which is not given through *Abschattungen*, (much as we can form a concept of color without extension), this concept cannot be fulfilled.[51]

Thus non-*abgeschattet* perception is included in the fulfillment conditions for experiences, but is ruled out by the fulfillment conditions for a physical object. This is quite different from a merely psychological impossibility, such as the impossibility of simultaneously imagining one hundred dots. Although we (or at least most of us) are incapable of producing the required image, we see how it would be brought about. It is also clear that such an image would be consistent with the fulfillment conditions implicit in the corresponding intention of one hundred dots.

Ideal and empirical impossibility can be distinguished phenomeno-logically by examining the relevant meaning formations themselves. Thus contra Tugendhat, it is not necessary logically to deduce ideal possibilities and impossibilities from empirical ones; they can be 'seen' directly. And if this language seems objectionable, it should be recalled that essential relations among meanings are immediately grasped in a manner analogous to the way purely formal analytic relations (e.g., identity) are immediately grasped, the 'seeing' of which latter not even Tugendhat would deny.

Yet as noted at the close of section three, if the conclusion of a consistent phenomenological approach is that physically objects *cannot* be adequately perceived even by God, then it seems to follow that phenomenologically considered, the physical world is not real. For Husserl correlates reality with the possibility of adequate *Evidenz*. Consequently, it might be thought that for Husserl only *Erlebnisse* are real and not physical things – a Berkeleyan conclusion, reached by different means.

However, this is not the conclusion reached by Husserl. The shift in the method for establishing ontology is accompanied by a corresponding refinement of the basic theory of truth. Thus Husserl argues that although eidetic variation demonstrates that genuine adequacy is impossible in the case of sensible perception, it also shows that we can still imagine a less rigorous kind of complete givenness in this realm. Here the most perfect possible *Evidenz* takes the form of an infinite continuum of *abgeschattet* presentations, of syntheses of fulfillment in which the object is presented from all sides and in all aspects, and in which its self-identity is har-moniously maintained. Of course, we cannot actually imagine the entire continuum in the concrete, but only certain parts and general features of it. For us, this complete givenness has the character of a regulative idea:

"**Complete givenness is nonetheless predelineated as an 'idea'** (in the Kantian sense) – as a **continuum of appearances** determined a priori... . More precisely defined, this continuum is infinite and consists in all its phases of appearances of the same determinable X, and this in such a way that ... each of the **lines** of the continuum, followed through in its continuous progression, presents a harmonious system of appearances ... in which the one and the same given X is determined continuously and harmoniously 'more closely' and never 'differently'."[52]

It is reasonable to think that the impossibility of concretely realizing the infinite continuum is a psychological impossibility (due, for example, to our finite life-spans), but not an ideal one ruled out by the meaning of a physi-cal object as such. For the impossibility we encounter here is analogous to that of imagining a very large number of dots: we can see how it would proceed, even though we ourselves cannot bring it about. Thus even in the realm of the physical, perfect givenness (in the sense of the infinite continuum) would be possible for an ideal consciousness. Indeed, although not explicitly stated in *Ideas I*, this is clearly Husserl's own view in the second edition of the *Prolegomena*, written around the time of *Ideas I*. In the second edition, the passage on ideal possibility quoted above appears in a significantly modified form. Here Husserl continues to maintain that an *adequate* and unitary perception of the entire world is ideally possible. However, the reference to molecules and atoms is deleted, and the original sense of the term 'adequacy' is greatly altered by the qualification that the requisite perception would actually be an infinite continuum of perception; or, thought as a unity, a Kantian idea:

> "Accordingly, a perception is **possible** which takes in the whole world with its boundless infinity of bodies in a **single** glance. Of course, this ideal possibility is in no way a real one which might be attributed to some empirical subject, especially since such a perception would be an infinite continuum of perception: thought as a unity, a **Kantian** idea."[53]

Thus the overall result of the phenomenological approach to ontology is not the exclusion of the physical world from the realm of true being, but a richer and more manifold notion of perfect *Evidenz*, and hence of true being itself. What constitutes perfect *Evidenz* will vary significantly from one category of entity to another, and will in many (if not all) cases fall short of adequacy in the strictest sense. The specific nature of *Evidenz* and its perfection cannot be posited in advance by a universal theory, but is to be elucidated by eidetic analysis of the relevant fundamental concepts.

Despite this significant change in conception, Husserl quite misleadingly continues to employ the terms 'adequacy' and 'adequate *Evidenz*', even where he clearly has a weaker, more manifold notion in mind than in the *Logical Investigations*. Thus towards the close of *Ideas I*, he presents an account of truth virtually identical to that of the *Prolegomena* and the Sixth Investigation. Once again it is asserted that truth and the ideal possibility of adequate perception are logically equivalent:

> "**To each 'truly existing' object** there corresponds in principle (according to the a priori of an unconditional, essential universal) the **idea of a possible consciousness** in which the object can be grasped **in original intuition** and thereby **perfectly adequately**. Conversely, if this possibility is assured, then *eo ipso* the object truly exists."[54]

However, in light of the multiplicity and also imperfection of the various forms of 'adequacy', a more accurate phrase than 'adequate *Evidenz*' in this context would be 'maximal *Evidenz*': the most perfect type of *Evidenz* which is in principle possible for an entity of a given type. For example, in the case of a physical object, maximal *Evidenz* takes the form of a perception of an infinite continuum of *Abschattungen*. By contrast, in the case of an immanent *Erlebnis*, maximal *Evidenz* takes the form of a non-*abgeschattet* retentive memory of the flowing reduced experience. Truth, then, according to the conception reached by the end of *Ideas I*, is the correlate of the ideal possibility of maximal *Evidenz*, where the precise nature of this maximal *Evidenz* must be investigated for each category of entity individually.

5. SUMMARY AND PROVISIONAL CONCLUSIONS

Of course, the mere formulation of a non-relative theory of truth cannot itself answer the question of relativism. For the relativist does not deny that such theories exist, nor even that there is a natural or culturally determined tendency to believe such theories. Rather, he questions their *validity*, despite their existence, prevalence, or naturalness. One of the most powerful arguments against a non-relative theory of truth is the epistemic critique: if a notion of non-relative truth is valid and not merely inadmissable speculation, then it must be possible for us to attain knowledge of such truths.

As we saw in section one, Cartesian objectivism falls prey to this epistemic critique, and so fails to answer the question of relativism. By contrast, the Husserlian analysis of truth is formulated from the outset with the demands of critical epistemology clearly in view. This analysis may be characterized as a reinterpretation of the traditional correspondence theory of truth. In the *Prolegomena*, truth is held to be the idea of the correspondence between the experienced meaning of an assertion and an experienced state of affairs. Similarly, according to the Sixth Investigation, a true judgment is one which corresponds to a state of affairs which can be given with adequate *Evidenz*. In *Ideas I* Husserl adds the qualification that 'adequate' or maximal *Evidenz* varies from one category of object to another, and in the case of physical objects in particular has the form of a Kantian idea. Thus the overall result of this analysis is to provide a further specification of the nature of the reality to which a true judgment must correspond: reality is that which is or can (ideally) be given maximally in intuition.

The contrast between Husserl's theory and Cartesian objectivism may then be formulated as follows. According to objectivism, the domains of what can be given in experience (the phenomenal) and of what exists in itself are disjoint. The phenomenal exists inside the subjective stream of experience, and stands in an immediate relation to the mind, while the real exists outside the stream of experience, and can appear to the subject only mediately (e.g., by causally interacting with the subject and so producing phenomenal presentations). By contrast, the Husserlian correlates of the phenomenal and the real are not disjoint. Instead, the real is a *subset* of the 'phenomenal', or rather the intentional. The realm of phenomenological being contains all objects and objectivities which can be given as intentional objects in experience, no matter what the degree or type of accompanying *Evidenz*. The realm of the real is then a subset of this first realm, consisting of those objects and objectivities in regard to which *maximal Evidenz* is ideally possible. Since true being is no more than a species of phenomenological being, the problem of how the subject, locked into its experience of a merely phenomenal world, is to come to know a reality apart from all experience, does not arise. According to Husserl's analysis, when a true object presents itself in experience, the subject then apprehends not a phenomenal object caused by this reality, but rather the reality itself: the apprehended object *just is* the true being, the being to which true judgments must correspond.

However, it could be objected that this does not yet suffice to overcome the epistemic critique. For in order to know whether a judgment is true in the Husserlian sense we must know whether a phenomenon, given with only some form and degree of *Evidenz*, could indeed be given with *maximal Evidenz*, at least to an ideal consciousness. But how are we to know this? For example, suppose I perceive an inkwell and form the judgment, 'the ink in this well is blue.' Following the Husserlian account, I must determine whether maximal *Evidenz* regarding this judgment is possible; that is, whether the infinite continuum of *Abschattungen* of the inkwell and its blue-colored ink is a possible perception-content for an ideal consciousness. However, since I myself am able to carry out only a few lines of the infinite continuum, and this only partially, it follows that no matter how thoroughly, or from how many different perspectives and in how many different lights I examine the inkwell, it remains a possibility that further investigation would produce a disharmonious perception of the well or the blueness of its ink, causing the intentional object of my judgment to 'break up'. Thus knowledge of the truth of the judgment, even in the Husserlian phenomenological sense, is not possible.

Yet against this objection, it is again necessary to distinguish between knowledge in the sense of certainty and knowledge in the sense of rationally justified belief. For Husserl grants and even strongly defends the view that in the case of transcendents such as physical things, certainty is not a possibility for us (nor for any finite being). This is because, as argued above, while we may carry out *some* of the lines of the continuum corresponding to the intentional object of a judgment, we are unable to carry out *all* of them. Thus it always remains possible that the further course of experience would demonstrate that not all the predelineated lines can be actualized, but rather a 'refuting' line can be. At the same time, knowledge in the sense of rational justification can be attained by us. Returning to the example of the inkwell, when I look in the well and see that the ink is blue, a certain degree of *Evidenz* is attained, and this *Evidenz* provides rational justification for my judgment 'the ink in this well is blue'. Similarly, if I carry out further syntheses of fulfillment (examining the well more closely, from another angle, in a better light, etc.), improving the degree of *Evidenz*, the degree of rational justification will correspondingly increase. Thus in the sense of rationally justified belief, knowledge of the (phenomenological) truth of the judgment is indeed possible.

Here it is important to emphasize the difference in this regard between the Husserlian and the objectivist accounts. For Husserl's alternate conception of truth renders claims to truth capable of rational justification in a way not possible when truth is conceived along objectivist lines. Taken in the objectivist sense, the claim that my judgment 'the ink in this well is blue' is true is not justified by my perception of the blueness of the ink. In order for this claim to be true in the objectivist sense, the real (objectivist) cause of my perception, existing apart from and outside of this perception, must be blue ink in a well. However, the fact that I perceive blue ink in no way demonstrates that the real cause of this perception is blue ink. By contrast, when it is held that this judgment is true in the Husserlian sense, what this means is that certain specific perceptions and series of perceptions are possible. My actual perceptions of the inkwell constitute a subset of the totality of perceptions which must be possible if the judgment is true. Thus the possibility of at least these is assured. Further, the possibility of the others can be grounded mediately, on the basis of motivating elements of the perceptual context. Hence, while certainty of the truth of the judgment is by no means attained, perception and experience do provide rational justification for affirmation of truth according to the Husserlian account in a way they do not on the objectivist one.

Husserl of course also asserts that at least in some domains knowledge is possible not merely in the form of limited rational justification, but as certainty. Correspondingly, here he holds that adequate *Evidenz* is really attainable. These claims are crucial both to the overall foundationalist project of establishing phenomenology on the basis of ultimate *Evidenz*, and for the more limited issue of relativism. This is because, as will be discussed in detail in subsequent chapters, Husserl treats intersubjectivity itself as a phenomenon with its own kind of *Evidenz*. Thus an important question is whether the *Evidenz* we have for the intersubjective validity of truth-claims is of the weaker or the stronger sort. That is, is the *Evidenz* of intersubjectivity merely limited rational justification which might in the end be overturned? Or is it absolutely adequate *Evidenz*, producing the highest certainty? The answer to this question depends upon Husserl's analysis of ultimate *Evidenz* itself, the *Evidenz* attained by phenomenological reduction, which will be addressed in the next chapter.

The present chapter has shown how and the extent to which the phenomenological theory of truth satisfies the demands of critical epistemology, thereby avoiding the skepticism to which Cartesian objectivism is prone. I will conclude this chapter with brief indication of the more direct implications of Husserl's theory of truth for the relativism problematic.

In section two it was argued that *Evidenz* (and hence truth) is indeed non-relative in the case of eidetic judgments. This is because this *Evidenz* is a consequence of meaning formations (essences) themselves. But this in turn implies that the resulting non-relativity insures only that the law of non-contradiction cannot be violated, and not that universal intersubjective consensus is in fact possible. Thus it is at least compatible with our analysis that judgments could be eidetically self-evident to some individuals or groups, but simply unintelligible or unverifiable to others. Further, here again the 'strength' of the *Evidenz* of this non-relativity remains to be evaluated: is it ultimate and certain, or only partial and subject to change?

The groundwork for addressing the issue of intersubjectivity in a positive fashion has already been laid with the *Evidenz*-theory of truth. Indeed, it could be argued that if the most important implication of the *Evidenz*-theory for relativism is its overcoming of Cartesianism and skepticism (which was in any case already in large measure accomplished by Berkeley and Kant), then the second most important contribution is its treatment of intersubjectivity itself as a phenomenon. An analysis of the *Evidenz* particular to intersubjectivity makes possible a phenomenological *demonstration* of whether consensus indeed obtains, could obtain, or could not. Thus the correlation of truth with *Evidenz* opens the way to a positive proof of universal intersubjectivity, or of its absence. Of course, here as before the strength of the phenomenological demonstration of the existence of intersubjectivity (its *Evidenz*) remains to be evaluated.

Husserl's theory of truth alone does not accomplish a definitive overcoming of relativism. However, it does lay the essential groundwork for a positive resolution of this question. In the next chapters we will examine how Husserl builds his position on this ground.

NOTES

1. The absolute priority and irreducibility of intuition is and remains the 'principle of all principles' of the Husserlian enterprise, as he explicitly states in *Ideas I*: "**every originally presentative intuition** is **a justificatory source of knowledge, everything** that is given to us **originally in intuition** ... is simply to be taken as it presents itself..." ("Daß *jede originär gebende Anschauung eine Rechtsquelle der Erkenntnis sei, daß alles was sich uns in der 'Intuition' originär ... darbietet, einfach hinzunehmen sei, als was es sich gibt...*"), *Hua III* 51/52 (*Id I* § 24).

    In this and subsequent references to the *Husserliana* edition of *Ideas I*, the page number before the slash gives the location of the passage in the Schuhmann edition; the page number after the slash, the location in the Biemel edition. Quotations follow the text of the Schuhmann edition.

2. Descartes does not affirm the view that the mind can be in immediate relation only to ideas and never to external things as consistently and unambiguously as, for example, does Locke. However, even if Descartes himself might have resisted this view, it does seem to be the logical consequence of his theory of perception and the distinction between primary and secondary qualities. For Descartes maintains that external things possess primary qualities only, and that secondary qualities exist solely as ideas in the mind. But all perceptions 'of' external things include the perception of secondary qualities, which are ideas only. Therefore according to Descartes' own account, perceptions of external things must be perceptions of ideas. For Descartes' account of the primary/secondary quality distinction, see René Descartes, *Principia philosophiæ*, in *Oeuvres de Descartes*, vol. VIII/I, edited by Charles Adam and Paul Tannery (Paris: Vrin, 1973), 22–23, 33–34, 42, 46, 318–323 (Part I, Articles 48, 68–70; Part Two, Articles 4, 11; Part IV, Articles 191–8); *Regulæ ad directionem ingenii*, in *Oeuvres de Descartes*, vol. X, edited by Charles Adam and Paul Tannery (Paris: Vrin, 1974), 412–19 (Rule 12); *Dioptrique*, in *Oeuvres de Descartes*, vol. VI, edited by Charles Adam and Paul Tannery (Paris: Vrin, 1973), 84–6 (Discourse One). For the causal theory of perception, see *Dioptrique*, 130–47 (Discourse Six); *Principia*, 315–6 (Part IV, Article 189); and *Passions de l'âme*, in *Oeuvres de Descartes*, vol. XI, edited by Charles Adam and Paul Tannery (Paris: Vrin, 1974), 336–7, 346, 354–5 (Articles 12, 23, and 34). For an unambiguous statement of Locke's representationalism, see John Locke, *An Essay Concerning Human Understanding*, edited by Peter Nidditch (Oxford: Clarendon, 1979), 525 (Book IV, Chapter I, § 1).

3. See *A Treatise Concerning the Principles of Human Knowledge*, in *The Works of George Berkeley*, vol. II, edited by A. A. Luce and T. E. Jessop (London and New York: Thomas Nelson and Sons, 1945), §§ 20, 26, 33; and *Kritik der reinen Vernunft*, A

30/*B* 45, *A* 250, *B* 289–290.

4. This empiricist justification of knowledge is generally the one proposed by Locke, not for knowledge of the mere existence of external material reality (which he holds to be certain), but for any specification of its properties. See *Essay Concerning Human Understanding*, 378–9 (Book II, Chapter XXXI, § 6) for the claim that any theory listing the primary qualities is nothing but a presumption, a best possible explanation of observed phenomena; and 537 (Book IV, Chapter II, § 14) for the argument that, unlike a specification of the primary qualities, the knowledge of the mere existence of external objects is past doubting.

5. For Berkeley's phenomenalist interpretation of natural laws, see *Principles of Human Knowledge*, §§ 30, 58, 62, 64. For the claim that the phenomenal content of our ideas can give no evidence whatsoever that their cause is not God alone, see § 53. A similar argument was common in the Middle Ages, as an elaboration of the omnipotence of God. For example, Ockham holds that God could produce all the subjective experiences we normally attribute to the external world, although we would not have any grounds for judging the difference. However, unlike Berkeley, Ockham is not prepared to assert that God does indeed do this. See *Ockham's Theory of Terms: Part I of the Summa Logicæ*, translated by Michael Loux, (Notre Dame, Ind. and London: University of Notre Dame Press, 1974), 182.

6. *Principles of Human Knowledge*, § 19. See especially the passage, "for though we give the materialists their external bodies, they by their own confession are never the nearer knowing how our ideas are produced: since they own themselves unable to comprehend in what manner body can act upon spirit, or how it is possible it should imprint any idea in the mind. Hence it is evident the production of ideas or sensations in our minds, can be no reason why we should suppose matter or corporeal substances, since that is acknowledged to remain equally inexplicable with, or without that supposition." For Locke's own admission that the posited causality is completely incomprehensible, see *Essay Concerning Human Understanding*, 545 (Book IV, Chapter III, § 13).

7. See *Kritik der reinen Vernunft*, A 391–4 (the general argument), as well as A 144/B 183 (the critical interpretation of causality).

8. *Principia philosophiæ*, 325–9 (Part IV, Articles 203–6). Similarly, in Part III, Article 43, Descartes argues that if we are to be justified in claiming that the hypothesized causes of planetary motion are ontologically true, it must be possible to deduce all phenomena from them, including local motions on earth. But Descartes grounds this inference from explanatory/predictive power to the nature of reality once again by appealing to God's justice: it is impossible that causes from which one can deduce all phenomena could be false, because God would not be so perverse (*ibid.*, 99).

9. Indeed, this seems to be the position of McCullagh, who thinks the mere possibility that our judgments are true in the traditional correspondence sense is sufficient to justify maintaining this concept, even if this rules out all possibility of rational justification: "The relativist may consistently hold that his beliefs about the world are true in a correspondence sense, while also insisting that they are culture-determined constructions. The claim that the world really is as we believe it to be is not one which the relativist is debarred by his doctrine from making, no matter what difficulty he would have justifying it" (McCullagh, 329). For Berkeley's argument against this very reduced version of Cartesian objectivism (i.e., which holds only that an external reality may exist, even if it is unknowable), see *Principles of Human Knowledge*, § 67.

10. For an earlier discussion of this combination, see Chapter One, section two, pp. 20 ff. above.

11. *Principles of Human Knowledge*, §§ 19, 53, 61. Berkeley's logic here is simply that of Ockham's razor, only applied more radically than by Ockham himself: whereas Ockham uses it to eliminate sensible and intelligible species, Berkeley employs it to eliminate the entire extra-mental world.

12. *Hua XVIII* 124–5 (*P A/B* 117–8).

13. See, for example, *Hua VI* 116–8 (*K* § 30).

14. Thus here is the possible reason for the tendency of Kantianism to become relativism, a tendency already mentioned by us in Chapter One (p. 24, n. 6): Kant's confusion about the proper method for establishing the a priori structures of experience, which in turn allows him to root them in the subjective faculties, and in general to accept the Lockean conception of the mind as 'forming' the material provided it by the senses.

15. *Hua XVIII* 183–4 (*P A* 180–2). (It should be noted that here and throughout this discussion, reference is to the first edition of the *Logical Investigations*. This is because the second edition contains a number of non-trivial revisions of the relevant passages, reflecting Husserl's attempt to reformulate his conception from the more purely phenomenological perspective attained by the time of *Ideas*. However, the language of the second edition is easily misinterpreted unless a general understanding of this phenomenological perspective has already been attained.)

16. *Ibid.*, 193–4 (*P A* 190–1). ("Das Erlebnis der Zusammenstimmung zwischen der Meinung und dem gegenwärtigen Erlebten, das sie meint, zwischen dem erlebten Sinn der Aussage und dem erlebten Sachverhalt ist die Evidenz, und die Idee dieser Zusammenstimmung ist die Wahrheit.") Here Husserl defines truth as the idea of the agreement between intention and perception. In other places, truth is variously conceived as the agreement itself, the correlate of the possibility of this agreement, and so on. These finer distinctions may be overlooked for the purposes of the present discussion. The ambiguities are resolved in the Sixth Investigation, where Husserl sets forth four distinct senses of truth. For a treatment of these, see page 79.

17. See Marvin Farber, *The Foundation of Phenomenology: Edmund Husserl and the Quest for a Rigorous Science of Philosophy* (Cambridge: Harvard University Press, 1943), reprint, (Albany: State University of New York Press: 1968); Elisabeth Ströker, "Husserls Evidenzprinzip. Sinn und Grenzen einer methodischen Norm der Phänomenologie als Wissenschaft," *Zeitschrift für philosophische Forschung* 32.1 (1978): 1–30; reprinted in *Phänomenologische Studien* (Frankfurt a.M.: Vittorio Klostermann Verlag, 1987); and Dallas Willard, *Logic and the Objectivity of Knowledge: A Study in Husserl's Early Philosophy* (Athens, Ohio: Ohio University Press, 1984). For an early statement in the *Philosophy of Arithmetic* of the distinction between authentic and unauthentic (symbolic) representation, see *Hua XII* 193.

A parallel analysis of the method for bringing the principle of non-contradiction to *Evidenz* is presented by Husserl in the *Logical Investigations, Hua XIX/1* 342–5 (*LU A* 318–9/B 334–6). Here he holds that we take any concrete instance of a logical contradiction (e.g., 'a square is round'), and then 'formalize' it: we vary the example freely in imagination, trying to bring any instance whatsoever of a contradiction to intuition. This allows us to 'see' the in-principle impossibility of doing so.

18. Similarly, as we have seen in Chapter One, Husserl holds that the self-evident truth of the principle of non-contradiction follows from the very meanings of 'truth',

'judgment', etc., and could not be (self-evidently) true for some beings and (self-evidently) false for others. See chapter one, p. 11 above and *Hua XVIII* 144 (*P A/B* 139).

19. *Hua XIX/1* 234–5 (*LU A* 228–9/*B* 231–3).

20. *Ibid.*, 255–8 (*LU A* 245–7/*B* 251–4).

21. Given the eventual need for Husserl to justify the universal intersubjectivity of truth, and hence the universal accessibility of at least some meaning formations, this is not a trivial reservation, as will be discussed further in what follows. However, in the context of the *Prolegomena* the non-relativity of *Evidenz* can only be taken in the weaker sense of the impossibility of contradictory *Evidenz*, and not in the sense of the certainty of universal intelligibility and consensus.

22. See David Michael Levin, *Reason and Evidence in Husserl's Phenomenology* (Evanston: Northwestern University Press, 1970), 209 ff. See also Alwin Diemer, "Die Phänomenologie und die Idee der Philosophie als strenge Wissenschaft," *Zeitschrift für philosophische Forschung* 13 (1959), 254 and passim. Diemer argues, similarly to Levin, that the unities of meaning which Husserl terms 'essences' are not eternal and invariant, and therefore eidetic analysis of them cannot give rise to universally and atemporally valid truths.

23. Levin, 210.

24. *Hua XIX/1* 51–3 (*LU A/B* 46–7). Husserl employs the terminology *'Bedeutung'* and *'gegenständlicher Beziehung'* for what in this passage I, following Frege, have termed 'meaning' (*Sinn*) and 'reference' (*Bedeutung*).

25. *Hua XVIII* 187 (*P A* 184). ("Da evidentermaßen die allgemeine Äquivalenz besteht zwischen den Sätzen, 'A ist wahr' und 'es ist möglich, daß irgend jemand mit Evidenz urteilt, es sei A'.")

   Günther Patzig mounts an elaborate argument to show that the correlation established in the *Prolegomena* commits Husserl to an *esse is percipi* form of idealism, and hence to a relativism of the most extreme and subjectivist sort. According to Patzig, the relation between *Evidenz* and truth is analogous to that between a ray of light and the image it projects upon a screen: the ray of light and the image are not identical, but the image exists when and only when the light-ray is present. Thus truth exists only insofar as it is experienced in a self-evident act of judgment. See Günther Patzig, "Kritische Bemerkungen zu Husserls Thesen über das Verhältnis Zwischen Wahrheit und Evidenz," *Neue Hefte für Philosophie* 1 (1971), 21. Unfortunately, despite its intricate argumentation, the Patzig interpretation has no basis whatsoever in the text.

26. The psychological limitations of humans in relation to *Evidenz*, and the implications of these limitations for mathematics in particular, were long of interest to Husserl. Schuhmann reports that at Husserl's doctoral examination in 1887, Husserl defended the thesis that we are able to count only up to the number three – in the genuine (i.e., intuitive) sense of counting. See Karl Schuhmann, *Husserl-Chronik. Denk- und Lebensweg Edmund Husserls*, Husserliana Dokumente, vol. 1 (The Hague: Martinus Nijhoff Publishers, 1977), 22. Further, both Farber and Willard have noted that one of the central projects of the *Philosophy of Arithmetic* is to establish with what justification we hold results in arithmetic to be true, despite the fact that we arrive at them almost wholly symbolically and mechanically, rather than intuitively. Indeed, Willard goes so far as to assert that "it is not a great or pointless exaggeration to say that the analysis of symbolic representation and knowing is *the* main problem for investigation

throughout Husserl's career" (Willard, 89). See also Farber, 43ff.

27. *Hua XVIII* 188 (*P A* 185). ("Was psychologisch unmöglich ist, kann ideal gesprochen sehr wohl sein. Die Auflösung des verallgemeinerten 'Problems der 3 Körper, sagen wir das 'Problem der *n* Körper', mag jede menschliche Erkenntnisfähigkeit überschreiten. Aber das Problem hat eine Auflösung, und so ist eine darauf bezügliche Evidenz möglich. Es gibt dekadische Zahlen mit Trillionenstellen, und es gibt auf sie bezügliche Wahrheiten. Aber niemand kannn solche Zahlen wirklich vorstellen und die auf sie bezüglichen Additionen, Multiplikationen usw. wirklich ausführen. Die Evidenz ist hier psychologisch unmöglich, und doch ist sie, ideal zu reden, ganz gewiß ein mögliches psychisches Erlebnis.")

28. *Hua XII* 218–9.

29. *Hua XVIII* 188 (*P A* 185).

30. *Hua III* 175/191, n.1 (*Id I* § 79). ("Die Idee Gott ist ein notwendiger Grenzbegriff in erkenntnistheoretischen Erwägungen, bzw. ein unentbehrlicher Index für die Konstruktion gewisser Grenzbegriffe, deren auch der philosophierende Atheist nicht entraten könnte.")

31. As will be discussed further in what follows and as emphasized by Kern, in *Ideas I* Husserl accords the role of determining the nature and limits of an ideal consciousness to free variation. See Iso Kern, *Husserl und Kant* (The Hague: Martinus Nijhoff, 1964) 133–4 and passim. Thus these limits are established not so much by the cognitive faculties as by the a priori structures of the objects themselves, and in the end everything is rooted by Husserl in meanings and not in faculties.

The emphasis placed here on the similarity between an ideal consciousness and our own is also largely in agreement with Kern, who writes: "The divine intellect set up by Husserl in contrast to [Kant's] *intellectus archetypus* is nothing other than an idealized human totality of knowledge, freed from all **factual** inadequacies. Thus this is a matter of 'God' as 'epistemic limit concept', which really is nothing other than the 'limit concept' of man. A difference of **essence** between this 'divine' knowledge and factual human knowledge therefore does not exist." ("Der göttliche Intellekt, den Husserl dem *intellectus archetypus* [Kants] entgegenstellt, ist nichts anderes als eine idealisierte, von allen faktischen Unzulänglichkeiten befreite menschliche Erkenntnis. Es handelt sich um 'Gott' als 'erkenntnistheoretischen Grenzbegriff', der in Wirklichkeit nichts anderes ist als der 'Grenzbegriff' des Menschen. Eine Wesensverschiedenheit zwischen dieser 'göttlichen' Erkenntnis und der faktisch menschlichen liegt also nicht vor"), Kern, 128.

However, Kern's view is somewhat too anthropomorphic to be genuinely Husserlian. It would be more in keeping with Husserl to hold that the limit concept is an idealization of the actual subject (where what this is remains to be determined purely phenomenologically), than that it is an idealization of a human being. For this latter version once again relativizes truth to a specific set of faculties or a particular, higher theory: a theory which establishes the nature of the human.

32. *Hua III* 326–9/346–8 (*Id I* § 141).

33. *Hua XVIII* 12 (*P B* XIII).

34. *Hua XIX/2* 566 (*LU A* 504/*B* 32). ("Wir erleben es, wie in der Anschauung dasselbe Gegenständliche intuitiv vergegenwärtigt ist, welches im symbolischen Akte 'bloß gedacht' war, und daß es gerade als das so und so Bestimmte anschaulich wird, als was es zunächst bloß gedacht [bloß bedeutet] war.")

35. *Hua XIX/2* 597–8 (*LU A* 537/B 65). ("In der Erfüllung erleben wir gleichsam ein *das*

ist es selbst. Dieses *selbst* ist freilich nicht im strengen Sinn zu nehmen.... Immerhin deutet uns die relative Rede vom 'mehr oder minder direkt' und von 'selbst' die Hauptsache einigermaßen an: daß die Erfüllungs- synthesis eine Ungleichwertigkeit der verknüpften Glieder zeigt, derart, daß der erfüllende Akt einen Vorzug herbeibringt, welcher der bloßen Intention mangelt, nämlich daß er ihr die Fülle des *'selbst'* erteilt, sie mindestens *direkter* an die Sache selbst heranführt.")

36. *Hua XIX/2* 647 (*LU A* 589–1/*B* 117–8). ("So weist die Erwägung der möglichen Erfüllungsverhältnisse auf ein abschließendes Ziel der Erfüllungssteigerung hin, in dem die volle und gesamte Intention ihre Erfüllung... hat .... Repräsentierender und repräsentierter Inhalt sind hier identisch eines. Und wo sich eine Vorstellungsintention durch diese ideal vollkommene Wahrnehmung letzte Erfüllung verschafft hat, da hat sich die echte adæquatio rei et intellectus hergestellt: das Gegenständliche ist genau als das, als welches es intendiert ist, *wirklich 'gegenwärtig'* oder *'gegeben'*; keine Partialintention ist mehr impliziert, die ihrer Erfüllung ermangelte.") Of course, as will be discussed in what follows, no perception or series of perceptions could provide a genuinely adequate fulfillment of a building.

37. *Ibid.*, 651–3 (*LU A* 594–5/*B* 122–4).

38. This account shows that the common objection that a phenomenological conception of truth cannot distinguish between genuine and illusory perception is completely unfounded. In one typical statement of this objection, Patzig argues that if a person sits in a train at rest, sees another train move out of the station, but experiences that *his* train is moving, then according to Husserl's view, for this person his own train *really is* moving, since he *sees* that it is moving. (See Patzig, 28.) However, the Patzig example, as all others of its kind, ignores the overall coherence of experience required for *Evidenz* in the case of physical reality. If the person's train were *really* moving on the phenomenological account, then upon continuing to look out the window, the person would see the landscape rushing by. Since he sees only the train station at rest, with the other train gone, the initial phenomenon ('my train is moving') breaks up, and is replaced by a new one ('my train is at rest, the other train was moving'). Thus it is not the case that, phenomenologically considered, the person's train is *really* moving simply because it is perceived to be moving in a single, isolated moment.

39. *Principles of Human Knowledge*, § 30

40. *Ibid.*, § 36. Indeed, here Berkeley goes so far as to say that orderliness and distinctness are what reality *means.*

41. Husserl's elucidation of the concept of truth in terms of the experience of the agreement between intention and perception is therefore in keeping with the early conception of the phenomenological project: to trace fundamental but abstract mathematical and logical concepts to elemental intuitive experiences, and to make these experiences as explicit and 'evident' as possible. A particularly clear statement of this project is contained in manuscript F I 26 of 1902/3: "Thus there arises the task of investigating the 'origin of knowledge'. That now means to obtain the most evident clarity for the fundamental concepts, on the one hand, and the psychological concepts corresponding to them, on the other, and this by going back to the intuitive experiences from which we derive them by abstraction. *Thus what is meant by 'concept', 'proposition', 'object', 'state of affairs', 'truth', 'falsehood', 'ground' 'consequence' and so forth? And what are the intuitive experiences which we indicate by the vague terms, 'perception', 'memory', 'representation', 'judgment', 'inference', 'self-evidence', 'absurdity', and so on,*

experiences in which logical forms are given to us? ... It is true that I understand what the word 'proposition' means very well: I possess more than the mere empty word, I can even give examples of propositions, such as the Pythagorean theorem. But for all that I do not get beyond merely symbolic understanding. I get beyond this only when I carry out some proposition in an authentic positing attitude, in a fully intuitive act of judgment, and when I attend to the moment in this concrete experience in which the symbolic attains its identifying verification. Only then have I answered the question of what I genuinely understand or intend by a proposition, and where it actually and authentically presents itself. The situation is precisely the same as in the case of a simple sensible concept such as red. Here I grasp the meaning of red when I attend to the moment of redness in an intuition and say to myself, 'that is it, redness is the universal of which this moment is an example.' What holds good of the logical idea of a proposition holds good for the other logical ideas and the accompanying questions..." ("So erwächst die Aufgabe den 'Ursprung der Erkenntnis' zu erforschen, das heißt jetzt, den fundamentalen Begriffen auf der einen Seite und den ihnen entsprechenden psychologischen Begriffen auf der anderen Seite durch Rückgang auf die Erlebnisse, denen wir sie abstrahierend entnehmen, evidenteste Klarheit zu verschaffen. *Was heißt also Begriff, Satz, Gegenstand, Sachverhalt, Wahrheit, Falschheit, Grund, Folge usw., und was für Erlebnisse sind es, die wir unter den vagen Titeln Wahrnehmung, Erinnerung, Vorstellung, Urteil, Schluß, Evidenz, Absurdität usw. ausdrücken, Erlebnisse, in denen uns eben logische Formen gegeben sind?* ... Ich verstehe zwar ganz wohl, was das Wort Satz meint, ich habe nicht den bloßen Wortschall; ich kann sogar Exempel angeben, wie den Pythagorischen Lehrsatz u.dgl. Aber mit all dem komme ich über das bloß symbolische Verstehen nicht hinaus. Erst wenn ich irgendeinen Satz in eigentlicher Setzung, im voll anschaulichen Urteilen vollziehe, und erst wenn ich auf dasjenige Moment in diesem konkreten Erlebnis achte, in welchem der symbolische seine identifizierend Bestätigung findet, erst dann habe ich die Frage beantwortet, was verstehe ich oder meine ich eigentlich unter einem Satz, wo läßt es sich wirklich und eigentlich aufzeigen. Es verhält sich dann damit genau so, wie ich bei einem einfachen sinnlichen Begriff, wie rot, den Sinn realisiere, wenn ich in einer Anschauung das Moment Röte erfasse und mir sage, das ist es, Röte ist das Allgemeine zu diesem Moment als Exempel. Was von der logischen Idee Satz gilt, gilt von den sonstigen logischen Ideen und den zugehörigen Fragen..."), manuscript page 73a, typescript pages 154–5.

42. *Principles of Human Knowledge*, §§ 33, 38, 39.

43. Berkeley attempts to demonstrate that *esse* is *percipi* by arguing that we cannot conceive of a phenomenal reality without having an idea of it, therefore such a reality cannot exist without the mind – or in Berkeley's terms, existence cannot be separated from perception in thought. (*Ibid.*, §§ 5, 23.) Yet clearly, here the conclusion does not follow from the premise unless 'exist' is simply equated with 'be conceived', which would be begging the question. The truth of the Berkeleyan argument is that existence as we conceive (intend) it in ordinary intentional acts does indeed contain a reference to perception, that is, perception is implicated in the very meaning of 'existence'. But contra Berkeley, the intentional implication contained in an existential positing is not of present perception but of possible perception.

44. John Stuart Mill, *An Examination of Sir William Hamilton's Philosophy* (London: Longmans, Green and Co., 1889), 227ff. With explicit reference to Kant, Mill correlates (physical) reality with possibilities of perception: "The conception I form of the world

existing at any moment, comprises, along with the sensations I am feeling, a countless variety of possibilities of sensation.... My present sensations are generally of little importance, and are moreover fugitive: the possibilities, to the contrary, are permanent, which is the character that mainly distinguishes our idea of Matter from our notion of sensation" (228–9). And again: "Matter, then, may be defined, a Permanent Possibility of Sensation" (233).

45. *Hua XIX/2* 599 (*LU A* 639/*B* 67). ("Denn die allseitige Darstellung vollzieht sich in solch einer synthetischen Mannigfaltigkeit nicht, wie es das Ideal der Adäquation fordert, in einem Schlage, als reine Selbstdarstellung und ohne Zusatz von Analogisierung und Symbolisierung, sondern stückweise und immerfort durch solche Zusätze getrübt.")

46. *Hua XVIII* 188 (*P A* 185) and Hua III 91–2/100–1 (*Id* I § 44).

47. *Hua XVIII* 188 (*P A* 185). ("Die Äquivalenz [der] Begriffe [individuelles Sein und Wahrnehmungsmöglichkeit] ist, wofern nur unter Wahrnehmung die adäquate verstanden wird, unbestreitbar. Es ist danach eine Wahrnehmung möglich, welche in EINEM Schauen die ganze Welt, die überschwengliche Unendlichkeit von Körpern mit allen ihren Teilen, Molekülen, Atomen und nach allen Verhältnissen und Bestimmtheiten wahrnimmt. Natürlich ist diese ideale Möglichkeit keine reale, die für irgendein empirisches Subjekt angenommen werden könnte.") It should again be emphasized that this passage is from the first edition. Understandably, it appears in the second edition in a substantially modified form. See p. 88.

48. *Hua III* 89/98 (*Id I* § 43). ("Gott, das Subjekt absolut vollkommener Erkenntnis und somit auch aller möglichen adäquaten Wahrnehmung, besitze natürlich die uns endlichen Wesen versagten vom Dinge an sich selbst.")

As in the *Prolegomena* passage, the position outlined in this passage actually combines two points: 1) God perceives entire objects, without *Abschattungen*; and 2) the objects perceived by God are very different from ordinary objects of sensible perception, and perhaps are similar to the entities described by physics. For the purposes of this discussion, we can restrict our attention to Husserl's critique of the first point. The critique of the second is treated in my paper, "Phenomenology and Scientific Realism: Husserl's Critique of Galileo," *The Review of Metaphysics* 44.1 (September, 1990), 67–94.

49. *Hua III* 91 and 92/100 and 101 (*Id I* § 44). ("Zur Dingwahrnehmung gehört ferner, und auch das ist eine Wesensnotwendigkeit, eine gewisse Inadäquatheit. Ein Ding kann prinzipiell nur 'einseitig' gegeben sein, und das sagt nicht nur unvollständig, nur unvollkommen in einem beliebigen Sinne, sondern eben das, was die Darstellung durch Abschattung vorschreibt.... Kein Gott kann daran etwas ändern, so wenig wie daran, daß 1+2=3 ist, oder daran, daß irgendeine sonstige Wesenswahrheit besteht.")

50. Tugendhat, 158–60.

51. This discussion may suggest that the truth of eidetic principles is therefore merely relative to 'our' own meaning formations. This objection has already been addressed in a preliminary way in section two (see pp. 70 ff). Its final resolution depends upon other elements of the Husserlian analysis, including the theory of the transcendental ego. For a further treatment, see Chapter 4, pp. 129 ff.

52. *Hua III* 331/351 (*Id I* § 143). ("Als 'Idee' [im Kantischen Sinn] ist gleichwohl die vollkommene Gegebenheit vorgezeichnet – als ein ... a priori bestimmtes Kontinuum von Erscheinungen.... Dieses Kontinuum bestimmt sich näher als all-

seitig unendliches, in allen seinen Phasen aus Erscheinungen desselben bestimmbaren X bestehend, derart ... daß jede beliebige Linie desselben in der stetigen Durchlaufen einen einstimmigen Erscheinungszusammenhang ergibt ... in welchem das eine und selbe immerfort gegebene X sich kontinuierlich-einstimmig 'näher' und niemals 'anders' bestimmt.")

53. *Hua XVIII* 188 (*P B* 185). ("Es ist danach eine Wahrnehmung möglich, welche in einem Schauen die ganze Welt, die überschwengliche Unendlichkeit von Körpern wahrnimmt. Natürlich ist diese ideale Möglichkeit keine reale, die für irgendein empirisches Subjekt angenommen werden könnte, zumal solches Schauen ein unendliches Kontinuum des Schauens wäre: einheitlich gedacht eine Kantische Idee.")

54. *Hua III* 329/349 (*Id I* § 142). ("Prinzipiell entspricht [im Apriori der unbedingten Wesens allgemeinheit] jedem 'wahrhaft seienden' Gegenstand die Idee eines möglichen Bewußtseins, in welchem der Gegenstand selbst originär und dabei vollkommen adäquat erfaßbar ist. Umgekehrt, wenn diese Möglichkeit gewährleistet ist, ist eo ipso der Gegenstand wahrhaft seiend.")

CHAPTER FOUR

Phenomenology and the Absolute

We have seen in the last chapter that a phenomenological understanding of truth effectively undercuts the extreme skepticism engendered by Cartesian objectivism, a skepticism which holds any rational justification of belief to be impossible. However, in the absence of a further demonstration that at least some *Evidenz* is absolute, Husserl's theory of truth remains compatible with a more moderate skepticism, one according to which all our beliefs are or might be false, even if rationally justified to some limited degree. Moreover, this potential weakness of Husserl's analysis in relation to skepticism will necessarily weaken it in relation to relativism as well. For unlike a formal approach (which, as we saw in Chapter One, can show only that relativism is inconsistent, and not that relativism's opposite is correct), a positive overcoming of relativism requires a justification of the possibility of knowledge of non-relative truth. This in turn presupposes a justification of the possibility of knowledge as such. Thus any positive overcoming of relativism can be no stronger than the overcoming of skepticism which supports it.

The Husserlian response to the epistemic critique reaches its high point in its analysis of the *Evidenz* attained by phenomenology itself, and it is upon the success of this analysis that the overcoming of skepticism ultimately depends. Phenomenology stands for Husserl as the realm of the absolute, in comparison to which he holds not only natural science but even logic and mathematics to rest on shaky ground. Indeed, much of the later development of the phenomenological method, including Husserl's rejection of the uneasy realism of the *Logical Investigations*, and the turn to the transcendental and the reductions, can be seen as the consequence of his systematic search for absolute *Evidenz*.[1] At the same time, absolute *Evidenz* functions not only as an end within the Husserlian project, but also as a means for establishing the foundations of other domains of knowledge, and the foundations of the sciences in particular. Thus the methodological developments at work in the transition from the *Logical Investigations* to *Ideas I* are shaped by two guiding aims: to provide a foundation for knowledge, both in general and in its specifically scientific forms; and to do so on a basis which is itself absolutely evident (transcendental phenomenology).

Yet to understand these determining motives of the transcendental method it is crucial to grasp 'foundation' in the proper sense. In particular, Husserl's phenomenological foundationalism is importantly different from the mathematical-logical foundationalism of Descartes. The aim of Husserl's foundationalism is not to provide a conclusive proof that specific knowledge-claims from domains other than phenomenology are in fact true, but rather to elucidate the sources of these claims in intuition, and so to clarify their sense, their justification, and also the limits of this justification. By contrast, for the early Descartes (e.g., of the *Rules*), knowledge is identical to absolute certainty, and thus to provide a foundation for the sciences can mean nothing other than to extend the certainty of immediately evident first principles to all scientific principles and results.[2] And while the later Descartes finds it necessary to weaken this equation and to introduce the category of 'moral' or pragmatic certainty, at least for lower-order principles of the natural sciences, even in his mature period (e.g., the *Meditations*, the *Principles*) Descartes still attempts to found the existence of the external world by extending the absolute certainty of the *cogito* to it. However, although Husserl also seeks to 'found' knowledge of the physical world, he does not attempt a definitive demonstration of the existence of the world, and moreover he believes such a demonstration impossible. As we saw in Chapter Three, Husserl argues that *Evidenz* of the physical world is always mediated by *Abschattungen* and syntheses of fulfillment, and therefore knowledge of it can only take the form of provisional, partial justification and never absolute certainty.

In many respects, Husserl's foundationalism is closer to that of Kant than to Descartes'. Similarly to Kant, for Husserl the problem of knowledge is not so much to establish certainty, but to make comprehensible how experience directed towards objects (i.e., intentionality) is possible at all, even in a fallible form. For both Kant and Husserl face the post-Cartesian question: given that all we ever have are our subjective representations, how is it nonetheless possible to have an experience of something objective, something which is (experienced as) independent of these representations? Kant solves this problem by arguing that the subjective manifolds of apprehension are able to take on the character of representing *objects*, existing apart from consciousness, only because these manifolds are subordinated by the subjective faculties of cognition to certain fixed rules or rule-forms, thereby ordering the contents of these manifolds in objective space and time. These rules constitute a priori conditions for the possibility of the experience of (what present themselves as) objects, and therefore for the (phenomenal) being of the objects themselves.[3]

Thus at least in the case of knowledge of sensible objects, the Kantian foundation of knowledge serves as much to clarify the very nature and limits of knowledge as to demonstrate its certainty. At the same time, Kant does claim a privileged epistemic status for those principles which are the a priori conditions of objects as such, and consequently for his founding theory itself. Husserl's analysis is similar to Kant's in both of these respects, although, as we will see in what follows, it remains importantly different in others.

In this chapter I present a critical evaluation of the *Evidenz* attained by phenomenology proper, the method conceived by Husserl to supplant the Kantian transcendental foundation of knowledge. The discussion will begin with a reconstruction of the essential elements of the phenomenological method, including the epoché and noetic-noematic analysis. This will then make possible an elucidation of the sense in which the results produced by this method are 'absolute', both in terms of certainty (against skepticism) and intersubjectivity (against relativism).

1. TRANSCENDENTAL PHENOMENOLOGY AND THE PATH TO ABSOLUTE *EVIDENZ*

1.1 *Inner Perception, Immanent Perception, and the Epoché*

The theory of the epoché, the transcendental attitude, and immanent perception presented in *Ideas I* contains the core of Husserl's justification for the claim that phenomenology attains *Evidenz* which is absolute. The move from descriptive to transcendental phenomenology is sometimes thought to be an abrupt and dramatic one. Yet far from representing a radical change, the line of thinking that will lead to the transcendental attitude is clear as early as the appendix to the *Logical Investigations* entitled "Outer and Inner Perception: Physical and Psychical Phenomena." Here Husserl traces the evolution of the notion of inner perception from Descartes and Locke to Brentano, concluding with a severe critique of the latter. Similarly to Brentano, Husserl is interested in inner perception as a source of absolute insight and absolutely reliable knowledge, and so as the most suitable foundation for other knowledge. However, Husserl attacks Brentano's conception of inner perception on the grounds that the *Evidenz* provided by it is no better than the (obviously deficient) *Evidenz* of outer perception. The *Logical Investigations* appendix identifies the specific sources of dubitability in inner perception as conceived by Brentano, but does not propose an alternative. This alternative is put forward in *Ideas I* in the form of immanent perception (the perception attained by the epoché), which is simply the inner perception of Brentano with the previously identified sources of dubitability put out of play.

According to the *Logical Investigations* appendix, common sense distinguishes between inner and outer perception in terms of the self: inner perception is perception of the self; outer perception, perception of what is other than the self. However, this distinction is insufficiently precise, because according to a naïve understanding, the self includes the body, something which is 'outer'. Husserl maintains that Descartes and Locke refine the common sense distinction by basing it on: (1) the type of object towards which the perception is directed; (2) the subjective cognitive faculties involved; and (3) the causal origin of the perception. On this version of the inner/outer distinction, an outer perception is one directed towards a physical body; the faculties involved include the organs of sense; and the perception arises from the causal operation of a physical object upon the sense organs, which then transmit this influence to the mind, producing a *cogitatum* or idea. In an inner perception, the objects are the mind's own activities or ideas, and the perceiving faculty is also the mind alone. Here the perception arises from the spontaneous activity of the mind, reflecting upon its own activities or ideas.[4]

Husserl points out that the inner/outer perception distinction as conceived by Descartes and Locke is unsuitable for identifying a domain of epistemically superior perceptions upon which to found other knowledge. This is because the distinction itself contains unjustified presuppositions, such as that the (objectivistically conceived) mind and physical bodies really exist and are distinct. Further, in order to decide whether a given perception is inner or outer, we must determine the nature of the non-phenomenal, objectivist cause of the perception, a determination which will always be speculative rather than self-evident. Thus even if inner perception as conceived by these thinkers were absolutely reliable, the determination of whether a perception is inner or outer would not be so.[5]

Brentano, by contrast, draws the distinction between inner and outer perception purely descriptively, detaching speculative considerations of causal origins and subjective faculties. According to Brentano, physical phenomena are objects and events which have the phenomenal character of being located in space; psychical phenomena (emotions, sensations, perceptions, etc.) are those which present themselves as mental states of a subject, as existing not in space but in consciousness alone. An outer perception is then one which has a physical phenomenon as its intentional object; an inner perception, one which has a psychical phenomenon as its intentional object. The status of the non-phenomenal causes of these perceptions is therefore irrelevant to the distinction as Brentano draws it.[6]

Clearly, Husserl follows Brentano in holding that the inner/outer distinction must be drawn purely descriptively if it is itself to satisfy the criteria of epistemic rigor it is subsequently supposed to enforce. However, Husserl argues that inner perception as conceived by Brentano is not epistemically superior to outer perception, but just as capable of deceiving and in precisely the same ways. As we will see, the crucial point noted by Husserl is that this allegedly 'inner' perception involves the intentional positing of worldly objects, objects existing in (intersubjective) space and time and independently of the specific acts in which they appear. But this means that the intention will always exceed the given in an act of inner perception, and this in such a way that the resulting perception will be no more adequate than a perception of an outer thing.

This objection can be elucidated by way of the example employed by Husserl in the *Logical Investigations* appendix: the perception of a toothache. According to Brentano, the perception of a toothache is an inner perception because a sensation of pain is a psychical state of a subject, an event existing in consciousness only and not in space. It would then follow that for Brentano this perception is infallible or at least significantly more reliable than the perception of outer things.

However, Husserl argues that in an ordinary perception of a toothache, the tooth itself is intended as a physical object with a specific location in intersubjective space, and the pain as well is intended as located in a specific part of an intersubjectively perceptible human body. In other terms, what might be characterized as 'beliefs' about the ontological status of the painful tooth become incorporated into the intentional constitution of the object perceived. However, as discussed above,[7] each of these intentional references to the physical world (e.g., a tooth, a human body) posits a manifold of further perceptions which must be possible if the initial perception is accurate. The complete intention is not adequately fulfilled in an isolated inner perception, nor could it be so by any finite series of perceptions. The 'inner' perception of a toothache can therefore deceive in precisely the same way as an outer perception. For perhaps the tooth is in fact a healthy tooth, or perhaps the tooth is in fact missing, in which case the further perceptions specified by the initial intention would be *im*possible, and the initial perception would itself prove to be an illusion. Such a case would be completely analogous to one of a deceptive outer perception in which, for example, I perceive a house although no house in fact exists. Therefore inner perception as conceived by Brentano does not provide the desired superior degree of *Evidenz*.[8]

Husserl does not undertake an elaboration of his own conception of genuinely self-evident 'inner' or immanent perception in the context of the *Logical Investigations* discussion. However, his critique of Brentano serves to trace the line of thinking which eventually leads to the notion of the immanent as presented in *Ideas I*, and to the phenomenological reduction as the method for attaining perception of the immanent realm. This notion is attained largely by the removal of the source of dubitability in inner perception as understood by Brentano: the implicit intentional positing of objects in the world. In the *Logical Investigations* example, an 'inner' perception of pain is shown to contain such implicit 'outer' intentional affirmations. Husserl argues more generally in *Ideas I* that an implicit positing of objects in the world arises in every case of Brentanoian inner perception because of the way the *subject* is intended. For although Brentano (much as the early Husserl) practices a neutral descriptive approach on the methodological level, he retains an underlying empiricist ontology of subjectivity, holding that the subject is an empirical subject, a human being with a body in objective space, and existing independently of the conscious processes in which the self appears to itself. This underlying ontology then infiltrates the allegedly neutral, completely self-evident content of inner perception itself. For an inner perception, according to Brentano, is a perception of one's own psychical state. But here the self is intentionally constituted as an empirical self, a person who is not only a subject but also an object in the world. The worldly objectivity of the self as intended means that although the perception is 'inner', the perception posits the existence of the world and objects in it. This perception will therefore necessarily be *inadequate*, failing to substantiate in intuition all that is posited in the intention. Husserl's strategy to produce genuinely adequate perception is then to 'bracket' all intentional positings which exceed the fully given (and thus all existence in the world), whether these positings relate to objects or to the subject itself.

It is the search for adequacy – the perfectly or maximally 'full' intuition upon which to found knowledge – that leads Husserl to replace the traditional notion of inner perception with his own conception of immanent perception. Husserl develops the notion of the immanent in *Ideas I*, where he employs at least three different guiding conceptions. According to the first, an immanent perception is one directed to a moment of the perceiving (the *cogitatio*) itself; a transcendent perception, to something over and above the perceiving and its parts.[9] This characterization is the one closest to the traditional notion that inner perception is of what is 'inside' and outer perception of what is 'outside', and it justifies the language of 'immanence' and 'transcendence'. However, in other moments Husserl emphasizes the epistemic motif and tends to equate immanent with adequate perception, and transcendent with inadequate.[10] Finally, once Husserl has established the epoché as the method for obtaining perception of the immanent, he then tends automatically to class any post-epoché perception as immanent, and any natural, 'worldly' perception as transcendent. Of course these various characterizations need not be incompatible, and the aim of the distinction will be accomplished if the epoché does indeed provide the desired 'absolute' *Evidenz*.

As noted above, the epoché functions by taking a given complex of perceptions and then 'suspending judgment' regarding whatever in the intention is not fully given in intuition. We can elucidate this by way of Husserl's example in *Ideas I*, in which we gaze with pleasure at a blossoming apple tree in a garden.[11] In the natural attitude, the apple tree is a three-dimensional object in intersubjective space, the pleasure is experienced as the state of an empirical human being, and further, certain causal relations are implicitly posited as holding between the tree on the one hand and the perceiving person on the other. Of course, this complex state of affairs is inadequately given in perception. According to Husserl, to transform this inadequate, transcendent perception into an adequate, immanent one, we 'bracket' the reality of the world, which means: we suspend participation in the thetic attitude positing those elements of the intended state of affairs which exceed the fulfillment provided. Thus, for example, we no longer straightforwardly participate in the attitude that posits that what appears to be a tree in intersubjective space is indeed so; or that the pleasure intended as a state of a full-blooded human being is in fact such; and finally, that certain causal relations exist between the perceived state of affairs and the person. It should be noted that this suspension of intentional affirmation is not merely an alteration of belief, a higher-order change in judgment that leaves the content of the perceptions themselves unaffected. Rather, the change in intentional attitude produces a corresponding change in perceptual content; or, in Husserlian language, the intentional contents are now constituted differently. Thus after the epoché, one is directed towards a new domain of entities (phenomena). Prior to the epoché, the intentional object is an ordinary apple tree, a physical thing with a back side, existing independently of this particular perception, available for perception by other observers. After the epoché, the intentional object is an 'apple-tree phenomenon' which exists only in this perception, a phenomenon which 'purports' to have a back side, and which is 'as if' it could be perceived by other persons, where these 'purportings' themselves have a motivating basis in the specific full content of the phenomenon. Similarly, the natural self-experience of oneself as a empirical person is transformed into an experience which 'purports to' be of a human being in the world. Here it is important to emphasize that Husserlian bracketing, unlike the hyperbolic doubt of Descartes, does not negate or deny the existence of the world, nor attempt to count all that is merely dubious as in fact false. Rather, in the epoché the ordinary intentional affirmation of worldly reality is simply suspended, and replaced by a neutral thetic attitude.[12] The end result is that a third type of entity is brought into view, an entity which is neither a physical object nor a psychical state of a human being. This new phenomenon has the same intuitive ('full') content as the original one, but a different ontological status and intentional nexus. And it is this phenomenon, according to Husserl, that is given with 'absolute' *Evidenz*.

Yet characteristically, immediately after emphasizing the adequacy of immanent, post-epoché perceptions as opposed to transcendent ones, Husserl notes that even here the fulfillment is less than perfect. The inadequacy of immanent perception is bound up with the general problematic of inner time consciousness. Because even a bracketed phenomenon is caught up in the unceasing temporal flow, the only way to examine this phenomenon is to retain the fleeting content in memory. But then what is actually given in perception is not the momentary phenomenon itself, but a retentive memory of it, separated from the original by varying and phenomenologically apparent temporal distances. Thus Husserl writes:

"Even an *Erlebnis* is not, and never can be perceived in its completeness, adequately grasped in its total unity. It is essentially a flux which we – directing our reflective gaze towards it – can swim after, starting from the now, while the stretches left behind are lost to perception. We are conscious of what has just concluded only in the form of retention, or in the form of a backwards-glancing remembrance."[13]

However, this imperfection in the adequacy of even immanent perception does not lead Husserl to conclude that he has drawn the immanent/transcendent distinction incorrectly, or that immanent perception is not the one sought for the 'absolute' foundations of knowledge. Rather, he argues that the inadequacy of immanent perception is of an entirely different nature from that of the transcendent. The one arises from the flowing temporality to which *all* perception, immanent and transcendent alike, is subject; the other from the mediated (i.e., '*abgeschattet*') mode of presentation proper to transcendent perception alone. Thus despite its imperfection in comparison with a limit idea of adequacy, immanent perception affords a markedly *higher* degree of adequacy than does transcendent perception, and therein lies its epistemic value.

Thus the immanent realm uncovered by the epoché remains the archetypical domain of adequacy, and the proper sphere of phenomenology itself, despite Husserl's own clear awareness that adequacy in the strictest sense is unattainable even here. I think the only conclusion to draw from this is that as in the case of the 'in itself', 'adequacy' in the Husserlian usage cannot be interpreted strictly and absolutely, but only comparatively and relationally. Thus, for example, when Husserl claims that perception after the epoché gives the phenomenon adequately, absolutely, and as itself, this should not be taken as a claim that such perception is flawlessly, ideally adequate, but rather that it is *comparatively* adequate, e.g., in comparison to natural or any other concretely imaginable forms of perception.

Indeed, despite the appearance of a paradox, I do not think it inaccurate to hold that in Husserl's usage, the qualifier 'absolute' has a *relative* character. It would be difficult to find a passage in which Husserl openly states as much, although, as we saw in Chapter Three, he does admit that the phenomenological 'in itself' is to be interpreted relatively.[14] The 'relative' or relational nature of Husserl's conception of absolute givenness can be inferred from his constant juxtaposing of claims, on the one hand, that a particular phenomenon is 'absolutely' self-evident or an 'absolute' in-itself, with claims, on the other, that the very same phenomenon is not quite absolute. If absolute givenness were non-relational, then a particular phenomenon would either be absolutely given or not. If, however, it is relational (as I believe), then whether a particular phenomenon is absolutely given will depend upon the other models of givenness to which it is being compared in a specific instance. A relational conception of absolute givenness could even be thought to be a *consequence* of a phenomenological approach. For interpreted phenomenologically, the assertion that a phenomenon is absolutely given can mean only that it *appears* absolutely given. But the appearance of absolute givenness will in turn be conditioned by the other (real or imagined) sorts of perceptions used as a basis of comparison. Thus, for example, compared to a natural perception of a house, the bracketed perception of an *Erlebnis* presents itself as absolutely adequate. However, compared to the idea of a non-flowing perception, even a post- epoché *Erlebnis* does not present itself as *absolutely* adequate, but merely as adequate to an unusually high degree, and possibly even to a *maximal* degree.

Thus in light of the in-principle impossibility of a perception which is absolutely adequate in the strictest sense (i.e., in relation to the intention), the absoluteness of adequacy must be measured in relation to other possible types of perception. Here, as before, Husserl's analysis would be less misleading if he had chosen the term 'maximal' instead of 'absolute' to characterize the adequacy of immanent perception.

1.2 *Noetic-Noematic Analysis: Husserl and Kant*

The epoché opens up the domain of intentional contents which is to form the field for (transcendental) phenomenological research. Were Husserl interested solely in adequacy as an end in itself, then his phenomenology could content itself with descriptions of arbitrary reduced phenomena. However, as noted above, for Husserl adequacy functions also as a means, a desideratum for the foundation of other knowledge. Husserl's further development of the phenomenological method may be characterized as an effort to provide an 'absolutely' self-evident means for specifying the structures which, as Kant noted, are necessary conditions for the possibility of the perception of objects, and so for the (phenomenological) existence of objects themselves. This method consists in the descriptive investigation of noetic-noematic correlations, after the epoché.

Husserl points out that the immanent domain as revealed by the epoché can be examined in two different ways, and correspondingly, that it presents itself as containing two different types of intentional contents. Examined one way, this realm contains *Erlebnisse*, intuitively full moments or experiencings comprising the '*reell*' content of the conscious stream. Examined the other way, this realm contains bracketed transcendent entities, entities of which the immanent *Erlebnisse* could be interpreted as apprehensions. For example, in a reduced perception of a house, the *Erlebnis* contains only the *Abschattung* in its full content and taken as the object of the perception itself, without any intentional reference to some further object of which it is the *Abschattung*. By contrast, the reduced transcendent also contains intentional references to sides and aspects which do not appear, although these references are bracketed. It should also be emphasized that the bracketed transcendent object, unlike the corresponding actually transcendent one, is itself *immanent* in consciousness in an important sense. The bracketed transcendent object is merely the correlate of the bracketed *Erlebnisse*, and not something (thought as) actually existing in the world, independent of its being thought or perceived in consciousness. Thus the bracketed object exists insofar as it is intended and precisely as it is intended, which is not the case for the transcendent one. For example, a transcendently perceived house may fail to exist, may prove to be an illusion, or prove to exist differently from the way in which it is intended. By contrast, once the house is bracketed it belongs to experience purely as an 'as if', as an intentional object with a certain descriptive character *defined* by the way in which it is intended in this particular experience. Thus even if the transcendent house is an illusion, this would not affect the bracketed one (its character or its existence) in the slightest. However, while the bracketed object is immanent in consciousness in this sense, Husserl emphasizes that it is not immanent in the same manner as the pure *Erlebnisse*. The pure *Erlebnisse* are one with the flowing conscious stream, contained *'reell'* within it (i.e., in an intuitively full manner, without even bracketed references to parts which exceed the given). The bracketed object is contained not *'reell'* within consciousness, but only intentionally, as the appearing object as such, with its transcendence suspended. Husserl sets forth the two sides of the reduced realm as follows:

> "Thus on the one side, we have to distinguish the parts and moments which we find through a **constitutive [*reelle*] analysis** of the immanent experience, an analysis in which we treat the experience as an object like any other, inquiring into its parts or the non-independent moments upon which it is constitutively [*reell*] founded. On the other side, however, the intentional experience is consciousness of something, and it is so according to its essence, for example, in the form of memory, judgment, volition, etc. Thus we can inquire into what can be said along essential lines from the side of this 'of something'."[15]

Husserl terms analysis which is directed towards the pure 'experiencings' *(Erlebnisse)*, 'noetic', and analysis which is directed towards the bracketed transcendent entity (that which the pure *Erlebnisse* are consciousness *of*), 'noematic'. Phenomenology is then concerned with investigating the immanent realm from these two sides, as well as the correlations between the two; that is, with what Husserl terms the 'noetic-noematic correlations'.

Finally, because the aim of phenomenology is not to give a descriptive account of immanent concrete particulars, but rather one of the *essential* principles governing noetic-noematic relations, the analysis is to be carried out eidetically. The immanent experiencings and intentional objects brought into view by the epoché are to be intended not as concrete particulars but as 'ideal' – as types whose tokens are just these concrete, particular *Erlebnisse* and their intentional objects. (This change in intentional attitude is the 'eidetic reduction'.) Phenomenology is then directed to specifying the essential characteristics of the pure *Erlebnisse* 'correlated' with an intentional object as fixed by a given intention; that is, it provides a descriptive specification of what is required in a complex of *Erlebnisse* for this complex to be able to be apprehended as an experience of an object meeting this intention. According to Husserl, the resulting set of descriptive specifications constitutes the a priori conditions for the possibility of the perception of an object of the type defined by this intention, and therefore of a priori conditions for the (phenomenological) existence of an object of this kind. Thus Husserl writes in the *Encyclopedia Britannica* article:

"For example, the phenomenology of the perception of bodies is not a report about factually occurring or to be expected perceptions. Rather, it is the setting forth of the invariant structural system without which perception of a body or a synthetically harmonious manifold of perceptions of one and the same body would be inconceivable."[16]

Here Husserl's guiding thought is that in order for a perception to occur which even purports to be a perception of an object, certain conditions must be satisfied. This is so that the flowing contents of the subjective stream of consciousness can be apprehended *as* perceptions of an object, something existing 'apart' from them, or only intentionally 'in' them. These conditions provide a descriptive characterization of what a manifold of *Erlebnisse* would have to 'look like' in order to be apprehended as an experience of an object of a certain type, or a temporally extended experience in which the (numerically) *same* object is given in different ways. If no such conditions existed, perception of this kind of entity would not be possible, since it would not be possible to distinguish between the flowing subjective *Erlebnisse* and the enduring, intersubjective object as that of which they are subjective apprehensions.

Husserl's obvious predecessor along this particular path of philosophical inquiry is Kant. It is useful to compare the Kantian analysis to the Husserlian one in order to clarify the distinctive features of Husserl's phenomenology. A clear grasp of the differences between Husserl and Kant is also crucial to understanding Husserl's efforts to overcome the variety of relativism either affirmed or engendered by Kant himself.

For Kant as well as for Husserl, the a priori is the answer to the crucial question of how the contents of consciousness can take on a reference to an object. Or to phrase this question in more Kantian language, how can a distinction and a relation be established between the subjective manifold of apprehension (for Husserl, the noeses) and the appearance or represented object (for Husserl, the noema)? The Kantian response is that the manifolds of apprehension take on a reference to an object because and only because the subjective faculties subordinate them to rules. These rules are then the a priori conditions for the possibility of experience of objects. Thus Kant writes:

"We have representations in us, and we can become conscious of them. But however far-reaching this consciousness may be, and however precise and accurate, we still have only representations... How, then, does it come about that we attach an object to these representations, and so, in addition to their subjective reality, as modifications, attribute I know not what kind of objective reality to them? ... If we investigate what new characteristic **reference to an object** confers upon our representations, and what dignity they thereby receive, then we find that it results only in making the connection of representations in a certain way necessary, and subordinating these representations to a rule; and conversely, that only insofar as a certain order in time is necessary for our representations do they acquire objective meaning."[17]

One example of such a rule, according to Kant, is the principle of causality. Kant demonstrates the necessity of this rule – that is, its role in making intentional reference to objects possible – as follows. How, he asks in the Second Analogy, is it possible for us to distinguish between subjective and objective succession, and so to experience a change in the content of perception not merely as a change in the subject, but as a change in the object? Put in other terms, how is a perception (which presents itself as) of an event, an *objective* succession, possible? Kant's response to this question is that perception of an event is possible only where the manifold of apprehension is subordinated by the faculties of cognition to the principle of causality. The crucial difference between a subjective and an objective succession, according to Kant, is that an objective succession is represented as necessary: its order is represented as tied down. But a cause just is something upon which something else follows necessarily in time. By representing the second element of a succession of apprehension as caused by something in the time of the first element, the temporal order of the succession becomes represented as necessary and irreversible, and therefore 'objective'. Thus, concludes Kant, the application of the conception of causality is an a priori condition for the possibility of experience of objects (in this case, of an event), and hence for their 'existence'.[18]

Husserl shares the general Kantian position in many respects. In particular, he agrees with Kant that: (1) knowledge is of objects satisfying the conditions for the possibility of experience, and not of things as they are in themselves, as conceived by objectivists (transcendental realists); (2) perception which presents itself as perception of something objective, existing apart from its actual appearance to consciousness, is possible only on the basis of certain a priori structures; and (3) knowledge of these a priori structures is in some sense privileged as compared with ordinary, straightforward knowledge of the perceived objects themselves.

However, in other respects, Husserl differs sharply with the analysis of Kant. For while Husserl suggests that Kant grasped the nature of intentionality and the relation between subjectivity and objectivity more accurately than any previous thinker, he also criticizes Kant as a dogmatic rationalist, a subjectivist, and as lacking a proper method. The most frequent target of attack is Kant's method, the manner in which he derives and justifies the a priori, which includes the specific Table of Categories, list of principles, and subjective cognitive faculties. Husserl characterizes the Kantian method as regressive, hypothetical, and even mythical, rather than intuitive and descriptive. Thus he writes in the *Crisis*:

"In fact Kant does fall into his own kind of mythical discourse, one whose words do indeed refer to something subjective, but to a mode of the subjective which we are in principle incapable of making intuitive to ourselves, whether by factual examples or through genuine analogies.... What would be required is a regressive method fundamentally and essentially different from Kant's own, which rests on unquestioned and apparently obvious assumptions; not a mythically and constructively inferring method, but a thoroughly intuitively disclosing one ..."[19]

In order to understand these criticisms of the Kantian method it is useful first to consider a related line of critique developed in the *Crisis*: Husserl's critique of Kant as a 'dogmatic' rationalist. Here Husserl charges Kant with remaining too much in the post-Cartesian rationalist tradition of Leibniz and Wolff, and consequently lacking the radicalness of British empiricists such as Hume. According to Husserl, Kant – much as the rationalists – simply takes for granted the validity of the 'truths of reason', including the principles of logic and mathematics. Husserl also maintains that Kant also never really doubts *that* valid knowledge of the world is possible, and that his problem is only to show *how* it is possible. That is, Kant's problem is: given that the truths of reason (mathematics, logic) are valid, how can these truths guarantee knowledge of things? Kant solves this problem by holding that the intuitively appearing world is a construct of the same faculties that create mathematics and logic. Reason then has two cognitive functions: its systematic self-explication (which yields logic and mathematics); and the rationalization of sensation (which yields the objective spatio-temporal world of phenomena).[20]

In this context Husserl also suggests that Hume is a more radical thinker than Kant, who presupposes so many things that Hume takes to be enigmas.[21] Kant, it is alleged, presupposes not only logic and mathematics, but even the lifeworld (the intuitively appearing world) itself. Now this latter claim could be interpreted to mean that, according to Husserl, the Kantian analysis of the subjective construction of experience applies only to the natural-scientific world, whereas Kant (unlike Hume, or Husserl himself) takes the being-for-us of the phenomenal world for granted.[22] However, this interpretation is clearly incorrect as an interpretation of Kant, and is also irreconcilable with Husserl's insistence that Kant takes the phenomenal world to be constituted by the subject.[23] Rather, I think that Husserl's charge that Kant presupposes the phenomenal world can only mean that Kant takes the *validity* of the phenomenal world for granted. That is, while Hume is willing seriously to doubt the existence of even a phenomenal world apart from our experience of it, and to question the validity of our judgments concerning anything objective, Kant never entertains such doubts. Instead, according to Husserl, Kant presupposes that there really is a phenomenal world, that there really are objects and not only subjective apprehensions, and that at least most or some of our judgments concerning these are valid. He then seeks ('regressively', or speculatively and hypothetically) for the conditions of the possibility of the validity of such judgments. The resulting Kantian justification of the a priori synthetic principles has the form: these principles must be true, because otherwise valid experience of objects would not be possible. The argument is then truly a transcendental/deductive and not a descriptive/phenomenological one: the demonstration of the a priori proceeds by arguing from the (presupposed) validity of experience to the validity of the a priori, rather than by merely exhibiting the a priori in intuition.

One could wonder whether Kant really does presuppose the validity of world- and object-experience, as Husserl alleges. For example, does the Second Analogy presuppose that we *really* have experience of changes in the state of objects, or only that we have experiences which *purport* to be of changes in the state of objects (something not even Hume would deny)? Certainly here it is important to interpret the 'real' objectivity and validity presupposed by Kant phenomenologically (or phenomenally), in terms of actual and possible perceptions, and not objectivistically. In the context of such an interpretation, to say that there 'really' are objects or objective successions, or that a judgment concerning something objective is valid, is to say that the further possible perceptions implicitly posited by this judgment are actualizable. Similarly, to assert that an event experience is valid is to claim that what purports to be a change in an object would not 'break up' in the further course of experience and turn into, for example, an illusion or hallucination (and hence a mere change in the subject).

Yet the presupposition of the reality of the phenomenal world in even the phenomenal sense of reality would be considered illegitimate by Husserl. For as we have seen in the previous chapter, Husserl argues that the validity of all experience of the world and of worldly objects must ultimately remain doubtful, so that we can never know with certainty that the world or anything objective really exists, even in the phenomenological sense of existence. The a priori therefore cannot receive its validity regressively from the validity of world-experience, since the validity of the latter cannot be presupposed.[24]

Husserl holds that this lack of methodological clarity leads in turn to an error on Kant's part as to the *source* of the a priori. For Kant roots the a priori in the contingent subjective faculties of cognition: experience has the form it does simply because we happen to possess the faculties of thought and intuition we do. Yet Husserl attacks the entire Kantian theory of the subjective faculties as 'mythical'; which here means: hypothetical, and not even open to philosophical justification via intuition. For again, the question remains: how is it that we attain knowledge of the nature of these faculties? In particular, how does Kant discover that the faculties are of just the number and kind he specifies, with precisely these categorial concepts, and further, that these faculties really exist and exercise causal influence over the raw data of experience? Husserl further suggests that Kant's theory of the faculties is the result of his dependence upon a Lockean psychology, and its naturalizing conception of the soul as 'wax tablet' and an agent with powers that combine the intuitive data received upon this tablet.[25]

In less polemical moments, Husserl does concede that the Kantian derivation or 'deduction' of the categories and the principles does contain some properly phenomenological elements, especially in the first edition of the First Critique, and that in general Kant's method is a mixture of logical, hypothetical, and phenomenological reasoning.[26] However, in contrast to Kant, Husserl emphasizes that the method for establishing the a priori must be *descriptive*, limiting itself to a self-evident account of the correlations between noeses (the manifold of appearances) and noema (the object).[27] In eidetic analysis, the correlation between noema and noeses (i.e., what is required in a complex of contents in order for it to be able to count as a presentation of an object of a given type) actually appears, and is not merely hypothesized. In addition to allowing a specification of the a priori, this procedure also provides a clarification of what knowledge *is* by showing the manner in which knowledge is accomplished in the case of a particular entity. That is, the phenomenological analysis shows how it is that the intuitive *Erlebnisse* come to have the meaning 'experience of an object of type x', and so how consciousness of something objective is attained.

The phenomenological elucidation of the a priori takes place without reference to a theory of the subjective faculties of cognition, hypothetical or otherwise. Whereas Kant roots the a priori in the contingent subjective faculties, Husserl holds that the a priori is contained in meaning formations (in the noetic-noematic structures themselves) and that this is the source of the a priori is itself evident in eidetic analysis.[28] A further result of Husserl's position is that, in contrast to the Kantian categories, the a priori structures do not constitute a very limited and predetermined set. Rather, for each type of experience and objectivity, another set of such structures is presupposed, and can be investigated phenomenologically. At the same time, however, Husserl emphasizes in *Ideas I* that it is of primary interest in phenomenology to undertake noetic-noematic investigations of the most basic, general categories of objects and objectivities in each of the various ontological domains (e.g., objects such as body, number, nature, spirit, etc.).

We have seen that Husserl criticizes the Kantian method as regressive. However, the Husserlian method is also a 'regressive' or a 'questioning-back' method in that it takes certain concrete experiences and experienced objects as given and then seeks the conditions for the possibility of such experiences.[29] The difference between Husserl and Kant here is that Husserl does not presuppose that these experiences are valid, nor that objects or the world really exist, even in the phenomenological sense of existence. The resulting 'justification' of the a priori therefore does not demonstrate its absolute necessity but only its contingent necessity. That is, it is shown that *if* experiences (which purport to be) of objects of a certain character are to take place, *then* these experiences must be governed by specific noetic-noematic correlations. The actual occurrence of the specified a priori correlations is contingent upon the nature of experience itself.[30]

Thus the main import of Husserl's noetic-noematic analysis is neither to demonstrate the absolute necessity of specific a priori principles, nor to demonstrate that what purports to be experience of worldly objects really is such. Rather, it is to elucidate the very *meaning* of knowledge and objectivity in specific cases, and this by exhibiting the constitution of such meaning in intuition. Against Kant's attempt to ground the validity of knowledge in a theory of subjective faculties, Husserl writes:

"[Kant] overlooked the fact that transcendental philosophy wishes and is permitted to wish nothing other than to elucidate the meaning of knowledge and its validity, and that elucidation here means nothing other than going back to the origin, to *Evidenz*, and so to the consciousness in which all epistemic concepts are made intuitively concrete."[31]

The aim of the phenomenological method of the epoché, the eidetic reduction, and noetic-noematic analysis is to provide an absolutely evident elucidation of the conditions for the possibility of knowledge of objects, and so of their 'being-sense' (*Seinssinn*). In what follows, I will address the issue of whether the *Evidenz* attained by this method is indeed 'absolute'.

2. ADEQUACY AND APODICTICITY

Our previous discussion concluded that phenomenology is the descriptive but eidetic study of noetic-noematic correlations displayed by transcendental (bracketed) consciousness. Here all positing of worldly reality is suspended, and the investigation is limited to an immanent specification of meaning structures, taken purely as phenomena. Clearly, the very method conceived by Husserl insures that phenomenological results will be evident to an unusually high degree. However, in order to evaluate the Husserlian assertion that the *Evidenz* of these results is 'absolute', it is necessary to introduce a distinction glossed over by us in our previous discussions. For Husserl's understanding of absolute givenness contains an important duality: the absolute as adequacy, and the absolute as apodicticity. Thus in asking the question about the absolute nature of specifically phenomenological *Evidenz*, we must ask, which sense of the absolute applies to phenomenology itself?

The two epistemic ideals can be briefly characterized as follows. Adequacy consists in the fullness and completeness of a perception, the exact correspondence of the perceived to what is thought or implied in the intention the perception fulfills. This perfect agreement of the given and the intended is the feature that gives a phenomenon the character of being the very thing itself. Apodicticity, by contrast, is the Husserlian notion of certainty: when *Evidenz* is apodictic it has the character of 'valid now and forever'. Thus adequacy corresponds to the traditional epistemic perfection of clarity and insight; apodicticity, of finality.

Yet although Husserl explicitly distinguishes between the two, in writings prior to the *Cartesian Meditations* he adamantly maintains that they always go hand in hand.[32] The correlation of adequacy and apodicticity has a certain logic to it, given the fundamental Husserlian principle that intuition is to be taken as the ultimate source of truth. It follows directly from this principle that what is fully given in intuition is also certain. Consequently, a judgment which limits itself strictly to the given (i.e., an adequate judgment) will be apodictic as well. Conversely, the sole authentic ground for certainty is complete insight, attained through givenness. Therefore adequacy is both necessary and sufficient for apodicticity.

However, despite the reasonableness of the correlation of adequacy and apodicticity given Husserl's basic intuitionism, the position encounters difficulties at the level of detail. These stem in part from the fact that Husserl develops the notion of apodicticity primarily in the context of eidetic judgments, judgments concerning general meaning structures and the ideal. By contrast, adequacy is a limit concept adapted to the perception of concrete particulars such as physical objects or *Erlebnisse*, objects which have various sides or parts, or which are given by way of *Abschattungen*. It is therefore unclear whether eidetic judgments could be adequately evident to the same degree as concrete particulars, or even what maximal adequacy would mean in the ideal realm. For example, an eidetic judgment such as $1 + 2 = 2 + 1$ does not have sides, parts, or *Abschattungen* in any straightforward sense, and therefore cannot be given more or less adequately in the manner of a sensible thing.

Now it could be held that in the case of eidetic judgments, adequacy is a function of the adequacy of the concrete intuitive illustrations upon which the eidetic intuition is founded. Yet even where the eidetic analysis is carried out on an immanent foundation (as occurs in the transcendental attitude), additional sources of inadequacy enter in. For example, if I begin with an ordinary perception of a red surface, and then consider this perception immanently, the resulting particular red phenomenon could be said to be *adequately* evident, in that it is not given by way of *Abschattungen*. However, if I now employ this concrete phenomenon to attain an intuition of red in general (i.e., by varying the content in imagination, producing a manifold of various fulfillments of the immanent intention, 'red'), the resulting *Evidenz* is *in*adequate (even relative to the founding intuitive illustration) in two respects. Because of the limits of imagination, I do not produce the entire manifold of possible fulfillments of red, but only a few of these, and even these in a rather 'pale', inadequate way. Further, in order to attain an intuition not merely of red as given in this particular perception, but of the *essence* of red, it is necessary to intuit a content which can present itself identically in an unlimited number of similarly constituted meaning acts. The possibility of infinite, identical repetition belongs to what is intended in any essence, and thus if the fulfillment of the essence is to be adequate, infinite repeatability must also be demonstrated in intuition. Husserl argues that this infinite repeatability does have its own kind of *Evidenz*, manifesting itself in the experience of the 'I can' (i.e., carry out the required meaning acts, without limit).[33] Yet even if it were granted that the *Evidenz* of the 'I can' is apodictic, it is surely not adequate in the limit, maximal sense, which would require an actual realization of the posited infinite number of acts. Thus it is not merely that adequacy in the strictest sense is unattainable for eidetic judgments; rather, even such adequacy as we can attain is of a lesser degree than that of concrete particulars.

Of course, in addition to the difficulty involved in claiming adequacy for eidetic judgments, there is the more general difficulty which Husserl's analysis must confront again and again: namely, that adequacy in the strictest sense is not attainable at all. As discussed in the first section of this chapter, because of the temporal flow of consciousness, even an individual reduced *Erlebnis* is not adequate in the strictest sense. Therefore insofar as Husserl ties apodicticity inextricably to adequacy, the discovery of the unattainability of perfect adequacy necessitates phenomenology's forsaking any claim to apodicticity as well.

Husserl attempts to resolve these difficulties in the *Cartesian Meditations*, where he renounces the position (affirmed or implied repeatedly in earlier writings) that adequacy and apodicticity always accompany each other. Instead, here he maintains that *Evidenz* can be apodictic even if *inadequate*, and further, that apodicticity is the *higher* of the two perfections.[34] Thus Husserl's later position seems to be that the results of phenomenological inquiry are apodictic but not adequate, at least not in the strictest or even in the maximal sense (which would be the sense applicable in the case of reduced particular *Erlebnisse*).[35]

Husserl's pronouncements on apodicticity have been unsympathetically received not only in the anti-foundationalist literature at large,[36] but even in the Husserl literature itself.[37] I think the main obstacle to a more sympathetic reception is that these critics do not understand apodicticity phenomenologically, but generally in a quasi-Cartesian sense of certainty. According to this latter interpretation, apodictic *Evidenz* is absolutely infallible, guaranteed for eternity and incapable of being overturned. The apodictically self-evident principles discovered by phenomenology can then be used to form the unchanging foundations of the edifice of knowledge.

Yet Husserl rails against precisely this interpretation of apodicticity in

Formal and Transcendental Logic, holding that it reflects a complete lack of phenomenological analysis. Rather, here he maintains that all forms of *Evidenz* alike are subject to error and deception, and that it is possible that in the further course of experience, what initially presented itself as an apodictic *Evidenz* could be 'refuted' ... by *another* apodictic *Evidenz*:

"Even an *Evidenz* which presents itself as apodictic can reveal itself to be a deception. However, this presupposes a similar *Evidenz* on which the initial one 'breaks up'.... The impediment which may have been continually sensed during this exposition lies solely in the usual, fundamentally wrongheaded interpretation of *Evidenz*, an interpretation made possible by a complete lack of a serious phenomenological analysis of the achievement common to all forms of *Evidenz*."[38]

Some commentators have attempted to salvage their Cartesian interpretations of apodicticity by hypothesizing a significant shift in the Husserlian position. Thus they allege that the later Husserl undermines and perhaps even abandons his foundationalist conception of knowledge, and of philosophy as a science. Similarly, it is maintained that at this later stage Husserl rejects the notion of apodicticity, or at least holds that it is an unattainable ideal. In short, the early Husserl conceives of apodicticity as infallibility, and the later Husserl abandons apodicticity either outright or as an actual attainment.[39]

However, I believe that such interpretations are clearly erroneous. As noted above, in the *Cartesian Meditations* (contemporaneous with *Formal and Transcendental Logic*) Husserl affirms apodicticity to be the primary criterion for scientific knowledge, and of even greater value than adequacy. Further, in *Formal and Transcendental Logic* itself he holds that an apodictic *Evidenz* can be refuted only by *another* apodictic *Evidenz*, which obviously implies that the notion of apodicticity has not been abandoned.

In the most detailed study of adequate and apodictic *Evidenz* to date, Levin attempts to solve these difficulties by suggesting that Husserl employs two distinct notions of apodicticity, a stronger and a weaker one. According to Levin, the strong notion is employed throughout all of Husserl's writings, and is the sole one employed up to the period of *Formal and Transcendental Logic*. By contrast, the weak one is employed in certain passages of the last works. In terms of the strong notion, what is once given as apodictically evident cannot be invalidated by any subsequent *Evidenz*. According to the weak notion, apodictic *Evidenz* appears especially compelling and unshakable, even though one realizes that such *Evidenz* might nonetheless subsequently be overturned. Levin sets out the two notions of apodicticity thus:

"According to the strong sense, apodictic knowledge is beyond all corrigibility, legitimated and guaranteed with the meaning, 'valid now and forever', come what may.... According to some weaker sense, it would merely be evidence of such lucidity and compulsion that, while the evidence is present, one cannot even conceive of doubt or cancellation; but one recognizes with regard to this evidence that, despite its compulsion, it is relative to subsequent evidential positions, and thus in fact may become subject to doubt."[40]

Levin concedes that the weak sense of apodicticity is the one more compatible with the *Formal and Transcendental Logic* passage. He nonetheless affirms that it is the strong sense that is consistently employed by Husserl throughout his earlier writings, and that is the decisive one for Husserl's thought.

Yet contrary to the Levin interpretation, Husserl's conception of apodicticity is phenomenological and not Cartesian, and as such can be compatible only with what Levin terms the 'weak' sense. Interpreted phenomenologically, that an *Evidenz* is apodictic can mean only that it *presents* itself as apodictic, and not that it *is* apodictic 'in reality', in some Cartesian, objectivist sense of the real. Phenomenological apodicticity is experienced, for example, in an intuitive enactment of $1 + 2 = 2 + 1$, or of 'no color without extension'. In such cases, while one carries out the intuitive fulfillment, this fulfillment is so lucid and appears to be of such enduring accessibility that the principle presents itself as always capable of conclusive intuitive demonstration, and never capable of intuitive cancellation. However, this phenomenological indubitability does not provide an absolute *guarantee* that the principle will in fact never be overturned (even though in the self-evident act of judgment, its cancellation is unimaginable).

In light of traditional hermeneutical principles, the temptation is great to hold that Husserl consistently maintains the 'weak', phenomenological sense of apodicticity throughout the various phases of his thought, rather than inexplicably reversing his position in selected passages of later works. However, since Levin's central thesis is that Husserl's notion of apodicticity is unacceptable, he denounces this more charitable interpretation as a thoroughly untenable view. Here Levin offers two lines of argument. The first line consists in the exhibition of numerous passages in which it is allegedly obvious that Husserl intends apodicticity in the strong sense. Rather than reviewing these many passages here, I will counter the Levin argument by selecting the single passage which appears most decisively to support the Levin view, and then demonstrating that, phenomenologically understood, this passage is wholly consistent with the weaker, fallibilist notion of apodicticity.

This apparently decisive passage occurs in an appendix to *Erste Philosophie II*. Here Husserl characterizes apodicticity as follows:

"An apodictic instance of knowledge <is> fully repeatable, with identical validity. When something is once given with apodictic *Evidenz*, this brings with it not only the possibility of recalling that this *Evidenz* was once possessed, but also the necessity of its holding as valid both for now and for all time: final validity."[41]

Now according to Levin, this passage asserts that what once presents itself with apodictic *Evidenz* can never be overturned by any subsequent *Evidenz*. However, this is very far from the case. Rather, examination of the context of this passage reveals that here Husserl is simply investigating the 'eidos' of apodicticity; that is, this passage offers a descriptive account of the features of (phenomenological) apodicticity. An apodictic judgment *presents* itself as capable of being demonstrated in intuition not only in one isolated instance, but again and again, without limit. For example, when a judgment such as $1 + 2 = 2 + 1$ is brought to *Evidenz* by intuitive illustration, this intuitive enactment *appears* fully repeatable; which is to say that it appears that I am able to carry out this demonstration not only at this particular moment, but also (in principle) at any moment, now and forever. The meaning of the *Erste Philosophie* passage is therefore: it belongs to the 'eidos' of apodicticity that in an apodictically evident judgment, the judgment has the descriptive character of 'valid now and forever', so that the intuitive fulfillment presents itself as repeatable *ad infinitum*.

However, this in no way excludes the possibility that a judgment which at one point in time presents itself as an instance of this eidos could subsequently be overturned. At one point in time, the *Evidenz* exhibited by a judgment could have the requisite descriptive character of 'infinitely repeatable', and yet later another *Evidenz* could cause the descriptive character of the first *Evidenz* to change, so that now it presents itself as 'not repeatable', or as 'canceled'. This does not imply that the notion of apodicticity is an incoherent one, but only that it is not guaranteed that what once presents itself as an instance of this eidos will always do so. Nor does it follow that there are no actual instances of apodicticity. Apodicticity is a phenomenon, a descriptive characteristic of judgments and not an objectivistically conceived state of affairs. Hence its existence or non-existence in concrete form can be ascertained only by examination of our judgments and such *Evidenz* as they possess. Further, that it is *possible* for an apparently apodictic judgment to be overturned does not mean that all concrete instances *will* be overturned, but only that their status as apodictic remains open to critical questioning. Thus, correctly interpreted, neither this nor the other passages put forward by Levin demonstrates that prior to *Formal and Transcendental Logic*, Husserl conceived of apodicticity in the sense of an absolute guarantee against fallibility, obviating the need for further criticism or revision.

Levin also presents a second line of argument in favor of his position. According to this second line, Husserl must intend apodicticity in the strong sense, for if apodicticity did not guarantee infallibility, then there would be no distinction between apodictic *Evidenz* and ordinary *Evidenz*, and the entire category of apodicticity would be superfluous. Thus Levin writes:

"Apodicticity must mean, therefore, an evidently guaranteed *infallibility*. If it were to mean a 'weaker' sort of claim, there would be nothing to distinguish it from certainty, plain and simple."[42]

However, because Levin does not recognize the phenomenological nature of apodicticity, he also fails to recognize that apodictic and ordinary *Evidenz* are clearly distinguished from one another phenomenologically. As characterized by Husserl in the passage from *Erste Philosophie II*, apodictic *Evidenz* presents itself as capable of being attained not only at the present moment, but also at any future moment – a characteristic which is not possessed by *Evidenz* of any arbitrary form or degree. Husserl also emphasizes that it is impossible to conceive of apodictic *Evidenz* being overturned. Now while this may seem to contradict the earlier claim that even apodictic *Evidenz* is fallible, the point here seems to be that in the case of apodictic *Evidenz*, it is impossible to imagine in a concrete manner a further positive *Evidenz* which would have the effect of invalidating the present one. Thus even though subsequent invalidation is possible, this possibility is phenomenologically an 'empty' one, a possibility posited without any positive or concrete imaginative illustration to fill it in. By contrast, although there is no reason to believe that ordinary, non-apodictic *Evidenz* will in fact be invalidated, it is at least possible to imagine specific sequences of perceptions which would have this result. Here the possibility of cancellation has a 'non-empty', although unmotivated, phenomenological character. Hence apodictic and non-apodictic *Evidenz* are clearly distinguishable phenomenologically, despite their shared fallibility.

Levin very briefly considers and rejects the possibility of interpreting apodicticity phenomenologically – i.e., in terms of apparent rather than objectivist infallibility – holding that to do so would be psychologistic: "Husserl's repudiation of psychologism makes it plain that we are *not* to understand these locutions in any psychological or subjective sense, referring merely to our relative capacities to *imagine* the evidence other than it is."[43] Yet this dismissal of a phenomenological approach is based upon Levin's incorrect equation of the subjective and the psychological, an equation to which Husserl's entire transcendental analysis is opposed. A psychological explanation roots what appears to consciousness in the contingent cognitive faculties of the subject, e.g., the faculties of a human being. Therefore a psychological account of apodicticity would indeed refer to 'our relative capacities to imagine', as Levin maintains. A phenomenological account of apodicticity is subjective insofar as it considers apodicticity as an actual or possible feature of experience (and hence in relation to subjectivity). Yet this account roots the impossibility of imagining other evidence not in a theory of the subjective faculties but in the phenomena, the contents of experience itself, and therefore it does not relativize this impossibility to 'our relative capacities'.[44]

Levin also protests that if apodicticity is interpreted in the weaker sense, then we cannot know with certainty that an apparently apodictic *Evidenz* 'really' is apodictic (i.e., that it will always appear apodictic in the future).[45] But this can seem to Levin to be a compelling objection to a phenomenological interpretation of apodicticity only because he implicitly demands from Husserl's foundationalism an absolutely unshakable basis for knowledge. Yet contrary to the Levin account, apodictic *Evidenz* as conceived by Husserl cannot be employed to form an absolutely immobile foundation for knowledge, secure for eternity, and in no need of further critical examination. However, at the same time, apodictic *Evidenz* does provide a higher and more perfect degree of *Evidenz* than the ordinary, non-apodictic variety, and indeed, the highest degree of certainty available. Levin is correct to note that the phenomenological conception of certainty has a certain 'weak' character to it, especially when set in contrast to the Cartesian one. Similarly, the foundations established on its basis will continue to be subject to criticism and possible revision. Thus Husserl's analysis demonstrates that foundationalism is not excluded by an anti-dogmatic, critical approach. Indeed, insofar as this approach discovers that there are relatively 'absolute' principles upon which to found other knowledge, it could be argued that a moderate foundationalism is its consequence.

To summarize the results of our discussion, phenomenology is 'absolute' firstly in the sense that it addresses the immanent realm, a realm which is *adequately* given to an exceptionally high degree; and secondly in the sense that the results it achieves, the eidetic specifications of noetic-noematic correlations, are *apodictically* self-evident.

This account grounds and also clarifies Husserl's claim in "Philosophy as

Rigorous Science" that phenomenology in the form of philosophy is 'scientific'. As discussed in Chapter Two, one of Husserl's principal criteria for scientific rigor is the degree and perfection of the *Evidenz* a discipline characteristically achieves for its results. Now because phenomenology is directed towards the immanent rather than the transcendent realm, it attains a higher degree of *Evidenz* than any 'worldly', transcendent-oriented discipline, whether this be a discipline such as physics (directed towards corporeal nature), or empirical psychology (directed towards empirical subjects and empirical consciousness). Further, in later writings Husserl asserts that the perfection of the *Evidenz* attained by phenomenology is superior even to that attained in 'eidetic', non-empirical positive sciences, such as mathematics. This is because, as noted in Chapter Three, virtually all of the *Evidenz* attained in mathematics is of a highly mediated kind, based on chains of reasoning with only certain elements capable of immediate intuitive fulfillment. By contrast, phenomenological inquiry proceeds not by chains of reasoning yielding mediate *Evidenz* as to the accuracy of the results, but rather by attainment of immediate *Evidenz* for each individual result. In addition, as will be discussed further in the next chapter, another relative imperfection of the *Evidenz* of the positive sciences stressed by Husserl in *Formal and Transcendental Logic* and the *Crisis* arises from their dependence upon idealization. Thus at least insofar as degree and perfection of *Evidenz* are taken as the decisive index of rigor, it follows that phenomenology is more 'absolute' than any transcendent-directed discipline, whether empirical or eidetic.

3. INTERSUBJECTIVITY: A FIRST APPROACH

The previous discussion established the sense in which the *Evidenz* of phenomenology itself is absolute, and so Husserl's strongest response to skepticism. In the present section, I turn to the relativism problematic proper, and hence to the issue of intersubjectivity. In Chapter Three it was argued that in the *Prolegomena* Husserl solves the problem of intersubjectivity via the notion of an ideal consciousness. According to this earlier solution, truth is the correlate of the possibility of maximal *Evidenz* for an ideal consciousness, and therefore does not vary from one subject to another. However, a full response to the epistemic critique must show not only that a conception of non-relative truth can be formulated, but also that we can attain knowledge of such truths and their non-relativity. This further question of knowledge was addressed in a preliminary way in Chapter

Three. There it was held that if eidetic *Evidenz* is possible for us then it would also be possible for an ideal consciousness, and therefore that when we attain eidetic *Evidenz*, knowledge of non-relative truth is also attained. But this treatment – following Husserl's own at this stage – ignores the problem of intersubjectivity implicit in the 'for us'. Is the *Evidenz* attained by phenomenology or elsewhere really *Evidenz* 'for us' and not just *Evidenz* 'for me'? And if the *Evidenz* that a judgment is non-relatively true is only *Evidenz* for me, unattainable by differently constituted subjects, is it really non-relative *Evidenz* at all? Consistent critical epistemology requires that if I hold a judgment to be non-relatively true then I also must hold that others can attain knowledge of it. Thus in the end the concept of an ideal consciousness cannot supplant a demonstration of intersubjectivity. In particular, if Husserl's claim that phenomenology overcomes relativism is to hold good, then the results of phenomenological analysis must be not only adequately or apodictically self-evident to the particular subject undertaking the inquiry, but also possible objects of intersubjective consensus.

The discussion in this section will have a negative and a positive part. In the first part, I will show how Husserl's conception of transcendental subjectivity undercuts a prevalent argument that intersubjectivity is *im*possible, an argument based on a dogmatic notion of subjectivity as such. In the second, I will take up the positive phenomenological analysis of intersubjectivity, and a preliminary evaluation of the nature and strength of the *Evidenz* of intersubjectivity itself.

3.1 *Intersubjectivity and Transcendental Subjectivity*

The Husserlian conception of transcendental subjectivity plays an important role in his treatment of the issue of intersubjectivity. As noted in Chapter One, one of the most prevalent arguments in favor of relativism and against the possibility of intersubjectivity depends upon a quasi-Kantian rooting of the a priori in contingent subjective faculties.[46] Where this conception of the subject and the source of the a priori prevails, it could be granted that a phenomenological principle is absolute in the sense of appearing apodictic to one subject, but denied that it would appear apodictic to all subjects.

According to this basic theory of subjectivity, the subject who carries out the epoché and eidetic analysis is a being with a contingent psychological constitution, and an historically conditioned set of concepts, beliefs, and modes of reasoning. All of these contingent features influence the perceptions and meaning formations available to this person, and hence also the so-called 'a priori' structures of this particular world of experience. The possibility of attaining *Evidenz* regarding specific eidetic principles is itself a function of contingent features of the subject, and what appears apodictically self-evident to one person will by no means appear so to another. For example, a sighted person possesses one sort of 'eidos' of a sensible body, from which one complex of noetic-noematic correlations follows. By contrast, a blind person would possess a different such eidos, with a correspondingly different complex of 'absolute' structures, equally apodictic, but only to *him* or to similarly constituted persons.

Thus this critique proceeds by returning to a non-phenomenological attitude, and then pointing out that from this attitude, the subject who carries out the phenomenological inquiry is a person with a specific, contingent physical, psychological, and historical constitution, and that the meaning formations which determine the character of the subject's experience and the results of phenomenological analysis are themselves products of this constitution and its contingent features. Therefore phenomenology is not and cannot be absolute in the sense of being intersubjectively valid, despite the apodicticity of its *Evidenz*.

Yet this critique turns upon the premise that the subject who carries out phenomenological inquiry is indeed an empirical human being, a person with a body governed by certain physical and biological laws, born on a certain date, raised in a certain historical context, influenced by certain ideas, beliefs and practices characteristic of this context. It is only because it is premised that the subject is all these things that it can be held that the meaning formations which appear in the phenomenological reduction are themselves contingent ones, products of a specific physical, psychological, and historical subjective constitution, and so accessible to and valid only for similarly constituted subjects.

Here again we see that the relativist argument turns upon the presupposition of a specific theory of subjectivity. Yet the tacit presupposition that this theory is non-relatively true not only contradicts the basic position that non-relative knowledge is impossible, but also simply presupposes the very possibility of knowledge which is in question, and which phenomenology is designed to demonstrate and to explain. *Before* the sense and the possibility of knowledge of transcendent objects has been elucidated, premises concerning the nature of the subject qua transcendent cannot simply be posited as valid. In order to carry out the demonstration of the possibility of knowledge of the transcendent in a non-circular fashion, it is necessary to begin with the epoché, the suspension of the affirmation of transcendent, worldly existence, and this not only of objects but of the subject as well.

After the epoché the self is a transcendental subject and not an empirical one. Much as a tree, for example, is perceived not as a tree in the world of objective space and time, but as a pure phenomenon immanent in consciousness, so too the subject is no longer perceived as a person with a body in objective space and time, born on a certain date, the product of certain objective historical influences, or as a person as defined by the sciences of anthropology, biology, or empirical psychology. Rather, the self is perceived as a realm of phenomena with a certain structured character, with its existence as an empirical human being not negated but 'bracketed', itself treated as a complex but immanent phenomenon.

The relativist argues that the a priori structures discovered by phenomenology are valid only for the limited cognitive background of the investigating subject. Yet considered phenomenologically, to say that these structures are relative can mean only that they *appear* relative. That is, *phenomenologically* relative structures are structures intentionally constituted with the sense 'a priori structures for this contingent form of experience', or 'valid for this limited cognitive background'. However, because the transcendental self is not constituted in experience as an empirical self with a contingent psychological-historical cognitive background, neither are the noetic-noematic correlations it discovers phenomenologically relativized to this background. And in general, for the a priori structures to be relativized phenomenologically at all, there must be some cognitive faculties (non-relatively) constituted in experience to which they may be relativized. But transcendental subjectivity does not posit itself as having the specific cognitive faculties or background attributed to the self by the empirical sciences, or even by common sense; if for no other reason than because such attributions go far beyond the adequately and apodictically self-evident, and hence claim 'too much'.

Now the empiricist will obviously protest that the subject *really is* a full-blooded person, whether he appears this way to himself or not, and it is absurd to think that what is no more than a mere alteration in reflective attitude could change this basic empirical fact.[47] However, if by 'really' the empiricist here means 'in reality as conceived by objectivism', then this claim must be rejected as employing a pre-critical conception of reality, the flaws of which were treated at length in Chapter Three. If, by contrast, it is held that even phenomenologically considered the subject is really an empirical human being, then this can be granted only in a qualified way. It is unquestionable that in the natural attitude we experience ourselves as beings 'in the world', and possessing a contingent cognitive background. However, this experience of ourselves is inadequate and dubitable in the way of the perception of all transcendents – even though we have no positive motive to believe that it is deceptive, or that it would in fact be overturned by the further course of experience. By contrast, after the phenomenological reduction the self is not given as an empirical human being, but rather as living, streaming consciousness on the basis of which it is possible to interpret or 'constitute' oneself as a human being. To reintroduce the claim at this level that 'really' the self is nonetheless an empirical human being would be both dogmatic and phenomenologically inaccurate. For the existence of the self as an empirical human being is given only very inadequately in experience (e.g., the body is perceived only by way of *Abschattungen*, as in the case of all transcendents). By contrast, the existence of the bracketed self – i.e., the complex of the stream of experiences and the intentional objects of these experiences (experiences which *purport* to be, for example, of a person with a body located in objective space and time) – is given far more adequately and indubitably. Thus while it is true that the subject really is a human being, all this 'really' means when interpreted in the critical-phenomenological sense of reality is that the self can (validly) *apprehend* or constitute itself as a human being, and this on the basis of the immanent *Erlebnisse* given in pure consciousness, and in accordance with the structural requirements for what can count as the appearance of an empirical, human self. However, the subject which *apprehends* itself to be an empirical human being is not itself a human being, but a complex phenomenon with a certain descriptive character.[48]

3.2 *The* **Evidenz** *of Intersubjectivity*

The preceding discussion was purely negative: it showed that a prevalent argument against the possibility of intersubjectivity is based on an inadmissible conception of subjectivity itself. However, this does not yet provide a positive demonstration that intersubjectivity is indeed possible. Accordingly, this chapter will conclude with a preliminary discussion of the resources provided by Husserl's phenomenology for mounting such a positive demonstration. Because a complete evaluation of intersubjectivity depends upon Husserl's analysis of the lifeworld, this issue will be addressed more fully in the next chapter.

In terms of a phenomenological conception of truth and reality, to 'be' intersubjective can only mean to be constituted (intended) as intersubjective, where this intention is itself capable of maximal harmonious fulfillment in the further course of experience (i.e., maximal *Evidenz*).[49] Thus to evaluate the justification for claims of intersubjectivity, we need to elucidate the nature of the *Evidenz* of intersubjectivity, and its strength.

Husserl's phenomenology provides two different paths to the *Evidenz* of intersubjectivity, corresponding to two different justificatory strengths. The first path is the one outlined in the Fifth Cartesian Meditation.[50] Here Husserl gives a phenomenological analysis of the constitution of the other in experience, and so of the *Evidenz* of the other's existence as well as intentional life. According to this analysis, the perception of the other's intentional life is an appresentation founded upon sensible perceptions such as, e.g., the other's body, the other's physical behavior, and possibly also, at a higher level, the other's speech. The appresentation or perceptual *Evidenz* of the other's intentional life is similar in some respects to the *Evidenz* of the non-appearing side of a physical object. In the case of a physical object, an 'absent' side is indeed immediately perceived and not hypothesized or deduced: this side belongs to the object as intentionally constituted and perceived, even though it is given only in an empty way and not in the full manner of the object's front sides. Similarly, Husserl argues, the intentional life of the other is perceived and not deduced, forming an intrinsic part of the overall constituted intentional object, 'the other', even though the specifically intentional component of the other is given in an empty way as compared to full givenness of the founding physical components.

However, the *Evidenz* of the intentional life of the other is quite different from the *Evidenz* of the back of a physical object, for the absent side of a thing can at some point become the front, present one, whereas someone else's thoughts and experiences can never be given in the full way of a physical object, or of my own. Yet Husserl argues convincingly that a harmonious further synthesis of fulfillment, and hence a perfecting of *Evidenz*, is nonetheless possible in the case of another's intentional life as well. Of course, here it cannot be a matter of 'going around the back' and seeing the previously emptily posited intentional life in concrete fullness. Rather, to each type of intentional life attributed to the other there corresponds a manifold of outward behaviors and expressions (not only but including linguistic ones) consistent with this attribution and which would count as further confirmation of its accuracy. For example, certain physical beings are attributed pain experiences because of specific behavior in the presence of injury (e.g., reaction, avoidance, and of course characteristic expressions for persons), and were these suddenly to cease, then the attribution itself would come into question.[51]

The *Evidenz* of consensus is just one form of the *Evidenz* of the intentional life of the other in general; i.e., the form in which the judgment of the other as appresented by me and my own judgment agree. The most common way for this *Evidenz* to be attained is through discourse, although it could also come about purely on the basis of outward behavior and facial expressions, or through a conjunction of these and language. Much as for any other concrete attribution of intentionality to the other, the positing of consensus brings with it a manifold of further perceptions (in this case also linguistic perceptions) which would be consistent with this appresentation and which would improve the degree of its *Evidenz*, and others which would be inconsistent with it. Intersubjectivity would then be the equivalent of the possibility of universal or some other suitably delimited consensus, and the fulfillment of the intended intersubjectivity of a particular judgment could be improved or diminished in the same way as the *Evidenz* of consensus between individuals: through discourse, observation of behavior, expression, etc.

However, while some degree of justification of claims to intersubjectivity is possible on this path, clearly the *Evidenz* attainable by it will be relatively weak. The source of this weakness is not merely the practical impossibility of engaging everyone else in discourse, and the concomitant need to extrapolate inductively from the (relatively) confirmed possibility of consensus within a small sample to the (relatively) unconfirmed possibility of universal consensus. Rather, the more serious difficulty is the imperfection of the *Evidenz* of consensus even in the case of a single 'other'. Husserl himself suggests that because of the essentially 'absent', founded nature of intersubjective appresentations, this *Evidenz* will always be less perfect and more highly mediated than even the always-inadequate *Evidenz* of physical objects.[52] Yet to put the issue more strongly, it could be argued that every kind of outer behavior and expression is at least minimally compatible with every intentional state, so that no language or behavior would be definitively excluded by the attribution of consensus to another and none would be unquestionable verifications of it. Although certainty may be unattainable in the case of physical objects as well, at least here the specific content of the harmonious manifold correlated with a specific state of affairs is much easier to define. And if to hold that appresentations of the intentional lives of others are wholly unreliable is going too far, it still must be emphasized that on Husserl's own account the *Evidenz* provided by such appresentations is only of the most probabilistic sort, worse than both the *Evidenz* of one's own intentional states and the *Evidenz* of the physical.[53]

Thus the first path offers the possibility of only a relatively weak justification of intersubjectivity (as well as the lack thereof), a justification which could be considered rational motivation of some degree or another, but far from certainty, even in the Husserlian sense. However, the second path to a justification of intersubjectivity seeks a far stronger demonstration. Because of the role played by the lifeworld on this second path, it will here be possible only briefly to indicate it. A full critical evaluation will be presented in the next chapter.

This second path proceeds not piecemeal, by individual interaction and discourse, but globally and monadically, by an eidetic analysis of subjectivity as such. According to Husserl, an investigation of the meaning structure 'subjectivity' through free variation in imagination reveals that certain features and forms of experience belong necessarily to it. For example, it could be claimed that eidetic analysis shows that temporality belongs essentially to subjectivity. Here again it should be emphasized that the 'essential' includes not only what belongs to the *intention* of a given phenomenon, but also to an intuitive *fulfillment* of this intention. Thus the claim that temporality is essential to subjectivity is not incompatible with the fact that we can *conceive* of a subjectivity whose experiences are atemporal. However, it is incompatible with the possibility that such atemporal experience could be *imagined*, or otherwise illustrated in intuition.[54]

The resulting specification of universal features of subjectivity can then be used to justify the possibility of universal consensus regarding specific judgments or phenomenological results (e.g., the analysis of subjective time consciousness). Because the structures under consideration are universal ones (as demonstrated by eidetic variation), the meaning formations and forms of experience necessary to attain *Evidenz* will be accessible to all subjects whatsoever. Further, as in the case of all eidetic *Evidenz*, the *Evidenz* of the possibility of intersubjectivity attained by this method arises purely from meaning structures, and so will be apodictic.

This second path could seem to represent a return on Husserl's part to a quasi-Kantian theory of the subjective faculties, and of the a priori as rooted in these. For what is being 'varied' and 'specified' in the eidetic analysis of subjectivity if not the subjective faculties, faculties similar to the Kantian understanding, judgment, and forms of intuition? The only difference between Husserl and Kant would then be the (questionable) Husserlian position that the faculties thus determined are universal ones, essential to subjectivity as such.

However, although the path to a strong justification of intersubjectivity does lead Husserl to develop a theory of (or method for investigating) the universal features of subjectivity as such, unlike Kant he does not root these features in faculties. Rather, Husserl holds that these features are merely structures found in experience, rooted as much in the 'outer' world as in the 'inner' subject. As we will see in the next chapter, in the end what is varied in eidetic analysis of subjectivity is not possible faculties of cognition 'internal' to the subject and in causal relation to the unsynthesized manifold of intuition, but possible realms of experience, possible *lifeworlds*.

Thus at least insofar as concerns intersubjectivity, in Husserl the lifeworld and its structures come to play the role that the subjective faculties of cognition play in Kant. The ultimate success of the strong justification of intersubjectivity then depends upon Husserl's arguments that the lifeworld itself has a universal structure. These arguments will be taken up in the next chapter, in the context of our general discussion of the implications of the lifeworld for the relativism problematic.

NOTES

1. I do not mean to imply here that Husserl is a realist throughout the *Logical Investigations*. While the *Prolegomena* is clearly realist, the second volume of the *Logical Investigations* is generally neutral or ambiguous.
2. *Regulæ ad directionem ingenii*, 362 (Rule 2).
3. See, for example, *Kritik der reinen Vernunft*, A 92–4/B 124–6, and A 387.
4. *Hua XIX/2* 751ff. (*LU A* 694/B 222ff.).
5. It should, however, be noted that Descartes and Locke do not themselves identify inner perception as here defined as the ultimate and infallible source of knowledge.
6. For Brentano's own statement of this distinction, see Franz Brentano, *Psychologie vom empirischen Standpunkt*, second edition (Leipzig: Felix Meiner, 1924), especially Book One, Chapter 1, and Book Two, Chapter 1.
7. See Chapter Three, sections three and four.
8. Husserl is actually much closer to Descartes on this point than he suggests in this text. For Descartes too notes that a pain sensation is an inner experience and certain only insofar as it is not referred to a part of the body or anything else existing outside the mind. See *Principia philosophiæ*, 22 and 32 (Part One, Articles 46 and 66–67). However, Descartes still differs from Husserl in believing that in at least *some* cases we can be absolutely certain about the nature of the external cause of a perception (e.g., in the case of primary qualities). It is this belief that allows him to draw the inner/outer distinction in terms of real causes rather than purely immanently, in terms of intentional reference.
9. *Hua III* 78/85–6 (*Id I* § 38).
10. *Ibid.*, 91–2/100–1 (*Id I* § 44). Where Husserl equates immanence with adequacy, the new concept begins to take on all the ambiguity and relativity of the old. Thus we find Husserl speaking of a reduced physical phenomenon (the noema, as opposed to the noesis) as an immanent transcendent, by which he seems to mean: a phenomenon which is given adequately in some respects and some relations, but inadequately in others. The pure ego is another example of something asserted to be a 'transcendence in immanence.' See *ibid.*, 124/138, 226–8/244–5 (*Id I* §§ 57, 97); *Hua I* 134–5 (*CM* § 47).

11. *Hua III* 203–4/220 (*Id I* § 88).
12. This point is stated by Husserl in a particularly clear way in *Hua III* 63–4/64 (*Id I* § 31). See also *Hua I* 60 (*CM* § 8).
13. *Hua III* 93–4/103 (*Id I* § 44). ("Auch ein Erlebnis ist nicht, und niemals, vollständig wahrgenommen, in seiner vollen Einheit ist es adäquat nicht faßbar. Es ist seinem Wesen nach ein Fluß, dem wir, den reflektiven Blick darauf richtend, von dem Jetztpunkte aus nachschwimmen können, während die zurückliegenden Strecken für die Wahrnehmung verloren sind. Nur in Form der Retention haben wir ein Bewußtsein des unmittelbar Abgeschlossenen, bzw. in Form der rückblickenden Wiedererinnerung.")
14. See *Hua XIX/2* 597–8 (*LU A* 537/*B* 65); and Chapter Three, p. 77–8 above.
15. *Hua III* 202/218 (*Id I* § 88). ("Auf der einen Seite haben wir also die Teile und Momente zu unterscheiden, die wir durch eine reelle Analyse des Erlebnisses finden, wobei wir das Erlebnis als Gegenstand behandeln wie irgendeinen anderen, nach seinen Stücken oder unselbständigen, ihn reell aufbauenden Momenten fragend. Andererseits ist aber das intentionale Erlebnis Bewußtsein von etwas, und ist es seinem Wesen nach, z.B. als Erinnerung, als Urteil, als Wille usw.; und so können wir fragen, was nach seiten dieses 'von etwas' wesensmäßig auszusagen ist.")
16. *Hua IX* 284. ("Z.B. die Phänomenologie der Körperwahrnehmung ist nicht ein Bericht über faktisch vorkommenden oder zu erwartenden Wahrnehmungen, sondern Herausstellung des invarianten Struktursystems, ohne das Wahrnehmung eines Körpers und eine synthetisch zusammenstimmende Mannigfaltigkeit von Wahrnehmungen als solchen eines und desselben Körpers undenkbar wären.")
17. *Kritik der reinen Vernunft*, A 197/*B* 242. ("Wir haben Vorstellungen in uns, deren wir uns auch bewußt werden können. Dieses Bewußtsein mag so weit erstreckt, und so genau und pünktlich sein, als man wolle, so bleiben es doch immer nur Vorstellungen... Wie kommen wir nun dazu, daß wir diesen Vorstellungen ein Objekt setzen, oder über ihre subjektive Realität, als Modifikationen, ihnen noch, ich weiß nicht, was für eine, objektive beilegen? ... Wenn wir untersuchen, was denn die Beziehung auf einen Gegenstand unseren Vorstellungen für eine neue Beschaffenheit gebe, und welches die Dignität sei, die sie dadurch erhalten, so finden wir, daß sie nichts weiter tue, als die Verbindung der Vorstellungen auf eine gewisse Art notwendig zu machen, und sie einer Regel zu unterwerfen; daß umgekehrt nur dadurch, daß eine gewisse Ordnung in dem Zeitverhältnisse unserer Vorstellungen notwendig ist, ihnen objektive Bedeutung erteilt wird.")
18. See *Kritik der reinen Vernunft*, B 233–40. In this argument Kant claims not only that if we subordinate the succession of apprehension to concept of causality, then our experience takes on a reference to an objective succession; but also that (1) our faculties actually do employ this concept; and (2) this is the *only* way that our experience of succession could take on an objective reference. It is these two latter claims that are particularly subject to the Husserlian charge – to be discussed in what follows – that Kant's procedure is 'hypothetical'.
19. *Hua VI* 116 and 118 (*K* § 30). ("In der Tat gerät Kant in eine eigene Art mythischer Reden, deren Wortsinn zwar auf Subjektives verweist, aber eine Weise des Subjektiven, die wir uns prinzipiell nicht anschaulich machen können, weder an faktischen Exempeln noch durch echte Analogie.... Hierzu bedürfte es einer grundwesentlich anderen regressiven Methode als der auf jenen fraglosen Selbstverständlichkeiten beruhenden Kants, nicht einer mythisch konstruktiv schließenden, sondern einer durchaus

anschaulich erschließenden...")

20. *Ibid.*, 93–100 (*K* § 25).

21. *Ibid.*, 99–100 (*K* § 25). For the view that Kant naïvely presupposes the validity of formal logic, see also *Hua XVII* 264ff. (*FTL* §100). That Kant does indeed presuppose the validity of mathematics is clear from his 'transcendental' argument for the ideality of space in the Transcendental Aesthetic (the third of the five 'metaphysical' arguments in the *A* edition, made into a separate section and entitled 'transcendental' in the *B* edition). Here Kant argues that if space were not ideal, we could have no necessary knowledge about it, and therefore the principles of geometry (e.g., there is always one and only one line connecting two points) would themselves be contingent, empirical truths, verified in experience up until now but not for all time. However, argues Kant, since the principles of geometry are necessary truths, space itself must be an a priori representation. This argument clearly just takes the validity of geometry itself (the necessary truth of its principles) to be beyond question. See *Kritik der reinen Vernunft*, A 24/B 40–1.

22. This is an interpretation at least suggested by David Carr. In a footnote to his translation of the *Crisis*, Carr holds that according to Husserl, Hume is the more radical transcendental philosopher because Hume understands that the *Seinssinn* of the lifeworld is a subjective construction, whereas Kant does not, because his transcendentalism does not penetrate to the lifeworld. See *The Crisis of the European Sciences and Transcendental Phenomenology*, translated with an introduction by David Carr (Evanston: Northwestern University Press, 1970) 69, n. 1.

23. Husserl frequently asserts that for Kant even the intuitively appearing world – the world prior to scientific knowledge – is a construct of the subjective faculties. See *Hua VI* 97–8, 102, 105 (*K* §§ 25, 27, 28). It is clear that this is also Kant's own meaning: his own example in the Second Analogy of something 'objective' (and hence 'constituted' or subordinated to the rules of the subjective faculties) is the event of a boat moving downstream – hardly something from the world of mathematical physics.

24. It is difficult to judge on the basis of the Second Analogy alone whether Kant presupposes that at least some of our experience of objective events is valid, in the specified phenomenological sense of validity. However, I think a clue to Kant's general position regarding the reality of the phenomenal world is to be found in the Refutation of Idealism. Here Kant attempts to provide a decisive proof that there really are objects and not merely subjective representations which are 'as if' of objects; or, in the language employed by us earlier, that we have some *valid* experience of objects. He does this by holding that consciousness of something 'outer' (i.e., of a phenomenal object) is a condition for 'inner' or subjective consciousness. (See *Kritik der reinen Vernunft*, B 275–9.) Although this *argument* for the reality of the world could seem to show that Kant *does not* merely presuppose the validity of the world, I think that the very fact that Kant attempts a demonstration of the existence of the phenomenal world is actually an indication that he *does* presuppose its reality – for otherwise he would not be so thoroughly convinced that such a demonstration is possible. By contrast, Husserl maintains that the existence of the phenomenal world or any worldly object cannot be made certain, and correspondingly that any demonstration of the sort attempted in the Refutation of Idealism is bound to fail. Further, contrary to Kant's position in the Refutation of Idealism, Husserl asserts that a consciousness which is not intentionally directed to a world is possible (or in Kantian terms, that there could be inner conscious-

ness without consciousness of anything outer). See *Hua III* 103–6/114–7 (*Id I* § 49); *Hua XVII* 258 (*FTL* § 99).

25. *Hua VI* 117 (*K* § 30). Husserl generally interprets Kant as conceiving of the faculties as causal agencies, an interpretation which is questionable, especially in light of the Kantian arguments against rational psychology in the Paralogisms. However, Kant's own language of 'faculties' and 'affection' makes it difficult to understand how the faculties *are* to be interpreted. For if the language of faculties is to be understood only functionally, as referring only to (phenomenally evident) activities which follow certain patterns, then it would be less misleading not to use this language at all.

26. See, for example, *Hua III* 133–4/148 (*Id I* §62), where Husserl holds "thus, for example, the Transcendental Deduction of the first edition of the *Kritik der reinen Vernunft* already really moves on phenomenological ground..." ("So bewegt sich z.B. die transzendentale Deduktion der ersten Auflage der Kritik der reinen Vernunft eigentlich schon auf phänomenologischem Boden ... ") This opinion is repeated in the *Crisis*, *Hua VI* 106 (*K* § 28).

27. In his insistence that the foundation itself must be established purely by intuition, Husserl is actually closer to Descartes than to Kant. And in general, Husserl's first principle that intuition is the ultimate source of *all* knowledge is a Cartesian and not a Kantian one.

28. For a similar analysis of the Husserlian a priori as grounded in meanings rather than subjective faculties, see Tugendhat, 164.

29. For Husserl's characterization of his own method as a 'questioning-back' ('*Rückfrage*') see *Hua VI* 170–1 (*K* § 49).

30. In agreement with this general interpretation, Tugendhat notes: "It is true that the Kantian a priori is relative to the human ego, but it holds good universally for this ego. By contrast, Husserl's a priori – considered in itself – does indeed hold good absolutely, but then only relative to the given state of affairs, which is not itself necessary." ("Kants Apriori ist zwar relativ auf das menschliche Ich, aber für dieses gilt es universal, während Husserls Apriori an sich zwar absolut gilt, aber nur relativ auf die jeweilige Sachhaltigkeit, die selbst nicht notwendig ist"), Tugendhat, 165.

31. *Hua VII* 356. ("[Kant] übersah, daß die Transzendentalphilosophie nichts anderes will und nichts anderes wollen darf, als den Sinn der Erkenntnis und ihrer Geltung aufklären und daß Aufklären hier nichts anderes heißt, als auf den Ursprung, auf die Evidenz zurückgehen, also auf das Bewußtsein, in dem sich alle Erkenntnisbegriffe intuitiv realisieren.") In a similar vein, Husserl writes in the *Crisis*: "No objective truth, whether in the prescientific or in scientific sense, that is, no claim about objective being, ever enters into our scientific sphere, whether as a premise or as a consequence." ("Keine objektive Wahrheit, ob in vorwissenschaftlichem oder wissenschaftlichem Sinne, bzw. keine Feststellung für objektives Sein tritt je in unserem Kreis der Wissenschaftlichkeit, ob nun als Prämisse oder als Folgerung "), *Hua VI* 178–9 (*K* § 52]).

32. The treatment in *Ideas I* suggests but does not unequivocally state that adequacy and apodicticity entail one another. See *Hua III* 317–8/337–8 (*Id I* § 137). Mutual entailment is emphatically asserted in *Erste Philosophie*, *Hua VIII* 35, 334.

33. See, for example, *Hua XVII* 195–6 (*FTL* § 74).

34. *Hua I* 55 (*CM* § 6).

35. However, this detaching of apodicticity from adequacy should not be interpreted as a complete abandonment of adequacy as an epistemic desideratum. Intuitive givenness

continues to remain an essential source of clarity and insight, even after the realization that complete givenness in the limit sense is impossible. The results of phenomenology have a high degree of adequacy, and a notably higher degree than those of other disciplines, and this constitutes one important sense in which its results are 'absolute'. Further, it is with the means of phenomenology itself that the impossibility of perfect adequacy is demonstrated, and this stands as a proof of the strength of the method in establishing its own limits, rather than relying on other disciplines or approaches to do so. Thus after the *Cartesian Meditations*, Husserl's claim that phenomenology is absolute must be interpreted as a claim *both* for the unusually high degree of its adequacy, *and* for the certainty of its results.

36. See, for example, Rorty, 166–9.
37. See, for example, Levin (*op. cit.*); Tugendhat (*op. cit.*); Maurice Merleau-Ponty, *Phénoménologie de la perception* (Paris: Gallimard, 1943); and Ludwig Landgrebe, "Husserls Abschied vom Cartesianismus," *Philosophische Rundschau* 9 (1962), 133–77.
38. *Hua XVII* 164 and 165 (*FTL* §§ 58 and 59). ("Selbst eine sich als apodiktisch ausgebende Evidenz kann sich als Täuschung enthüllen und setzt doch dafür eine ähnliche Evidenz voraus, an der sie 'zerschellt'.... Der beständige Anstoß, der bei dieser Darstellung empfunden werden dürfte, liegt nur an der üblichen grundverkehrten Interpretation der Evidenz vermöge des völligen Mangels einer ernstlichen phänomenologischen Analyse der durch alle ihre Formen gemeinsam hindurchgehenden Leistung.")
39. This is the view of Landgrebe as well as Merleau-Ponty, who interprets the *Formal and Transcendental Logic* passage as follows: "The substance of what is said in *Formal and Transcendental Logic* (p. 142) is that there is no apodictic evidence." ("Il n'y a pas d'évidence apodictique, dit en substance la *Formale und transzendentale Logik*, p. 142"), *Phénoménologie de la perception*, xi, n. 2. Tugendhat suggests that Husserl verged upon and should have abandoned apodicticity as an actual attainment, although he never quite could bring himself to do so. See Tugendhat, 195–6.
40. David Michael Levin, "A Critique of Husserl's Theory of Adequate and Apodictic Evidence," Ph.D. diss., Columbia University, 1967, 200–1. For a more cursory explanation of this distinction by Levin, see his *Reason and Evidence in Husserl's Phenomenology*, 109–10.
41. *Hua VIII* 380. ("Eine apodiktische Erkenntnis <ist> vollkommen wiederholbar, in identischer Gültigkeit. Was einmal apodiktisch evident ist, ergibt nicht nur mögliche Wiedererinnerung, diese Evidenz gehabt zu haben, sondern Notwendigkeit der Geltung auch für jetzt, und so für immer: Endgültigkeit.")
42. Levin, "A Critique of Husserl's Theory of Adequate and Apodictic Evidence," 183.
43. Levin, *Reason and Evidence in Husserl's Phenomenology*, 84–5.
44. For a further discussion of the difference between psychological and ideal impossibilities of imagination, see Chapter Three, pp. 85 ff. above. For the issue of the role of the subjective faculties, see section 1.2 of this chapter, especially pp. 118 ff., and section 3.1 below.
45. Levin, *Reason and Evidence in Husserl's Phenomenology*, 109.
46. See note 6 on page 24.
47. Perhaps the archetypical example of such a realist student of Husserl's phenomenology is Farber, who protests as follows against Husserl's unrelenting refusal to admit without

bracketing into the phenomenological realm what stand for empiricism as basic truths: "To retort that this is 'naïve' or a 'dogma', as Husserl insisted, is an indication of the astonishing length to which a philosopher confined to his special 'cave' could go. Surely it is not naïve or dogmatic to refer to Husserl's own parents as antedating his revered 'phenomenological reduction'" (Farber, viii). However, Farber refuses to recognize that Husserl's epistemic requirements are far more stringent than those of empiricism. In light of these requirements, the simple belief asserted above, while reasonable in its own way, is indeed naïve.

48. A similar objection to the Husserlian account is raised by Heidegger in his notes to the *Encyclopedia Britannica* article, although in a phenomenological rather than an empiricist or objectivist form. Here Heidegger argues that the self is always and everywhere *really* a human self, even where this self carries out the epoché or employs other special methods of self-interpretation. Thus, for example, where Husserl writes of the non-humanity of the self after the epoché: "If I carry out [the epoché] in relation to myself, then I am not a human self..." ("Tue ich so für mich selbst, so bin ich also nicht menschliches Ich ..."); Heidegger objects: "Why not? Is not this activity a possibility of a human being?" ("Warum nicht? Ist dieses Tun nicht eine Möglichkeit des Menschen ... ?"). See *Hua IX* 274–5 and 275, n. 2

   Heidegger's objection differs from the empiricist one in that his notion of the human self (Dasein) is allegedly won purely phenomenologically, from an 'eidetic' analysis of what it is to exist as a self, rather than being dogmatically taken over from anthropology, biology, or history. Heidegger claims that a phenomenological analysis of the 'constituting' self itself reveals that traits such as mortality, facticity and historicity belong to Dasein's essence, traits which therefore cannot be removed by the epoché. However, there is clearly a paradox in attempting to derive a relativist conclusion from the Heideggerian position: if the results of phenomenology are only relatively true, then so is his existential analytic of Dasein, phenomenological demonstration of facticity, and all the rest. The question of whether transcendental subjectivity is indeed conditioned and contingent even considered purely phenomenologically will be taken up in greater detail in the next chapter (see pp. 181 ff. below).

49. Or more precisely, to 'be' intersubjective is to be *capable* of maximally evident constitution as intersubjective, independently of whether this intersubjectivity is in fact intended or not.

50. See especially *Hua I* 138–41, 143–5 (*CM* §§ 50, 52).

51. Scheler challenges the view (defended by Husserl) that the self and its experiences are what are given primarily, and my apprehension of the thoughts and feelings of others are constituted only on the basis of my own. Rather, Scheler maintains that at the most basic level of experience – the level which forms the constitutional foundation for experience of the other – there is no differentiation between 'mine' and 'thine'. Thus at this level all thoughts and feelings (including those which may eventually be assigned to another self) are given with equal immediacy. Further, to the claim that *all* of these thoughts and feelings, including those eventually assigned to another, must also be assigned to me, as *my* experience of the thoughts and feelings of another, Scheler replies that this 'me' is a purely formal unity of consciousness, not something experienced, nor my 'own' self, which latter can be constituted only in contrast to some 'other' self. See Max Scheler, *Wesen und Formen der Sympathie*, edited with an afterward by Manfred S. Frings, in Gesammelte Werke, vol. 7 (Berlin and Munich:

Francke Verlag, 1973), 238–40, especially the note on page 240.

I think Scheler is actually in agreement with Husserl in his claim that at the 'ultimate' level, the level at which all others and references to others have been bracketed, there is no distinction between 'mine' and 'thine'. This is the implicit meaning of the assertion in the *Crisis* that the transcendental ego (the ego after the others have been bracketed) is called 'I' only by equivocation – i.e., because there is no 'Thou' to whom it could be contrasted. (*Hua VI* 188 [*K* § 54 b]). However, contra Scheler, this 'I' is not merely a formal unity and nothing experienced, nor is there no self or self-experience without experience of the other. Rather, even without the experience of other subjects, the self is experienced as the unitary awareness persisting through the flow of perspectival presentations, and which grasps these as presentations *of* something which endures. Thus intentionality itself, as directedness towards objects rather than *Erlebnisse* (the *cogitata* rather than the *cogitatio*) is sufficient to give an ego-experience. (See *Hua I* 134–5 [*CM* § 47] and *Hua VI* 173–5, 188–9 [*K* §§ 50, 54 b].) Of course, this is not a full ego-experience in the sense of 'one ego among many', much less 'a person in the world, a possible object of experience for others'. These latter ego-experiences are possible only on the basis of the (constitutionally prior) experience of the other. However, Husserl's point is asserting the priority of the self to the other is to claim that ego-experience in the former, less complete sense is prior to other-experience. This claim is not refuted by Scheler's critique.

52. *Hua I* 139 (*CM* § 51).

53. A complete pessimism about the possibility of knowledge of the intentional life of the other is characteristic of Sartre. According to Sartre, I apprehend the other-as-subject (as opposed to the other-as-object) solely as an absence, a 'hemorrhage' in the world. See *L'être et le néant* (Paris: Gallimard, 1943), especially 312–4 and 354. But Sartre is not able to show that simply because the mode of givenness of the other's intentional life is *different* from the mode of givenness of objects or of my own intentional life, this givenness always amounts to no more than the registering that something (i.e., the thoughts of the other) is *not* given. This could sometimes be the case, as when, for example, another person is speaking a foreign or unintelligible language. However, in general the intentional life of others is given with far more content than this, and this content is also reasonably evident.

54. Of course Kant maintains that space and time are forms of intuition for human subjectivity and not necessarily for other types of subjectivity, such as God. (*Kritik der reinen Vernunft*, A 27/B 43, B 72.) Husserl's objection against this position is that not only do we not have the intuitive insight into the allegedly atemporal divine subjectivity necessary to justify claims that it is indeed atemporal (as Kant himself admits), but it can be shown that the givenness of an atemporal experience is in principle impossible. Where all intuitive givenness is impossible, assertions are too speculative to be admissible in the light of critical thinking.

CHAPTER FIVE

Relativism and the Lifeworld

According to the prevailing view, Husserl is and remains a virulent absolutist. Our discussion in the preceding chapters has shown that this view is not without its grounds. We have seen that through the time of *Ideas I* Husserl fiercely attacks relativism both on theoretical (*Prolegomena*) and ethical/social grounds ("Philosophy as Rigorous Science"). We have also seen that one of the central motives guiding Husserl's development of phenomenology itself is precisely the desire to overcome relativism (and skepticism) in the most convincing and ultimate fashion possible. Yet although Husserl himself is almost universally acknowledged to be an absolutist, the same is not the case for the phenomenology he developed to provide an epistemically sound foundation for this absolutism. Rather, it has been suggested that relativism arises as an unexpected and undesired consequence of Husserl's own phenomenology, and its analysis of the lifeworld in particular. Thus it is alleged that Husserl remained an absolutist out of pure dogmatism, while the later heirs of the phenomenological tradition were truer to phenomenology itself, and so became relativists.[1]

In this chapter I will propose a different interpretation both of Husserl and of the implications of phenomenology for the relativism problematic. First, I will argue that the later Husserl explicitly embraces a limited version of relativism – relativism at the level of the concrete lifeworld – and this as a consequence of his phenomenological approach. Thus contrary to the prevailing view, the later Husserl exhibits a growing sympathy for relativism, and does not remain dogmatically opposed to it in all shapes and forms. At the same time, this does not mean that Husserl abandons the absolute, or the idea of philosophy as a foundational discipline capable of attaining this absolute (whether as absolute givenness or as universal intersubjectivity). The uncharacteristically poignant passages of the *Crisis* clearly testify to Husserl's continued belief that a phenomenological defense of the absolute is possible, and indeed essential to save humanity from the irrationality sweeping Europe and the world (an irrationality which Husserl interprets as the consequence of Cartesian objectivism and skepticism). Rather, the final position which emerges from Husserl's phenomenology is an attempt to reconcile and demonstrate the validity of both a relative and a non-relative conception of truth.

In fairness to the received view of Husserl as an unrepentant absolutist, it should be admitted that this final reconciliation of relativism and absolutism is nowhere systematically expounded as such. Much as is the case for other issues, Husserl's writings on relativism retain their provisional, 'on the way' character to the last. Thus my main claim is not so much that the final position reconstructed here is one Husserl actually and univocally embraces, but rather that this is the position he should have embraced, and the one most consistent with the other tenets of his phenomenology, and the truth. Further, in many writings Husserl himself suggests and is sympathetic to a position of this sort.

The discussion of this chapter falls into five parts. The first part is largely historical, providing a transition from the analyses of the earlier chapters. Here I briefly sketch the emergence of the lifeworld thematic within the overall context of Husserl's thought. This reconstruction also aims to undermine the common view that the 'turn' to the lifeworld is a late development motivated by extrinsic historical factors, and to show instead that the lifeworld is a recurrent, internal theme for Husserl from the time of *Ideas* onward. In the second section I examine how the analysis of the lifeworld leads to an affirmation and justification of relativism in a specific form. Contrary to the prevalent interpretation holding that Husserl conceived of the lifeworld as single and universal, I maintain that the lifeworld is culturally and historically relative: even according to Husserl's explicit analysis, there is not one concrete lifeworld but a plurality of them, each relative to a limited intersubjective community. In the third section I elaborate the notion of lifeworld truth, set in contrast to universally intersubjective, ultimately justifiable 'scientific' truth. An explication of the relativity of lifeworld truth in terms of its limited intersubjectivity, justification, and exactness, as well as its overall pragmatic character, serves to show how in the case of lifeworld truth, the very *sense* of truth varies depending upon the intentional horizon of the judgment. In the fourth section I address Husserl's position that the lifeworld is prior to the world of science. This position is of significance for our discussion both because it strengthens Husserl's affirmation of relativism, and also because it presents a major difficulty for his continued defense of a scientific, non-relative notion of truth. In the fifth and concluding section, I set forth the final resolution of the problem of relativism. Contrary to recent suggestions in the literature that the analysis of the lifeworld should have led Husserl to abandon the absolute conception of truth altogether, I argue that his phenomenology makes possible a reconciliation and a positive defense of both a relative and a non-relative notion of truth. Thus the relativization of the lifeworld is shown to be not an end but a starting-point, opening the possibility for a more perfect knowledge of what is common.

1. HISTORICAL INTRODUCTION: THE 'TURN' TO THE LIFEWORLD

Why *does* Husserl, the philosopher of transcendental consciousness and the epoché, find himself compelled to address something as concrete and 'presupposition-laden' as the lifeworld? Because of a tendency of Husserl scholarship to fall into two camps – scholarship of the early Husserl on the one side, and of the late Husserl on the other – this question is often not even raised. Writings on the early Husserl fail to mention the lifeworld altogether, whereas writings on the late Husserl start right in with the lifeworld thematic, without troubling themselves about its sources in what went before.[2]

According to one popular view, the theme of the lifeworld represents a dramatic change in Husserl's thinking around the time of the *Crisis*. This change is allegedly motivated largely by extrinsic historical factors, such as the demands of Husserl's audience in the thirties for a more concrete, 'relevant' philosophy, or by his desire to rebut or even to borrow from Heidegger's wildly popular *Being and Time* (published in 1927), with its affirmation that Dasein is always Being-in-the-world, and never a pure, worldless transcendental consciousness. However, contrary to this popular view, Husserl's writings reflect a virtually uninterrupted concern with themes surrounding the lifeworld from the time of *Ideas* onward. To demonstrate this, I will preface my analysis of the implications of the lifeworld for relativism with a brief sketch of these early discussions. Because the concern here will be simply to set out the lines of the early history of the lifeworld concept in Husserl's thought, this preliminary treatment will of necessity be quite schematic. The substantive issues relating to the relativism problematic will be taken up in detail in what follows.

The earliest documented occurrences of the term *'Lebenswelt'* in Husserl's writings are contained in Appendix XIII to *Ideas II*, dated 1917.[3]

However, not too much weight should be placed on the occurrence of this particular term. Although historically this term has been the most influential, overemphasizing its importance for Husserl's own analysis can only have the effect of obscuring the continuity of his thought.[4] Rather, Husserl regularly discusses the themes associated with the lifeworld under many other headings, including *'Umwelt'*, *'natürliche Umwelt'*, *'natürlicher Weltbegriff'* (from Avenarius), *'Erfahrungswelt'*, *'Alltagswelt'*, and *'Lebensumwelt'*, among others. This is not to say that Husserl's conception of the lifeworld is without ambiguity or development. However, the texts provide no grounds for correlating a particular stage or a particular conception with a particular term. To the contrary, Husserl is exceedingly loose with his terminology, often employing terms such as *'Umwelt'* or *'Erfahrungswelt'* interchangeably with *'Lebenswelt'*. Indeed, up through his very last writings, one finds Husserl simply substituting one term for another in a single train of thought.[5] Therefore any analysis of Husserl's conception of the lifeworld must take into account the discussions formulated in *all* these terms.

As soon as the emphasis on the specific word *'Lebenswelt'* is removed, it can be seen that the lifeworld turns up as early as *Ideas I*. Here it is entitled the *'natürliche Umwelt'*, and is characterized as the world of the natural attitude, the world in which we find ourselves prior to the epoché. The *Ideas I* analysis is quite cursory, since at this stage Husserl is not at all interested in the study of this world in its own right, but only in making clear the factual starting-point of the reductions. Nonetheless, the *'natürliche Umwelt'* is easily recognized as the lifeworld from the brief description provided: (1) it is spread out in space and time; (2) it is bounded by a horizon (only a small part is 'bodily' present, the remainder is anticipated, shrouded in mist, indeterminate but determinable in progressive stages); (3) it is a world not of mere sensible things but rather of cultural objects, persons, practical concerns, books, friends, servants; (4) it is a world which is intersubjective in a qualified sense: the objects in it present themselves as 'there for others', although the others may experience them in a somewhat different manner than do I.[6]

Although the lifeworld as a phenomenon is clearly familiar to Husserl as early as *Ideas I*, the first motivation to make this phenomenon into a theme in its own right arises in *Ideas II*, in the context of Husserl's attempt to provide a phenomenological foundation for the distinction between the *Naturwissenschaften* and the *Geisteswissenschaften*. Dilthey had already shown that the two domains of inquiry could not be distinguished simply on the basis of their *objects*, since the proper objects of the human sciences –

human beings and human products – are studied by the natural sciences as well. Rather, Dilthey had emphasized that the distinction must lie in the different *manner* in which the very *same* objects are studied, the different ways in which they are apprehended and determined in each of these domains of inquiry. For example, in physiology a human being is determined as a conglomeration of tissues, organs, and nerves, governed by causal laws; in history as a person to be understood 'from the inside out'.[7] The analysis of Part 3 of *Ideas II* can be taken as Husserl's supplement to Dilthey's beginnings of a phenomenological foundation for the distinction between the natural sciences and the human sciences. The theory of the epoché had already demonstrated to Husserl that highly significant differences in modes of givenness can result simply from a change in intentional attitude. Consequently in *Ideas II* he attempts to correlate a specific intentional attitude with each type of science and its mode of objectification of the human. The natural-scientific objectification of the human (and indeed, of the world in general) is correlated with the 'naturalistic' (*'naturalistische'*) attitude; the human sciences with the 'natural' or 'personal' attitude. In the first case, the world is intended as a mathematizable, causally ordered 'in-itself', and what is given in experience is constituted as the (caused) appearance of this underlying substrate. By contrast, argues Husserl, the human sciences are based on a study of human beings and the world as they are given (objectified) in the *natural* (also termed 'personal') attitude, the attitude of everyday life. Thus the despised natural attitude and natural *Umwelt* of *Ideas I* are rehabilitated in *Ideas II* as providing the intuitive material for the basic theoretical concepts of the human sciences, and as such highly worthy of phenomenological analysis in their own right.

A number of points of the *Ideas II* analysis are of particular note. As in *Ideas I*, Husserl again emphasizes that the world as experienced in the natural attitude is not a world of mere sensible things, much less of electrons and waves, but rather of persons, cultural objects, social institutions, and values. Further, every person lives in and has experience of a surrounding world, and this is one of the defining features of selfhood as such.[8] The *'Umwelt'* is a '*we-Umwelt*', a world I share with a community of other persons whom I recognize as other persons and who recognize me as such, and with whom I can communicate, agree and disagree.[9] The notion of an *Umwelt* belonging to myself alone can be reached only by a process of abstraction from this concrete, intersubjective world of everyday life.[10] Finally and perhaps most importantly, Husserl here presents in the strongest terms the position generally associated with the *Crisis*, according to which the lifeworld (the *'personale Umwelt'*) is not and cannot be superseded by the world as understood by the natural sciences, but rather precedes and founds the latter. The objectification of the world in the form of a mathematical nature is possible only as the result of intentional operations (abstraction, mathematization, idealization) carried out on the basis of what is given at the level of the lifeworld.[11] Thus the lifeworld is prior to the world of science in the (particularly Husserlian) order of *'Seinsgeltung'*: if we did not have experiences in which the everyday world attains existential validity, then neither could the world of science attain existential validity, and hence it would not 'exist' for us.[12]

Thus Husserl's attempt in *Ideas II* to provide a phenomenological foundation for the *Geisteswissenschaften* results in a striking ontological pluralism: it is not that a human being 'really' is a mass of bones, nerves, tissues and ganglia, or 'really' is a person such as is given in everyday life, but rather that each of these different objectifications is a phenomenological datum, valid as the harmoniously verifiable correlate of the attitude from which it arises.[13] However, at the same time Husserl grants a certain priority to the natural attitude and the everyday world, harshly criticizing that interpretation of science which holds only scientific nature to be real. For every person lives in an *'Umwelt'* (including the practicing natural scientist), but some individuals or cultures are innocent of the world of science. Further, as noted above, the natural-scientific world (or rather, its *Seinssinn*) is constructed as the result of intentional operations carried out on the basis of the everyday world, and in this sense, the former depends upon the latter.[14]

The theme of the *'Umwelt'* recurs frequently within Husserl's manuscripts on intersubjectivity, dating from at least 1915.[15] In light of the position attained in *Ideas II*, at least one motivation for these further reflections is clear. According to *Ideas II*, the sciences are founded upon the personal *Umwelt*, the everyday world in which each person lives and on the basis of which higher-order theoretical objectifications are carried out. Now the sciences claim that the world they describe is an 'objective' world, and this objectivity implies, according to Husserl, universal intersubjective verifiability. But further analysis reveals that while *Umwelten* have a limited intersubjectivity, they may also differ more or less drastically from one community to another (or even from one individual to another), and further, that this variation is itself phenomenologically ascertainable. Thus the question arises: with what justification can it be asserted that the world addressed by the sciences is a universally intersubjective world? Phenomenologically considered, the problem of justifying claims to universal intersubjectivity, including those of phenomenology itself, comes to rest upon the problem of explaining how it is possible for a domain of objects to be constituted in experience with the meaning, 'there for everyone', despite the (phenomenologically evident) variations in individual and social *Umwelten*.[16]

2. THE PLURALITY AND RELATIVITY OF THE LIFEWORLD

Despite his early attacks against relativism, Husserl's analysis of the lifeworld results in an affirmation and a phenomenological justification of relativism, albeit in a form quite different from the one refuted in the *Prolegomena* and discussed here in Chapter One. Thus the usual interpretations of Husserl as dogmatically opposed to relativism are inaccurate in terms of his later writings.

In my view, one of the main reasons that Husserl's affirmation of relativism at the level of the lifeworld has been overlooked is confusion about the nature of the lifeworld itself. Much debate exists in the literature as to the precise content of the lifeworld. In particular it is asked, does Husserl conceive of the lifeworld as a full-fledged cultural-historical world, complete with all the sedimentation of past theoretical activity that this implies, and hence varying more or less dramatically from one culture and period to another? Or rather, does he conceive of the lifeworld as a stripped-down perceptual-natural world containing sensible objects only, a pre-theoretical world without any culturally or historically specific attributes, and hence conceivably a world which is the same for all subjects (or at least for all 'normal' human beings)?

In *Phenomenology and the Problem of History*, David Carr argues that Husserl vacillates between these two crucially different conceptions, mixing them up, and in general not even aware of the distinction between them: "Rather than explain the lifeworld in its own terms, Husserl gives us only a derivative and rather blurred concept, lumping together under one term many levels of experience – like perceptual and cultural – that need to be distinguished."[17] Carr nonetheless suggests that Husserl's *dominant* conception is of the lifeworld as a sensible-natural world. But this, argues Carr, is phenomenologically indefensible, since the *life*world, the world in which we actually live, is obviously a concrete, historical-cultural world, and not a world of pure perception uninformed by theory.

However, Carr presents a revised position in a later essay. According to this modified position, in writings *prior* to the *Crisis*, Husserl understands the lifeworld in the phenomenologically more authentic sense of the subject-relative conception or apprehension of the world (the 'world-view'), conditioned by culture and history. By contrast, continues Carr, the *Crisis* presents a significant shift in Husserl's thinking. Here there can be no talk of 'lifeworlds' in the plural, for now the lifeworld is the unitary natural-perceptual world which *precedes* all historically and culturally conditioned world-views.[18]

Rather curiously, Kern draws a similar distinction between lifeworld qua concrete, cultural-historical world and lifeworld qua pre-theoretical, natural-perceptual world, and then proposes a chronology exactly the *opposite* of Carr's and Brand's. According to Kern, the notion of the unitary pre-theoretical world of natural experience is dominant in the Husserl of the 1920's; whereas in the *Crisis*, the lifeworlds are many rather than one, and are relative to the various cultural contexts.[19]

However, contrary to the views of Carr and Brand on the one side, and of Kern on the other, examination of the texts reveals that it is not the case that at one historical stage Husserl operates with one of these two conceptions of the lifeworld, and then at another stage, with another. Nor is it the case, as held by Carr in *Phenomenology and the Problem of History*, that Husserl is simply unaware that there is any distinction to be drawn here at all. Rather, in numerous passages Husserl *does* explicitly distinguish between the two senses of the lifeworld, and also indicate their relations.[20] Summed up in a rough fashion, the position presented in these passages is as follows. The *concrete* lifeworld, the world as apprehended in everyday life (or, as Husserl rather misleadingly puts it, the world as given in the 'natural' or the 'personal' attitude) is indeed a full-fledged cultural-historical world, a world containing language, practical objects, persons, works of art, and so forth, and not, e.g., colored bodies and variously-pitched sounds. However, this lifeworld in its full concreteness contains various levels of objectification, layers which can be separated out by a process of abstraction. In particular, it is possible to abstract from the non-sensible attributes of the pre-given concrete lifeworld, leaving a spatio-temporal world of perceptual things (the so-called *'anschauliche Dingwelt'*). For example, at the level of the *concrete* lifeworld, the piano before me is *my* piano, it is constituted in my apprehension as something for making music, an instrument invented at a certain point in history, producing a pleasant sound, and so on. However, although concretely the piano is constituted as all these things, I can nonetheless undertake to abstract from all the non-sensible attributes (e.g., 'mine', 'pleasant', 'for music') and direct my attention only to the sensible attributes contained in the complete concrete phenomenon (e.g., 'reddish-brown', 'solid', 'heavy', etc.). Here the essential point emphasized by Husserl is that the perceptual object is reached by a process of *abstraction* from what is given at the level of the concrete lifeworld. Thus he unambiguously asserts that the cultural-historical world is the one in which we find ourselves when reflection begins, and upon which reflection must operate (whether by abstraction, idealization, mathematization, or whatever). In this sense, Husserl is in full agreement with Carr (as well as the obvious truth of the matter) that the world in which we live is a cultural and not merely a sensible world.[21]

Now insofar as the lifeworld is understood as the *concrete* lifeworld, Husserl unquestionably maintains that the lifeworld is relative: there is not one concrete lifeworld but a plurality of them, and each is intentionally referenced ('relativized') to a specific intersubjective community as the group for which this world is 'there'. Statements of this position are found even in Husserl's major published works, although here they tend to be overshadowed by assurances that the concrete lifeworlds nonetheless contain a universal structure or nucleus of experience.[22] By contrast, in Husserl's personal manuscripts the relativity of the concrete lifeworld is asserted repeatedly in the clearest and most unambiguous terms.[23]

For example, in manuscript A V 9 of 1927 entitled *"Umwelt und 'Wahre' Welt"*, Husserl writes:

"Thus for the Zulu, the things *we* know and experience as the sciences, scientific works and literature, are simply not there as books, journals, etc., although the books are there for the Zulu as things, and possibly as things imbued with this or that magical property; that is, with interpretations which in turn are not there for us. If we take what presents itself in the subjective consensus [*subjektiv-einstimmig*] of experience, or in the consensus of experience nationally or socially in the historical community, if we take this to belong to the concrete world of experience of this human community, then we must say: every such human community has a different concrete world."[24]

Husserl asserts the limited intersubjectivity of many objects of the concrete lifeworld again in A V 10 of 1925, entitled *"Zur Beschreibung der Umwelt"*:

"We do not share the same lifeworld with all human beings. Not all humans 'on the face of the earth' have in common with us all the objects which constitute our lifeworld and determine our personal acting and striving, even when these persons come into actual contact with us, as they can at any time.... Objects which are there for us – although admittedly in changing, now harmonious, now conflicting apprehensions

– are not there for them, and this means, the others have no apprehension of them, no experience at all of them as these objects. This is the case even when they see them, and as we say, see these same objects of ours.... If we add a Bantu to this human community, then it is clear that faced with any of our works of art, he does see a thing, but not the object of our surrounding world, the art work. He has no opinion, no apprehension of it – as this object, the art work – that is in 'our' world as the David of Michelangelo with the 'objective' determinations belonging to this work.... Thus we have to distinguish among various human 'worlds', the world of the Europeans, the world of the Bantu, etc., and these worlds are themselves changeable in their personal ('we-') reference."[25]

Thus Husserl explicitly affirms both the plurality and the relativity of concrete lifeworlds. As these passages make clear, pluralism and relativism are not simply equated by Husserl but asserted to accompany each other. The pluralism of the lifeworld consists in the different *contents* and horizons of the worlds themselves; the relativism in the reference to a specific 'we' (or 'they') that comes to belong to the intentional constitution of this world and its contents, as the limited intersubjective community which lives in this world (i.e., for which this world has *Seinsgeltung*). Thus it is not merely that each individual lives in several worlds (which would be pluralism only) but also that some worlds are (constituted as) 'there' for one community of individuals and not for others.

This clear statement of the plurality and relativity of concrete lifeworlds might seem surprising in light of Husserl's persistently harsh attacks against relativism,[26] even though the general style of the position adopted here is by no means unique to Husserl.[27] Now claims to the effect that different persons, cultures, or beings live in different 'worlds' are often subject to attack. For example, in one common style of objection, it is held that even if there were other worlds or alternate conceptual frameworks, we could never recognize them as such, and therefore talk about 'other worlds' and 'alternate conceptual frameworks' is empty, or even unintelligible.[28]

However, one of the more interesting features of Husserl's specifically phenomenological analysis is that it makes explicit the way in which the plurality and relativity of worlds is actually intended and given in experience. Thus it is shown that talk about multiple worlds is not unintelligible, nor merely empty speculation about the possible existence of realities wholly incommensurable with our own. It should be emphasized that Husserl's justification does not provide a demonstration of the existence of multiple worlds in the way of objectivism: i.e., that there 'really' are or could be other worlds, independently of the possibility of *Evidenz*. Rather, as in the case of all phenomenological analyses, the demonstration is a descriptive/regressive one: it begins with the fact that we already have experience (which purports to be) of subject-relative worlds, and then investigates the way in which this sense ('relative world') is constituted in experience. This clarification of the nature of the *Evidenz* of the relativity of the lifeworld then permits an evaluation of its strength, and so, eventually, a further perfecting of such *Evidenz* of it as we presently possess.

Let us elucidate this analysis by way of an example. Suppose I now make the world thematic as it presents itself in the everyday attitude. I am in a room with various objects, lamps, plants, pictures, books, and so forth. Further objects are not actually given in present perception but implicit in my world-horizon, e.g., other New Yorkers, subways, skyscrapers, as well as many other higher-order objectivities (e.g., social institutions, electrons, etc.). Now *that* these objects present themselves as *objects* or objective states of affairs (as opposed to mere appearances in my individual stream of experience) means that they are constituted with the sense, 'there for everyone'. The world of everyday experience is not a solipsistic, I-world, but rather a common, shared world (and this holds good whether or not other persons happen to be present). For example, when I pick up a book, the book is perceived by me as an object, which means it presents itself as 'there for others', a possible object of '*Wechselverständigung*' for an entire community of persons.[29] *I* perceive the book only from a particular angle, in a certain light, from a certain distance, etc. But insofar as I am intentionally directed towards the *book*, these perception-contents count only as appearances, as my particular apprehensions of the object which is 'there for everyone'. Other persons can come into the room, see the book, touch it, and the book will then be given differently in each person's appearance-system (as when, for example, a group of persons stand in a ring about a single object). But all of these different apprehensions can be synthesized into a single manifold of perception of the same object. The same is the case for the other objects and states of affairs in the surrounding world. These have the meaning 'objective' only insofar as they are (intended and perceived as) 'there' for all the members of the community, i.e., as possible objects of mutual comprehension, intersubjective discourse and consensus.

However, in some cases the harmonious synthesis of reference to a single object breaks down. The failure of straightforward synthesis can be motivated by the other person's descriptions of what he perceives, by his actions, by his outward appearance, etc. In the example given by Husserl, what is 'there' for me as a book is 'there' for the old-style Zulu as the embodiment of some spirit. Thus here the object as constituted in my experience and the object as constituted in my *appresentation* of the intentional life of the other cannot be synthesized into a single manifold of the same object, the book. In an ordinary case of intersubjective consensus, my appresentation of what is perceived by the other is formed simply by substituting my anticipation of how the object would present itself *to me* if viewed, e.g., from the position where the other is standing (an anticipation implicit in my own initial perception).[30] By contrast, my 'relativized' appresentation of what the Zulu perceives is constituted by abstracting from one or more of the constitutional layers of the object as constituted in my own perception, then superimposing other layers or modifying the remaining ones by analogy. In this particular example the appresentation is attained by abstracting from the cultural attributes of the book, leaving only its sensible properties (color, shape, texture, weight, etc.), and then superimposing other cultural-spiritual attributes on the sensible substrate (e.g., 'spirit of my ancestor').

But what is essential here is that the book *loses* the sense 'there for everyone', and this sense is now gained instead by some stratum of the fully constituted book. This stratum is 'there for everyone' across cultural boundaries, it maintains itself identically through the manifold of different cultural apprehensions (e.g., I perceive it as a book, the Zulu as an ensouled being), and it is (intended and perceived as) an object of possible mutual comprehension and consensus within the wider intersubjective community. This realization of the limited intersubjectivity of the book has the consequence that the book, qua book, 'is' (in the phenomenological sense) no longer an objective reality in the strict sense of 'there for everyone' but only in the subject-relative sense of 'there for the we'. In this particular example, the object in the strict sense 'is' now the sensible body, and the book-appearance is simply the way the sensible body appears to, e.g., adult Westerners, whereas the embodied spirit-appearance is the way the sensible body might appear to Zulus.[31]

Generalizing this account, the relativity of the lifeworld consists in its being (intentionally constituted as) 'there' for a limited community, a matter of possible *Evidenz* and consensus for some individuals but not for others. Of course a world is different from a particular object such as a book. According to Husserl's account, a world is neither a particular object nor a collection of particular objects, but a context together with its 'final' horizon.[32] Before explication, this horizon simply has the character of 'and so on', that there is more than the particular context presently in view, and that this 'more' is determinable in progressive stages. Once explicated, the horizon contains anticipations of the specific content of the 'more', as well as a general typical determination of its overall character, content and structure. Thus the constitution of a lifeworld as relative requires a thematization of the horizon of this world, and its referencing to a limited community.[33]

As in the case of other phenomenological demonstrations, the Husserlian justification of relativism consists not merely in the claim that limited intersubjectivity is *intended*, but also in an elucidation of how it is given or 'verified' through *Evidenz*. The *Evidenz* of relativity is a particular instance of the *Evidenz* of the intentional life of others, discussed in section three of Chapter Four. As noted in this earlier discussion, an appresentation of the other's intentional life is founded upon physiognomy, behavior and speech, and each attribution of intentional life to another is correlated with a manifold of further perceptions (including linguistic ones) which would be harmonious with this attribution and would serve to increase its *Evidenz*. For example, in the case of the Zulu, the attribution of visual and tactile experience of the book is based upon his (evident) human physiognomy and visual/tactile behavior, and possibly also on discourse.[34] Similarly, the *Evidenz* of the 'absence' of the specific book-qualities from both the Zulu's present perception and from his world horizon could be founded upon behavior or language. (An appresentation of this kind could also be founded simply on inherited opinions, prior to any first-person perception or discourse, but in this case the *Evidenz* would be mediate and would depend upon the possibility of immediate, first-person *Evidenz* for its validity.) If the Zulu were to pick up the book and (evidently) begin to read from it, then this *Evidenz* would be seriously undermined, if not overturned. As already noted in Chapter Four, *Evidenz* of this kind has a fairly weak, probabilistic character. However, this is equally true both for *Evidenz* of the presence as well as the absence of intersubjectivity, so that the justification of relativity is as strong as that for non-relativity, at least insofar as it is attained following this route.

Now an important further question in relation to this justification of relativity is whether the evident limitation on intersubjectivity is a provisional or definitive one. That is, when it is evident that certain elements of one lifeworld are not elements of another, and hence not possible objects of *Wechselverständigung* for members of the other community, what is the precise nature of this impossibility? Is it a provisional impossibility, an impossibility given the current situation and the resources provided by it alone for establishing consensus? Or is it a definitive impossibility, an impossibility even supposing the opportunity for dialogue, education, and increased familiarity through shared experience? This is an important question, because it could be argued that if Husserl does not provide a justification for the second, stronger sense of the impossibility of intersubjectivity, then the phenomenology of the lifeworld does not provide a demonstration of 'relativism' in any important sense at all. Rather, all that would be shown is that universal intersubjectivity and consensus, although always possible, are more difficult to attain in some cases than others.

I think the only legitimate phenomenological response to this question is to examine the nature of the impossibility of intersubjectivity as it actually is (or could be) constituted in experience, and to evaluate its *Evidenz*. Clearly, in many cases this impossibility is constituted as provisional, a limitation only given certain background conditions as fixed, and surmountable by further dialogue and experience. Husserl's own examples of the book and the Zulu, and the sculpture and the Bantu, tend to fall into this category. The *Evidenz* for the eventual possibility of mutual understanding and consensus could be grounded either on past success in similar cases, or on insight into the existence of sufficient common ground between the two lifeworlds to construct a path from this to the hitherto 'inaccessible' meaning structures and intentional objects. For example, in the case of the old-fashioned Zulu and the book, the existence of language and communication even in a lifeworld without writing could provide such a ground. Thus the Zulu would understand what language and communication are and what signs are, and on this basis could come to (the intentional constitution of) written language, and to a book as a form of communication employing this language. The book would then belong to his lifeworld much as to our own.

However, there are certainly cases in which the impossibility of intersubjectivity is (constituted as) far more definitive, and this definitiveness has its own *Evidenz*. Here we can distinguish among several different types and degrees. Probably one of the most common grounds for the evident impossibility of intersubjectivity is the personality of the participants. A person must be open to dialogue, in possession of certain cognitive flexibility and sensitivity to otherness in order for *Wechselverständigung* to be established. Where these traits are evidently lacking, the impossibility of intersubjectivity will be (constituted as) definitive.

Yet despite the overwhelming practical importance of this source of lived 'incommensurability', it is of relatively little theoretical significance. This is because here the impossibility, although in some sense definitive, is still an empirical and not an in-principle one. That is, it arises not from the content or nature of a lifeworld as such, but from contingent features of a particular individual.[35] We could still imagine that another individual with the same concrete lifeworld could enter into a *Wechselverständigung* with us and that eventually we would come to share a single lifeworld. The theoretically interesting case is one where intersubjectivity is (constituted as) impossible even where the variable pragmatic conditions are ideal, or at least maximally favorable.

A fertile ground for examples of this sort is of course provided by religion. As in the example of the Zulu, Husserl frequently points out that the lifeworld of 'primitives' is populated by demons, spirits, and other fantastical beings, beings which have communal *Seinsgeltung* for them but not for us. What he does not point out it that it is not necessary to look to non-Western cultures to find such examples. The most cursory acquaintance with Western religions reveals similar beings here too (e.g., angels, demons, not to mention the divinities themselves), as well as even more complex intentional constitutions (e.g., the Eucharist). Without trying to defend a relativism of religion in general, I think that at least with respect to these specific beings, intersubjectivity in the relevant sense is not possible, and this not because of lack of hermeneutical tact, but because of differences in the content of the concrete lifeworlds that serve as starting-points. Clearly it is possible for, say, a modern Western anthropologist to form an excellent appresentation of the lifeworld of the primitive, including its spirits, and 'mythical' gods and beasts. Similarly the Zulu could arrive at an understanding of how the wine and wafer are constituted in the intentional life of a Christian. But it is one thing to have an *appresentation* of a foreign lifeworld, and quite another to live in it. Intersubjectivity and *Wechselverständigung* in the relevant senses require not merely the former but also the latter. For it should be emphasized that in the concrete lifeworld these 'superstitions' are not only posited and believed but also *perceived*, have their own *Evidenz* and correlated harmonious manifolds of experience, and so are indeed real in the phenomenological sense of reality.[36] A person who appresents the intentional life of another while failing to constitute its world as real *for himself* (or *tout court*) may indeed understand the other, but does not agree with him. Nor does the content of each lifeworld offer any promising path to a resolution of this disagreement and the establishment of a single concrete lifeworld ontology.[37] At best consensus would consist in the acknowledgement of relativity: these beings belong only to our lifeworld, and those to theirs, without a demand or need for a resolution of this difference.

This is only one example. Similar examples could be developed in ethics or by considering beings with non-human perceptual faculties. Supposing we could communicate with beings with different perceptual faculties, it might then be possible to come to a consensus as to the structure of the 'scientific' world. However, no degree of dialogue or experience will enable us to share a single concrete lifeworld in its full sensible givenness, to 'see' and perceive what these beings do. Again, at most here consensus would mean the acknowledgement of relativity on both sides: the constitution of our sensible lifeworld as *our* world, and not theirs.

Thus Husserl's analysis does not exclude the possibility of irreducible differences in lifeworlds, but rather provides a method for elucidating their grounds and justification. This is not to say, however, that his analysis allows for a *complete* incommensurability of lifeworlds, as we will see in what follows.

3. THE LIFEWORLD AND TRUTH

Once the relativity of the concrete lifeworld has been established, the question arises as to the implications of this relativity for truth. Are judgments about objects and states of affairs encountered within the concrete lifeworld *true*? Or, expressed ontologically, do these objects and states of affairs constitute 'reality'? Now a physicalist objectivist could simply dismiss these variations in concrete lifeworlds, holding that the phenomenal objects given at the level of the lifeworld (e.g., books, works of art, spirits, mythical figures) are in any case not really real, but only subjective appearances. By contrast, according to the physicalist, the real is the mind-independent, subject-irrelative physical nature or reality underlying the culturally and historically relative phenomenological 'reality'. Similarly, a non-physicalist objectivist could claim that, for example, the book really is a book, even though some persons or cultures cannot (presently) recognize it as such. Because on these views truth is conceived as correspondence with a subject-invariant reality, variations in concrete lifeworlds in no way undermine the posited non-relative nature of truth.

However, in light of Husserl's rejection of an objectivist conception of truth in favor of a phenomenological one, the relativity of the lifeworld is not so easily dismissed. Here we see the phenomenological tendencies in Husserl's thinking coming into conflict with the subject-irrelativity of the traditional, logical-mathematical conception of truth with which he begins. (This conflict is ironic insofar as the phenomenological interpretation of truth was originally meant to *save* the traditional conception, together with its subject-irrelativity, by rendering it immune to skepticism and the epistemic critique.) As discussed in Chapter One, according to Husserl's position in the *Prolegomena*, it belongs to the very meaning of truth that what is true is true for all beings, whether men or gods, and this is the only sense intended by 'us all' whenever we speak of truth. Indeed, in the *Prolegomena* Husserl goes so far as to hold that anyone who uses expressions such as 'true for this or that subject' might as well be using the term 'proposition' to refer to trees.[38]

But the *fundamental* tendency of the phenomenological interpretation of truth is not to equate being with the *intersubjective*, but rather with the *given*, with what is evident, in no matter what manner and to no matter what degree.[39] 'True being' is then being which can be verified in further harmonious syntheses of experience, being for which the harmonious manifold of fulfillment predelineated in the initial intentional act can successfully be carried out. This analysis does not prejudge whether the manifold is (intended as) a universally intersubjective one, a partially intersubjective one, or a solipsistic one, but rather directs us to intentional acts themselves to discover this, and so to determine our ontology from the 'things themselves' and not from preconceptions. Now objects and objectivities of the lifeworld are certainly given, and are in no way illusions. Here too there are harmonious fulfillment conditions implicit in the acts in which the objects are constituted, and here too a distinction can be drawn between 'true' being, objects for which these conditions can be satisfied, and illusions. In the case of a lifeworld object such as a book, there is a manifold of syntheses of fulfillment which would confirm or refute whether this really is a book (and not, say, a mirage created by lights), whether it was written by a certain author, etc. Further, these syntheses of fulfillment can be carried out by any of the different members of the limited community for which books are 'there', and consensus can in principle be established. Thus Husserl is led to reject the position of the *Prolegomena* and to affirm that there are two kinds of objectivity: objectivity relative to a restricted subjective community; and objectivity in relation to the total community of cognitive subjects.[40]

Together with the affirmation of the objectivity of what exists at the level of the lifeworld, Husserl suggests a notion of lifeworld truth (in the sense of true judgments). This is developed parallel to the earlier notion, now characterized as 'scientific' truth. Although many remarks concerning lifeworld truth and its relativity are scattered throughout Husserl's writings, especially the *Crisis*, no systematic explication is provided. Indeed, Husserl actually attributes several different kinds of relativity to lifeworld truth without ever distinguishing among them or indicating their interrelations. In light of the incomplete and shifting character of Husserl's treatment, our reconstruction of lifeworld truth will necessarily be a projection beyond the various lines of thought found in the texts.[41]

Four main characterizations of the relativity of lifeworld truth can be discerned in the various discussions: (1) limited intersubjectivity; (2) limited justification; (3) inexactness; and (4) situational character.[42] In addition to explicating each of these senses of relativity, I will argue that the first three types of relativity (limited intersubjectivity, justification, and exactness) can be understood as particular forms of the fourth (situational character). In brief, when a judgment is affirmed as true at the level of the lifeworld, a whole array of situational qualifications concerning the extent of intersubjective verifiability, justification, and exactness of this judgment belong to the intentional horizon of the affirmation itself, and so determine the particular sense in which the judgment is held to be true. Further, while lifeworld truth is indeed relative (e.g., of limited intersubjectivity), it is not the case that the very same judgment with the very same meaning could be true at some times or for some lifeworlds but false relative to others. (This is important if the particular notion of relative truth suggested by Husserl's discussions is to survive the sort of formal critiques presented in the *Prolegomena*, and discussed in Chapter One.)

The first sense in which lifeworld truth is relative was discussed in the previous section: its limited intersubjectivity. As noted above, certain elements of the lifeworld (e.g., cultural-historical objects, religious institutions) come to be experienced not as 'there for everyone', but as 'there for this or that intersubjective community'. Thus what is meant when it is affirmed that a judgment about such objectivities is true is that it is true for a particular intersubjective community, the community able to comprehend and verify this judgment and to come to a mutual understanding and consensus (*Wechselverständigung*) concerning its truth or falsehood.

However, it is not the case that the same judgment could be true relative to one community but false relative to another. Rather, at most a judgment would simply be unintelligible to members of the other community, or they would not be able to carry out the intentional acts in which the objects under discussion are made evident. Thus, for example, Husserl argues that judgments about Michelangelo's David are neither true nor false relative to the Bantu, because the conditions for the constitution of the object under discussion are not met:

"Every existing object is the correlate of certain 'apperceptions' which belong generally to it and its type of objectification. Further, every distinction between agreement and disagreement, and finally between the correct and the incorrect, presupposes the relevant kind and specificity of apperceptions to which it refers back.... We can argue with each other about truth and falsehood, being and non-being, in our world, but not with the Bantu, because he, as a member of his 'we', has another surrounding world."[43]

The second sense in which Husserl characterizes lifeworld truth as 'relative' is its limited justification. Even at the level of the lifeworld, argues Husserl, judgments are formed, doubts occur, grounds are provided, and decisions are made concerning truth and falsehood. However, here the justification sought and attained is by no means a final one, nor even a best-possible one. Rather, the extent of justification is fixed by practical interests and needs: judgments are rendered as secure as necessary for the practical projects of life.[44]

Thus at the level of the lifeworld, what is *meant* when it is affirmed that a principle is true is that this principle is justified relative to a specific set of interests and projects, and over a specific range of situations. That is, the truth-affirmation itself contains an implicit reference to these limiting initial conditions, and this reference (together with a specification of the conditions), although generally not thematic, itself belongs to the intentional horizon of the affirmation. This truth-affirmation is then justified or unjustified (and hence true or false) over this limited range of interest-situation complexes; outside of them it has no application and makes no claims. Now this does not imply that a judgment really is justified at the level of the lifeworld simply because one thinks it is so, nor that a judgment which at one time counts as justified cannot later be overturned. Rather, the point is that the justification can be overturned only by failing to apply in the same contexts and for the same interests as those for which it is affirmed to hold good. For example, suppose Husserl's trader has certain trading practices and principles, and that these count for him as justified or 'true' (i.e., effective in bringing about the desired practical ends). The affirmation of their truth does not hold without qualification, but rather contains an implicit reference to certain interests (e.g., making a reasonable living) and situations (e.g., the size and type of business, the city in which it is located, etc.). Therefore in order to be overturned, the principles would have to be seen to fail even relative to the very interests and situations for which they were held to hold good. The justification would be overturned if, for example, the trader's business thrived for a few years and then failed, but not if a much larger business in a different city were ruined by their application. Thus while it might *seem* that these principles are true, e.g., relative to the trader, but false relative to a Wall Street brokerage house, in fact these principles are neither true nor false relative to the latter, since the situation of the latter is not encompassed in the intentional horizon of the truth-affirmation itself.

A third relativity of the lifeworld is given special emphasis by Husserl in the *Crisis*: its inexactness. Here he argues that unlike the idealized objectivities of mathematics and science, the things of the lifeworld have only rough, approximate shapes, weights, colors, and other properties, properties which are more or less but not absolutely determinate. Nowhere in the lifeworld does one find a perfect line, an exact circle or plane. Rather, one finds, for example, a table, something with an edge which is more or less straight, a surface that is more or less flat, a base more or less round. Thus 'round' at the level of the lifeworld does not denote an exact, geometrical figure, but a typical range of approximate forms.[45]

Husserl argues that while mathematical exactness has no place in the lifeworld, there is nonetheless a practical, pragmatic sense of exactitude. A specific determination of a property of a lifeworld object counts as 'exact' at this level insofar as it is accurate to the degree fixed by the practical interests governing the particular situation, and the available technological means.[46] Much as in the case of lifeworld justification, in the case of determinations of measurements, each truth-affirmation has an intentional horizon implicitly specifying the situations, interests, and technological means relative to which the measurement is asserted to hold good. For example, the shopkeeper does not assert that his determination of weight is true universally for all situations, interests, and technological means, but only for those similar to his own. It is therefore inappropriate to characterize his measurement of weight as true for him, but false relative to, say, a goldsmith or a physicist. For understood properly (i.e., with its horizon partially explicated) his truth-affirmation has the meaning, "This determination is exact relative to situations, interests, and means of the following general type ...", and makes no claim at all about the weight of the object for a goldsmith, much less the weight of the object 'in itself'. This judgment, understood with its horizon, may be either true or false. It cannot, however, be true relative to some persons and false relative to others.

The final sense in which lifeworld truth is relative, its situational or occasional character, is the one which runs most consistently through Husserl's scattered remarks. An occasional judgment is defined by Husserl as one whose meaning depends upon the situation the judging person has in view, as in the case of judgments employing indexicals.[47] Further, in the assertion of such a judgment all of the manifold relevant elements of the situation are intended along with the judgment itself, but this only implicitly, only in the 'background' (i.e., in the intentional horizon of the judgment). These elements are not even thematic in the intention of the judging person, and can only be elucidated subsequently, bit by bit. Because the meaning of the judgment is not carried in the words alone, but determined essentially by innumerable unexpressed situational elements, the intelligibility of the judgment depends upon the typical similarity of situations within a common lifeworld: persons who share the same lifeworld will be familiar with the typical elements of the situation in view, and hence the judgment will be understood even when its meaning is not explicitly set forth.[48]

In light of this characterization of a situational judgment and of our preceding discussions of limited intersubjectivity, justification, and exactness, it can be seen that in the case of a lifeworld truth-affirmation, the very *sense* in which the judgment is held to be true varies from one judgment to another, and is itself contained implicitly in the intentional horizon of the judging person in the act of judgment. When a lifeworld judgment is held to be true, it is not held to be true for all subjects and all times, and finally justifiable in the way of logical truth. Rather, it is held to be true in a qualified sense and with a limited range: e.g., justifiable relative to certain practical interests and technological means; intelligible, verifiable, and a matter of possible consensus for a certain limited intersubjective community. Further, the specific sense of truth cannot be determined in advance for all judgments, but can only be uncovered by a subsequent explication of the horizon of such judgments as present themselves as true.[49]

The emergence of the notion of lifeworld truth therefore presents a significant self-critique of Husserl's earlier 'absolutist' conception in the *Prolegomena*, according to which the absolute conception is the one 'we all' intend *whenever* we talk about truth. To the contrary, a more careful examination of the intentional horizons of the truth-affirming judgments we actually carry out reveals that, in many cases, truth is (implicitly) intended as a pragmatic verifiability of limited intersubjective availability. Thus the analysis of lifeworld truth provides a phenomenologically more accurate characterization of the sense in which many judgments are held to be true. By contrast, the position of the *Prolegomena* now appears to be the result of an unjustified universalization of the logician's conception of truth to all domains of judgment, an attempt to determine the nature of truth by means of a philosophical theory, rather than by the phenomenological analysis of such 'truths' as actually turn up.

Thus in *Formal and Transcendental Logic* Husserl maintains that it is neither necessary nor possible to determine the general nature of truth (and, in particular, its absolute or relative character) by way of a philosophical theory or philosophical argumentation. Rather, we can only consult experience and examine the evidence it presents. It is the particular task of phenomenology, he argues, to carry out a systematic explication of the horizons – the limits, ranges, qualifications, and presuppositions ordinarily veiled from view – of whatever objectivities or judgments present themselves as true in the naïve course of experience, whether these be the truths of the logician, the natural scientist, or of everyday practical life. This explication of the horizons yields a superior degree of rationality not in that it further assures that what gives itself as true actually is true, but rather in that it makes plain the *sense* of the truth which one already has, together with its range, presuppositions, and limits: "We have the **truth** then, not as falsely absolutized, but rather in each case within its **horizons**, horizons which do not remain overlooked or veiled from sight, but which are systematically explicated."[50]

The above remarks make possible an important clarification of the strategy adopted in Chapters Three and Four to 'defend' Husserl's phenomenological elucidation of truth. There I argued that the phenomenological conception of truth is preferable to the objectivist correspondence theory because it does not fall prey to skepticism and relativism. Yet such an argument could appear illegitimate on Husserl's own account, for it attempts to establish a philosophical theory of truth 'from above', imposing preconceived criteria (e.g., truth should be conceived so as to avoid skepticism and relativism) rather than by deriving the conception of truth from experience itself.

However, although the rhetorical structure of my earlier argument could suggest that Husserl's conception of truth receives its justification philosophically 'from above', this is not the case. As noted in Chapter One,[51] three steps are involved in the phenomenological justification of a concept: its derivation from experience; a demonstration of its formal consistency (which shows that the concept can be thought); and a demonstration that the concept can be *given*, fulfilled in intuition (which shows that instances of this concept are possible existents). Thus, for example, the concept 'color without extension' fulfills the criterion of formal consistency but not that of consistency with fulfillment conditions, and hence instantiations of it cannot exist.[52] Now Husserl's position with respect to the phenomenological conception of truth is that it is not at all an abstract philosophical theory but rather the conception of truth (or the generalized form of the various particular conceptions) actually shaping lived experience. Arguably, the traditional correspondence theory of truth (even in the objectivist form) is also sometimes actually employed in judgments. Further, both conceptions of truth are logically consistent. However, the objectivist theory of truth fails to meet the third criterion, the criterion of fulfillment in intuition. As argued in Chapter Three, 'truths' or 'realities' objectivistically conceived cannot be given in experience. Accordingly, the earlier exposition of the sense in which the phenomenological conception of truth avoids skepticism is not an argument 'from above' but a demonstration that this conception, unlike the objectivist one, meets the third justification criterion. Similarly, the final justification of either a relative or a non-relative conception of truth would consist in a demonstration that truths of this sort can be given evidently in experience.

Clearly, in terms of Husserl's general conception of conceptual justification, the validity of a relative conception of truth cannot simply be ruled out from the start. A further phenomenological analysis reveals that such a conception does indeed meet the three justification criteria.

4. THE PRIORITY OF THE LIFEWORLD

Husserl's assertion of the priority of the lifeworld is significant in the context of this discussion in two respects. Firstly, it strengthens his support of relativism insofar as the relative lifeworld is held to be prior to the non-relative world posited by science. Further, it provides a crucial weak point for his continued defense of the traditional conception of truth, as will be discussed in detail in section 5.

Although Husserl's thesis of the priority of the lifeworld is generally associated with the *Crisis*, it can be found in much earlier writings as well. Arguments for the priority of the lifeworld can be found in *Ideas II*, the lectures on phenomenological psychology, and *Experience and Judgment*, as well as the *Crisis* itself.[53] Three different senses of priority can be distinguished. The lifeworld is prior historically, both in human history in general and in the development of the individual. Further, the lifeworld is universally given, whereas the world of science is not: not all cultures or persons have the concepts and methods through which the world of science comes to be 'there' for them. By contrast, every culture lives in a lifeworld and possesses its everyday, practical truths, and this is the case just as much for societies with modern science as for those without it.[54] However, the third and much stronger sense of priority which Husserl attributes to the lifeworld is priority in the order of *Seinsgeltung*. That is, he argues that the world as posited and described by the sciences is a higher-order construction attained by abstraction, idealization, and (in the case of the natural sciences) induction starting from the concrete intuitive bases provided by the lifeworld. Thus if there were no lifeworld attaining *Evidenz*-grounded existential validity for us, then neither could the world of science have existential validity and so 'be' for us: the abstract or theoretical entities of the sciences could not be thought and given in intentional acts.

In the *Crisis* Husserl argues that the basic concepts of geometry arise from an idealization of the always rough, merely approximate forms given in sensible perception or imagination. What is actually given in intuition is not, for example, the straight line of geometry, but the edge of a table, something only imperfectly and roughly straight, something finite rather than infinite. Even in the imagination, only imperfect, approximate fulfillments can be generated, and not exact fulfillments of what is intended by a geometrical line. Rather, the concept of a geometrical object is a limit concept attained by imagining a series of increasingly more exact intuitive forms, extended by an 'and so forth' past the bounds of the imagination to the ideal. As in his earlier writings Husserl continues to maintain that there is indeed *Evidenz* regarding mathematical objects. But if, as Husserl here asserts, intuition of mathematical objects is possible only by way of idealization of lifeworld objects or images thereof and not directly, then without the lifeworld it would not be possible to arrive at mathematical concepts. Similarly, neither would it be possible to attain *Evidenz* regarding those fundamental principles upon which the bulk of mathematical knowledge is erected by symbolic thinking. Therefore if there were no lifeworld, the world or worlds posited by mathematics would be (phenomenologically considered) nothing for us. Lifeworld evidence does not determine which mathematical principles are true, but it makes mathematical evidence and therefore mathematical truth possible.

The dependence of the natural sciences (e.g., mathematical physics) upon the lifeworld is even greater. In addition to employing mathematics and therefore depending upon the lifeworld in the same way as this discipline, the natural sciences also have recourse to the lifeworld for empirical verification of their theories, verification which is necessary if these theories are to attain the status of truths. Thus if there were no observation statements counting as true at the level of the lifeworld, then no theoretical statements could come to count as true in the sense of scientific truth, i.e., as 'true for all subjects and all times'.

It should be noted that Husserl's category of priority in the order of *Seinsgeltung* is *neither* the traditional category of epistemic priority, *nor* that of ontological priority, but a specifically phenomenological category that is to supplant them both. Thus it should not be thought that what is being asserted here is simply the priority of the lifeworld to the world of science in the order of *knowledge*. This latter is a priority which any objectivist scientific realist could easily grant, but then dismiss as trivial. The non-phenomenological scientific realist would admit that we need to know about the lifeworld in order to know about the 'true' (i.e., subject-irrelative) world investigated by science. Nonetheless, this realist would hold that the world of science is prior to the lifeworld in the order of *being*. Because the lifeworld is no more than the appearance of the true, scientific world in subjective experience, if the scientific world did not exist, neither would the lifeworld itself. Thus the objectivist scientific realist would maintain that the world of science is prior in the more significant sense.

However, once one rejects an epistemically naïve objectivism, a strict distinction between order of knowledge and order of being can no longer be maintained.[55] As discussed in Chapter Three, according to the phenomeno-logical elucidation of reality, to exist is not to exist 'in itself' apart from all possibility of knowledge, nor to exist as an object of knowledge for God. Rather, reality is a modalization of appearance (or better, of phenomenality). A reality is a phenomenon which is constituted with the sense, 'capable of maximal *Evidenz* or verification in accordance with the immanently specified fulfillment conditions', and a true reality is a phenomenon actually capable of such maximal fulfillment. Thus in order to be even a *candidate* for reality in the phenomenological sense (i.e., for *Seinsgeltung*), something must first be a phenomenon, or an 'object of knowledge' in the traditional sense. Therefore there is no order of being wholly detachable from the order of knowledge. Further, it is not merely that we must experience the lifeworld as an unmodalized phenomenon in order for the world of science to be experienced as a phenomenon. Rather, the lifeworld must attain *Seinsgeltung*, it must be experienced as a *reality* in order for the world of science to be experienced as a reality.

Still, it could be objected that what count as verifying observation statements or 'phenomena' in science are not simply descriptive characterizations of lifeworld objects (e.g., 'the needle moved to the left', 'there were three clicks'), but rather statements that are themselves products of theories. For example, Newton takes Kepler's laws as 'phenomena' or observation statements in demonstrating the law of gravity, although obviously Kepler's laws are not evident at the level of the lifeworld: we cannot look into the sky and 'see' the planets travelling in ellipses about the sun in the way in which one 'sees' a passing cloud. Therefore it could be argued that scientific evidence is founded upon scientific evidence, and not upon lifeworld evidence. Or phrased alternately, the distinction between observation sentences and theoretical sentences does not hold up.[56]

But in response to this objection it should be pointed out that it has not been claimed that all statements which count as observation statements in science are in fact statements evident or verifiable at the level of the lifeworld. The claim is also not that lifeworld-level observation sentences *guarantee* the truth of scientific sentences, nor that they uniquely determine which theoretical statements or higher-order observation statements can count as true. Rather, the position is the much more limited one that lifeworld evidence is a *necessary* condition for any scientific demonstration at all, and therefore for the (phenomenological) truth of any scientific sentence (whether a theoretical or an observation statement) and for the *Seinsgeltung* of the entities it posits. For example, returning to the previous case of Newton, Kepler's laws count as true on the basis of Tycho's numerical data, and this data in turn counts as true on the basis of certain perceptions of the planets carried out in ordinary sensible perception. Similarly, a physicist who determines the location of a star on the basis of an x-ray photograph (a determination which then counts as an 'observation sentence' at a higher level) does not perceive the star in sensible perception. But he must perceive *some* lifeworld objects (e.g., the lines and patterns on the photograph), and these objects must count for him as intersubjectively verifiable if the determination of the location of the star is to count for him as 'true' in the sense of science.

This shows that the claim of the priority of the lifeworld is independent of the distinction between observation and theoretical statements. However, it does make use of the distinction between lifeworld evidence and lifeworld objects on the one hand, and scientific evidence and scientific objects on the other. Husserl himself seems willing to admit a certain fluidity in this distinction, conceding in *Experience and Judgment* that received scientific theories themselves appear as sedimentations in ordinary experience, fusing with and conditioning the lifeworld.[57] Yet despite this interaction between the two, important differences remain. As discussed in Chapter Two, scientific *Evidenz* always has the character of subject-irrelativity, whereas lifeworld *Evidenz* is often subject-relative. Similarly, in general scientific *Evidenz* is more exact and fully justified than that of the lifeworld. By contrast, lifeworld *Evidenz* has a greater degree of intuitive fullness and immediacy than scientific *Evidenz*, at least in the case of the 'worldly' sciences (which include not only physics but also mathematics and logic). Finally, scientific *Evidenz* is *founded*, occurring only on the basis of perceptions of other objects which are given with greater adequacy. For example, we can compare the two judgments, 'the planets travel in ellipses' and 'a cloud is overhead'. The latter judgment can be made evident by merely looking, and is not founded on the perception of another domain of objects. This is not the case for the judgment that the planets travel in ellipses. If we employ the Newtonian demonstration, the *Evidenz* of elliptical planetary orbits requires observations made with special instruments; the supposition of the truth of other laws (e.g., Newton's three laws of motion); and numerous mathematical principles (either of geometry or calculus). It should be emphasized that the principle of elliptical planetary orbits is not highly abstract, especially in comparison to principles of atomic or sub-atomic physics. Yet because its *Evidenz* involves mathematics it is still mediate, founded upon the *Evidenz* of an order of objects given more fully in intuition and not mentioned in the judgment itself.

To summarize the results of our discussion, Husserl holds that the lifeworld founds the sciences in the sense of providing the intuitive bases on which concepts are formed and *Evidenz* is attained, and thus the bases which make possible the intentional constitution of the entities and principles posited by the sciences. Lifeworld truths do not guarantee that scientific truths are really true, but rather are necessary conditions for the verifiability of scientific principles and so for their (evident) holding as true. Thus the lifeworld is prior in the order of *Seinsgeltung* or intentional constitution.

Now Tugendhat suggests that there might be yet another sense in which, according to Husserl, the lifeworld is prior to the sciences. Tugendhat argues that Husserl does not merely affirm the priority of the lifeworld in *Seinsgeltung*, but that he takes the further step of asserting lifeworld truth to be the more *authentic* of the two kinds of truth. Tugendhat then attacks Husserl for taking this step, holding that it goes against the proper meaning of truth. For according to Tugendhat, it belongs to the proper meaning of truth that the more subject-irrelative an object or state of affairs, the more true the judgments about it. Now the objects of the lifeworld have a certain degree of independence from subjective modes of givenness, but they are more subject-relative than the 'world in itself' posited by science. Thus, concludes Tugendhat, it must be granted that scientific truth is the more authentic.[58]

But in response to the Tugendhat objection, it must be asked whether the category of 'authenticity' could have any meaning in terms of Husserl's analysis of truth. As noted above,[59] Husserl argues in *Formal and Transcendental Logic* that the sense of truth is to be derived by analyzing such evidence as comes up, and not by universalizing to all domains a notion of truth that is appropriate only to some. Now Husserl does characterize the lifeworld as the '*Letztbegründende*', in the sense that if there were no concrete, everyday world, it would not be possible to carry out the intentional acts in which the theoretical entities of science attain *Seinsgeltung*. Yet at the same time that he claims greater intuitiveness and 'originality' (i.e., genetic priority in intentional constitution) for the lifeworld, Husserl constantly emphasizes the greater intersubjectivity, exactness, and certainty of scientific truth. But once these distinctions have been drawn, the question of degrees of authenticity has no place. Scientific truth is authentically true, and so is lifeworld truth, although each has its own proper character.

However, perhaps Tugendhat is motivated to insist on a further ranking of the two truths by another worry. Perhaps he is concerned with the question of the 'really real': is the world really as it appears to us in everyday life, or is the world really as it is described by the sciences?[60] It could be argued that it is not possible to adopt a neutral position on this issue. For both the sciences and everyday life present claims about the same objects, and these claims often conflict. For example, in everyday experience my lamp is perceived to be a solid, impenetrable object, whereas modern science teaches that the lamp is in fact largely empty space. Thus it is not possible to hold that the lamp is described equally correctly or 'authentically' by both everyday and scientific judgments. Because the two judgments are mutually inconsistent, we must hold *either* that the lamp is really as perceived in ordinary experience, *or* that it is really (or at least more authentically) as described by science.

However, the guiding presupposition of this argument, i.e., that lifeworld truth and scientific truth could conflict, cannot be granted. This is already demonstrated by the fact that the lifeworld continues to be 'there' for us even when we take up theoretical activity as scientists, and is not canceled or 'broken up' by the affirmation of scientific judgments. For example, at the level of the lifeworld the lamp is solid, and its everyday solidity does not vanish when I become acquainted with or even come to believe the theories and discoveries of science (as would occur if, for example, I discovered that what seemed to be a lamp is in fact an illusion produced by hidden mirrors or lights). For the sense contained in the intentional horizon of my judgment, 'this lamp is solid' is that, for example, if I touch the lamp, I feel resistance; if I drop it on a glass table, the table will break; no matter what angle I choose, I cannot see through the lamp, etc., and the same holds good for other normal persons. By contrast, when science claims 'this lamp is not solid', what is meant is that, for example, if a beam of particles is shot through the lamp, most of them will pass undeflected. But even if this latter judgment is granted, it in no way contradicts the judgment made at the level of the lifeworld, when this is understood with the meaning implicit in its horizon. Thus both assertions, 'the lamp is solid (in the everyday sense)' and 'the lamp is not solid (in the scientific sense)' are true, each understood in terms of its horizon.

The whole tendency of Husserl's phenomenology is to dissolve the question of the 'really real.' It is not that *either* there are tables and lamps, *or* there are electrons and waves (*or* there are immanent *Erlebnisse*). Rather, each type of object has its own mode of givenness, and counts as real in its own manner and within its own horizon. Some categories of objectivity are more intuitively evident than others, some are prior in the order of *Seinsgeltung*, some have greater certainty, intersubjectivity, or exactness. But the question, over and above these various differences, as to which is the more *authentically* or really real has no sense in terms of Husserl's analysis.[61]

5. THE PHENOMENOLOGICAL OVERCOMING OF RELATIVISM

The previous discussion shows that a limited version of relativism emerges as a consequence of Husserl's analysis of the lifeworld, together with the phenomenological elucidation of truth. Yet despite the affirmation of relativism at the level of the lifeworld, Husserl continues to defend a non-relative conception of truth, albeit now only for certain object-domains such as logic, mathematics, natural science, and philosophy qua phenomenology, and perhaps even here only as a regulative idea. However, it has recently been suggested that in light of the relativity and plurality of the lifeworld, the traditional 'scientific' conception of truth should simply have been abandoned by Husserl, even if this was a step he himself was unwilling or unable to take. A consistent development of phenomenology would then lead to the kind of relativism allegedly characteristic of the later heirs of the phenomenological tradition.[62]

In what follows I will offer an alternative to the view that abandonment of non-relative truth is the legitimate consequence of Husserl's phenomenology. I will begin with a critique of recent interpretations advanced in the literature in support of this view, and then attempt to provide a positive and properly phenomenological justification of an absolute conception of truth.

5.1 *Phenomenology as Relativism?*

According to the traditional conception of truth, truth is as it is 'in itself', the same always and for everyone. But in light of Husserl's rejection of an epistemically naïve realism in favor of a phenomenological conception of truth, what it means for a judgment to be true 'in itself' is that it is of *universal* intelligibility and verifiability, across diverse lifeworlds, and not merely true within one lifeworld but meaningless or of indeterminate truth-value outside it.[63]

Yet it could be thought that the most consistent development of Husserl's own position would actually lead to the *abandonment* of the traditional conception of truth. This is because even a restricted defense of the traditional conception encounters a serious difficulty unearthed by Husserl's own analysis: the lifeworld, the foundation of the sciences, is itself relative. Thus the very realm which is to provide the founding meanings and evidences for the higher-order, universally accessible concepts and evidences of the sciences is not itself universally intersubjective, but culturally and historically relative. How then can the sciences validly take the notion of truth 'in itself', in the sense of universally intelligible and verifiable judgments, even as a goal-idea?

Husserl is clearly aware of this difficulty. For example, he writes in the *Crisis*:

"[The lifeworld] is the spatio-temporal world of things as we experience them in our pre- and extra-scientific life and as we know them to be experienceable beyond what is [actually] experienced.... Things: that is, stones, animals, plants, even human beings and human products; but here everything is subject-relative [*subjektiv-relativ*], even though normally in our experience and in the social group united with us in the community of life, we arrive at 'secure' facts.... But when we are thrown into an alien social sphere, that of the Negroes in the Congo, Chinese peasants, etc., we discover that their truths, the facts that are for them fixed, generally verified or verifiable, are by no means the same as ours."[64]

As is well known, Husserl mounts a massive effort to overcome this difficulty with the argument that while the *concrete* lifeworld of each human community may vary, nonetheless the various lifeworlds share a common general structure. This shared structure of all lifeworld experience can then provide the foundation for the formation of higher-order concepts and evidences (e.g., concerning physical bodies, numbers, geometrical shapes) of *universal* intelligibility and verifiability. Thus Husserl continues the *Crisis* passage:

"The embarrassment [of the relativity of the lifeworld] disappears as soon as we consider that the lifeworld does have, in all its relative features, a **general structure**. This general structure, to which everything

that exists relatively is bound, is not itself relative."[65]
Yet the position that the multiplicity of concrete lifeworlds possess a universal structure has been found an inviting target of attack. David Carr sets up his critique of this position by distinguishing two importantly distinct claims made by it. The first claim is that the sciences *presuppose* the existence of universal lifeworld structures. For example, the natural sciences presuppose that despite cultural-historical differences there is basically a single normal human experience of the spatio-temporal realm of sensible bodies. Thus the empirical verifications carried out by a member of a particular lifeworld could in principle be carried out by a member of any lifeworld, and the judgments of natural science are (at least potentially) of universal intersubjectivity. Similarly, the mathematician and the logician presuppose that the concepts employed in their judgments are universally accessible, and that the judgments themselves can be re-enacted again and again, in any historical period or cultural context and always with exactly the same meaning and always attaining the same *Evidenz*. But if mathematical and logical concepts are themselves formed by abstraction from and idealization of the concrete intuitive objects of the lifeworld, then the assertion of the universal intersubjectivity of mathematics and logic also presupposes that there is a common structure running through all lifeworlds.[66]

It should also be emphasized that Husserl's claim that phenomenology is capable of addressing universally intersubjective truths can be held equally to depend upon the presupposition of an a priori of the lifeworld. Consider, for example, the case of the phenomenological analysis of time. According to this analysis, time is experienced as a living present with a 'before' in retention and an 'after' in protention. But Husserl's implicit claim that this analysis can be understood and also verified in experience by all cultural-historical groups (and not merely, say, by contemporary Westerners) presupposes that there is a single structure of lived time characteristic of all lifeworlds whatsoever. If this were not the case, then the phenomenological analysis of time would be of merely local verifiability and intersubjective validity, and similarly for all other phenomenological analyses, eidetic or otherwise.

Now the second element of the Husserlian position identified by Carr is the much stronger claim that all lifeworlds *actually possess* universal structures. Knowledge of these structures would then provide an ultimate justification for the employment of the traditional conception of truth.[67] However, while Carr agrees with Husserl regarding the first claim, he denies the demonstrability of the second. Further, he argues that the plausibility of the claim that universal structures actually exist is seriously undermined once we realize that the lifeworld includes not only things and persons but also the sedimentation of historically contingent philosophies, religions, sciences, and other cultural formations. These penetrate so deeply into our way of apprehending reality, maintains Carr, that not only the content but also the very structure of experience is affected. Thus even at the most basic levels of sensible perception, lifeworlds may differ fundamentally depending upon the theories and interpretations prevalent in them.[68] In particular, Carr criticizes Husserl for asserting that the distinction between things and persons is a universal structure of all lifeworlds. Rather, suggests Carr, in some societies, such as those dominated by animism or totemism, there might be no experience of purely corporeal, spiritless things, and thus here the thing/person distinction might not be a structure of experience at all. Perhaps this distinction is itself no more than the contingent product of Western culture and its objective science.[69]

Yet the Carr analysis suffers from a number of flaws. Probably the most serious of these is its employment of an unphenomenological form of the presupposition/reality distinction, the consequence of an implicit unphenomenological conception of reality as such. As noted above, Carr grants that the sciences *presuppose* universal lifeworld structures, but denies that such exist (or at least that their existence has been demonstrated). Now while it is true that Husserl himself employs the language of 'presupposition' versus 'reality', it must be recalled that the meaning of such language on a phenomenological account is significantly different from its meaning on an objectivist one. According to the phenomenological conception of reality, where a 'presupposition' is so entrenched in the very character of experience that it itself becomes a feature of what is given in perception, then this is not merely a presupposition but also a reality, something that is evident.[70] Thus if features of the lifeworld are actually intended and perceived as universal, then according to a phenomenological account they are not *merely* presupposed to be universal. At the same time, we may validly require a critical evaluation of the degree and reliability of the *Evidenz* of their universality before naïvely admitting that such universality is indeed even phenomenologically real. Where the *Evidenz* of universality falls short of maximal adequacy or apodicticity, the universality is still not 'merely' a presupposition (since it is at least partially justified), but it is a presupposition in relation to the ideal of maximal justification. Thus the phenomenological distinction between presupposition and reality is a somewhat fluid one.

By contrast, Carr's emphasis on a hard-and-fast distinction between presupposition and reality suggests that he is not employing a phenomeno-logical conception of reality at all. Yet if Carr's objection against Husserl is that he fails to demonstrate that universal lifeworld structures exist in the *objectivist* sense of existence, then clearly Husserl would completely agree with him. However, Husserl neither attempts such a demonstration nor believes one possible.

Thus the first flaw of the Carr argument is to demand from Husserl a demonstration which his own analysis shows in principle impossible. However, another strand in Carr's argument suggests that if we are willing to accept partial evidence as justification, then what we find is that we have better evidence to the effect that universal lifeworld structures do not exist than that they do. In order to evaluate the merit of this strand of the Carr argument, it will be useful to reconstruct it as consisting of three separate claims:

(1) Anthropology teaches that some societies (e.g., animistic ones) do not distinguish between persons and things;

(2) All experience and perception of reality is contingent theory-laden, both in content and in structure;

(3) There are no universal, trans-cultural structures of the lifeworld.

How do these various claims function together within the argument as a whole? Clearly, (3) follows from (2): if all structures of experience are conditioned by contingent theories, then there are no universal structures of the lifeworld. But the crucial question to raise in relation to this argument is: what is the justification for (2)? That is, on what grounds can it be concluded that *all* experience and perception of reality is contingent theory-laden? Although Carr does not admit this explicitly, it is in fact (1), Carr's anthropological evidence of the non-universality of the thing/person distinction, which provides the grounds for (2), the claim that all perception is contingent theory-laden. Carr's implicit argument is that anthropology reveals that populations with different religious, philosophical, or scientific views also experience and perceive the world in markedly different ways. Further, similar findings on the part of psychology, sociology, and history could be adduced to provide additional justification for (2). Thus in the Carr argument, the burden of the justification of the principle of the theory-ladenness of perception is carried by the results of empirical sciences such as anthropology.

Now it could be objected against Carr that although anthropology and other sciences teach that different societies experience the world in different ways, it is not at all the case that anthropological studies demonstrate or even suggest that there are *no* universal structures of experience. Which anthropological study concludes that there is a population with no experience of space and time, or of the world of sensible things as belonging to a single spatio-temporal order? Indeed, even Carr's claim that anthropological findings show that members of societies dominated by animism draw no distinction between persons and things is questionable.

However, yet another objection can be brought against the Carr position. For, as argued above, Carr's central claim of the theory-ladenness of perception depends upon empirical sciences for its justification.[71] But then the assertion of this claim presupposes the *validity* of the results attained by these sciences. However, the claim of any science to attain intersubjectively valid results itself presupposes that there are universal structures running through all lifeworlds, structures which make the intersubjective intelligibility and verifiability of these principles possible. Therefore, *either* Carr must hold that the results of anthropology suggesting the theory-ladenness of all perception (presuming there are such) are valid only, e.g., for certain Western intellectuals of the post-war period; in which case he would have to hold the same for the claim that there are no universal structures of the lifeworld. *Or* Carr can hold that the results of anthropology are valid across lifeworlds; in which case it would follow that (3) is false. Clearly Carr's implicit position is the latter and not the former, and therefore the argument is self-refuting.

Thus the Carr critique fails because it encounters the same difficulty as arguments in favor of relativism. In order to mount even qualified evidence in support of the claim that there is no common structure running through all lifeworlds, and hence that Husserl's continued defense of the traditional conception of truth is unjustified, Carr surreptitiously employs the very principle he seeks to undermine.

A related attack against Husserl's assertion that all lifeworlds have a common structure is mounted by Bernhard Waldenfels.[72] Waldenfels notes that according to Husserl, the basic lifeworld stratum which is to provide the general foundation for the sciences is the spatio-temporal world of sensible bodies.[73] Further, Husserl claims that the lifeworld (including this founding stratum) differs from the idealized world 'in itself' posited by the sciences in that the lifeworld is given intuitively in experience. However, argues Waldenfels, it follows from Husserl's own theory that this universal stratum is not the object of intuitive experience but a *construct*, the product of an abstractive analysis.[74] By contrast, insofar as space and time are taken as the concrete, *lived* space and time of the lifeworld, they are not single but manifold in structure. The way space presents itself in experience varies depending upon forms of social organization, historical tradition, circumstances, and even education. A painter, for example, may experience space differently from a layman. Similarly, time is experienced differently again depending upon circumstances, mood, whether one lives in an urban or a rural environment, the prevailing standards of time-measurement, and so forth.[75] Thus, concludes Waldenfels, it is only an abstraction to speak of a single, universal *lifeworld* spatio-temporal structure. Further, there would be no difference between this structure and the objective space and time posited by science. Rather, there are *many* lived space and time structures, structures which may variously intersect and overlap, but which – insofar as they are taken as actually given within the lifeworld – retain their distinctness.[76]

Yet in response to this objection, it should first be noted that Waldenfels makes extensive use of the results of sociology and psychology to support his claims that the experience of space and time varies from one culture or situation to another.[77] Waldenfels is clearly maintaining that these results are themselves objectively valid, intersubjectively verifiable ones, and therefore that his claim of the non-universality of experienced space and time is such. If Waldenfels agrees with the Husserlian position that the evidence of the sciences is founded on the lifeworld, then his assertion of the intersubjectivity of psychology and sociology presupposes the existence of universal lifeworld structures Waldenfels denies. If, by contrast, he rejects the Husserlian claim that the sciences are founded on lifeworld (as indeed seems the case), he is still in no position to attack Husserl's continued maintenance of the claim to universal intersubjectivity, a claim Waldenfels himself continues to employ.

Moreover, in contrast to the Waldenfels characterization of Husserl's analysis of the lifeworld as overly universalist, and even 'violently' so, it should be emphasized that this analysis in no way ignores or is intolerant of differences in concrete experiences. Such differences as exist and can be given phenomenologically are to be fully acknowledged and not to be trivialized by abstractions, and this includes differences in the experience of, e.g., bodies, spatiality, and temporality. Yet the question which must be asked is whether the *denial* of the existence of universal structures is the less violent position, the one truer to the character of the lifeworld as concretely given. In particular, the recognition that space and time can be experienced in different ways does not demonstrate that there is *no* common structure or layer of spatio-temporal experience running through all lifeworlds. Indeed, the very perception that there are differences in the ways space and time are experienced at the level of the lifeworld already reflects that there are some common elements to these experiences. For when we perceive that two concrete lifeworld experiences are *different* experiences of time, we also perceive that they are both experiences *of time*, and hence that despite their differences, they both exhibit the same noetic-noematic correlations that make an experience an experience of time.

Following Wittgenstein (and the Waldenfels argument seems to move in this direction), it could be thought that the various experiences of temporality exhibit only a family resemblance, and not an essential common structure.[78] The force of the Wittgensteinian 'family resemblance' argument seems to be that when various individuals are grouped under a single term there need be no property common to them all. Rather, different similarities are shared by different subgroups of the complete set. For example, in a family some individuals may have a similar build, others similar eyes, others a similar complexion, and so on, although no single feature is shared by all the family members. The same could be the case for concrete experiences of space and time.

However, this objection is based on an un-Husserlian conception of an 'essence' or universal structure. As discussed in Chapter Three, a Husserlian essence is not a list of identifying 'marks', but rather a highly complex and largely implicit set of rules governing the manifold of possible fulfillments for a given intention. While some explicit limit conditions can be derived from essential intuition (e.g., no color without extension), an exhaustive explicit statement of the content of an essence is in general not possible. Husserlian essential structures provide 'rules' in a way closer to schemata in the Kantian sense than to essences as conceived by Wittgenstein: we can recognize whether a given intuition satisfies them, although we often cannot explicitly state precisely what properties are required to do so. The essence can be elucidated, but only by exhibiting a manifold of possible instantiations in intuition and examining the noetic-noematic correlations, not by listing necessary and sufficient properties.[79]

Thus Husserl's essentialism consists in the claim that a common *schema* is in effect whenever we judge ('perceive' or 'recognize' is better) a particular experience to be temporal. The Wittgensteinian example of family resemblance does not contradict the existence of such a common schema. For such a schema must also be in effect when we determine whether an individual is a member of a family or not. This schema could either take the form of a general definition of blood and marital relations, or it could be a 'universalized' family appearance schema. But it could not be the case that we proceed wholly without a schema, simply appending members to the family on the basis of any arbitrary resemblance to any arbitrary existing members of the group. For then there would be no sense in which the group would be a family at all: the resemblance relationship is intransitive, so some members would have absolutely nothing in common with each other, whether with respect to blood relations or appearance. Indeed, the entire analysis of 'family resemblance' functions by tacitly combining the intransitive and relatively loose notion of 'resemblance' with the transitive and relatively firm notion of 'family' (understood in terms of blood and marital relations), thereby securing an identifying schema without admitting it. The notion of blood and marital relations is tacitly used to determine whether individuals are members of the family, and then it is pointed out that although these individuals form a single group no uniform resemblance relation is shared by them.

Now Waldenfels also maintains that even if we possess a notion of a universal spatio-temporal order, this notion is merely an abstract, idealized construction and not something actually given in experience. Yet here we must challenge Waldenfels' claim that his assertion that there are only various intersecting, overlapping spatio-temporal structures is the more phenomenologically accurate one. For granted that we experience now this particular space, now that, now as conditioned by this mood or these circumstances, now by others, it nonetheless is also the case that we experience all these spaces as being part of the *one* world-space. Further, the unity of world-space is *given*, and not merely thought in the way of, e.g., the geometrical curved space of mathematical physics. Much as a sensible object is perceived by way of *Abschattungen*, so (what presents itself as) the one world-space is perceived by way of more limited, particular spaces, all of which present themselves as partial, particular views of the one lived-world space.

To illustrate this, let us consider the somewhat analogous case of the perception of a very large object, such as a stadium. Suppose we are standing on the ground outside the stadium and walking around it. Each perception presents only a very tiny part of the stadium, and this from a certain perspective, in a certain light, and so on. It would nonetheless be descriptively inaccurate to hold that what are given in perception are only the variously overlapping, intersecting stadium-*Abschattungen*, whereas the stadium is merely a construct and not given. Rather, what is given in each of the series of perceptions is the *stadium*: the object constituted in our intentional acts is a single, unified one, and the various *Abschattungen* are merely 'lived through', taken as partial perspectives of the one thing, the stadium. Now an analogous situation occurs in the perception of world-space. Although the world-space is given only a tiny bit at a time, and also from various perspectives and in various ways, nonetheless all of these particular spaces can be experienced as 'space-*Abschattungen*', partial perspectival views which are 'lived through' in intentional directedness towards the one world-space. Were it granted that Waldenfels' argument demonstrates that a universal space is not given in experience but is merely a construction, then it would follow that the ordinary objects of sensible perception are not given either but are only constructions, and what are really given are their variously intersecting, overlapping *Abschattungen*. Yet both of these claims are clearly refuted by an examination of the intentional objects of experience. In experience, we are or can be directed to a unitary whole only partially present, whether this is the stadium or space. This whole is not *merely* constructed, but also intentionally *given*.[80] Thus neither Carr nor Waldenfels is able to provide a phenomenological refutation of the Husserlian claim of the existence of universal lifeworld structures. Correspondingly, they fail to show that the consistent development of Husserl's phenomenology would lead to the abandonment of an absolute, 'universalist' conception of truth.

5.2 *Phenomenology of Universality*

Despite the inconclusiveness of the Carr and Waldenfels critiques, they remain valid as challenges, posing a legitimate demand for a positive justification of universal structures. Of course in terms of a phenomenological conception of truth, a justification of universal lifeworld structures can only mean an intuitive exhibition of their *Evidenz* and an evaluation of the strength of this *Evidenz*, and not a proof of their existence in the objectivist sense.

As in the case of intersubjectivity itself (discussed at the close of Chapter Four), Husserl's phenomenology offers a number of different approaches to the *Evidenz* of universal lifeworld structures, with correspondingly diverse justificatory strengths. The primary approach adopted by Husserl is eidetic analysis of the lifeworld as such.[81] According to this approach, we begin by immersing ourselves in ordinary experience of the pre-given world. For example, I find myself in a room filled with various furnishings, books, plants, pictures, and so on. Examining the horizon of this experience, I find it contains anticipations of further possible perceptions of the specific objects presently in view, of other objects not presently in view, as well as of the general style of any further experience. Now if I freely vary the anticipated further experience in imagination, certain structural elements and categories of objects stand out as belonging necessarily to world-experience as such: space and time, things, persons.[82] This procedure, according to Husserl, yields structures which belong not only to the particular, contingent lifeworld in which *I* live, but to any lifeworld whatsoever.[83] This is the case because these structures are conditions for the constitution of a lifeworld-noema: anything which did not possess them could not be constituted *as* a lifeworld.

Now it could be objected against Husserl that eidetic analysis alone cannot possibly provide the requisite demonstration of the universal structures of the lifeworld. For, as argued above, the validity of all claims to universal intelligibility and verifiability itself *depends* upon whether all lifeworlds share a common structure. Further, this includes the validity of such claims not merely on the part of geometry, logic, or the empirical sciences, but those of phenomenology as well. Thus until the demonstration of the existence of a universal structure has actually been accomplished, the claim to universal validity of the results of eidetic analysis remains merely a claim. To use eidetic analysis itself to justify this claim is circular, simply presupposing what is supposed to be demonstrated. Perhaps my eidos of the lifeworld is merely *my* eidos of the lifeworld, specifying 'essential' structures which are indeed necessary for a noema to be constituted as a lifeworld *by me*, but not by other subjects. Yet if the results of eidetic analysis of the lifeworld are not themselves universally intersubjective, then they do not provide a demonstration that *all* lifeworlds share a common structure.

However, against this objection it is important to insist that the question of whether *my* eidos of the lifeworld is *merely* my eidos of the lifeworld should be addressed phenomenologically and not objectivistically. Rendered phenomenologically, this is the question of whether the eidos is constituted as 'there for me (or for us), but not there for others'. This could indeed sometimes be the case. As argued in section two of this chapter, features of the concrete lifeworld can come to be constituted with a reference to a limited intersubjective community. Insofar as my concept of the lifeworld remains closely modeled after my own particular lifeworld, retaining contingent features of it, then it too will be constituted with the sense 'my concept, but not a universal one'.

A second source of (phenomenological) limited universality is the manner in which the self is constituted. If I apprehend myself as possessing contingent cognitive faculties or a contingent cognitive background, then 'my' concept of the lifeworld will be constituted with the sense 'the lifeworld concept of a subject with such-and-such contingent cognitive background', and hence will be a (phenomenologically) relativized concept rather than a universal one.

Yet Husserl's position is clearly that the correct attitude for carrying out eidetic analysis (whether of the lifeworld or anything else) is the transcendental and not the natural one. As argued in section three of Chapter Four, in the transcendental attitude the self that performs eidetic analysis is not (constituted as) an empirical human being, and does not possess faculties with respect to which the eidos could be relativized. Rather, these faculties and background elements appear only as phenomena belonging to the phenomenon of the worldly self. To attribute such a background to the *transcendental* ego is to assume too much. Far from representing a neutral or even a skeptical position in relation to the possibility of non-relative truth and cognition, it would in fact be covertly to presuppose both of these in the case of the subjective background itself.

At the same time, even a phenomenological account would have to admit some contingency to transcendental subjectivity. For although the transcendental ego is not itself a part of the world or in the world, it still possesses a contingent 'home' lifeworld, the concrete lifeworld in which the self found itself prior to the epoché and which then serves as the starting-point for eidetic analysis of the lifeworld as such. Now the contingency of the home lifeworld is itself *phenomenological*, made evident if by no other means then by the juxtaposition of this particular lifeworld and other possible lifeworlds, a juxtaposition which necessarily occurs in eidetic variation. Thus it could be argued that the self experiences itself as contingent (i.e., possessing a contingent home lifeworld) even from the transcendental point of view, and therefore that its eidos of the lifeworld (as well as all other eidoi) is similarly infiltrated with (phenomenological) contingency and relativity. These are then constituted as eidoi for a subject with this home concrete lifeworld, and not for all subjects whatsoever.[84]

Yet the consequent Husserlian response to this objection is that although the home concrete lifeworld is contingent, the eidos of the lifeworld is not. The eidos, the universal, is not patterned directly after the concrete particular with all its contingencies, but rather is derived from an analysis in which the contingent and the necessary are distinguished. Indeed, the home lifeworld can be constituted *as* contingent only because it is seen to contain elements not required by the eidos. Hence phenomenological contingency *presupposes* phenomenological necessity. Further, contingency does not seep from the self-apprehension of transcendental subjectivity to its eidoi. Although transcendental subjectivity in fact possesses a contingent home lifeworld, the possession of this particular lifeworld is itself contingent and not essential to this transcendental subject. What is essential to transcendental subjectivity is a realm of phenomena with a certain structure, not a specific content. Further, the individuation of a transcendental subject and its distinctness from other subjects is based not upon the particular contingent content of the phenomena experienced by it, but upon the immediacy of these phenomena: the 'self', one's 'own' phenomena are identifiable because they are apprehended immediately and without appresentation, whereas the intentional lives of other subjects must be appresented. If the contingent home lifeworld of a transcendental subject were abruptly to undergo an extreme alteration, this subject would not lose its identity qua transcendental subject, because some phenomena would continue to have the character of mineness, whereas others not. In short, individuation, although essential to transcendental subjectivity, is independent of the contingent concrete content of the lifeworld or the phenomena experienced by this transcendental subjectivity.[85]

The eidetic analysis of the lifeworld removes all (phenomenological) contingencies, whether of the concrete lifeworld or of transcendental subjectivity itself. The resulting lifeworld eidos is therefore (constituted as) universal, and not merely as valid for a contingent subject possessing a contingent lifeworld. As discussed in Chapter Four, these results are also 'certain' in the specifically phenomenological sense of apodicticity, although not in the Cartesian sense of indubitability. In the case of a phenomenologically apodictic principle, it is impossible concretely to imagine a course of experience which would lead to the overturning of this principle. Thus while the truth of the principle is not finally guaranteed, the possibility of refutation is an 'empty' one. Certainly we can speculate in an empty way that there might be beings whose lifeworld is not temporally structured, or which is temporally structured in a way 'radically' different from our own. However, in order for this foreign lifeworld to attain *Seinsgeltung*, it would have to be not merely conceptually hypothesized but also given in intuition. But an atemporal or a radically different temporal experience is unimaginable, and therefore the possibility that the principle 'temporality is a universal lifeworld structure' could be overturned is an empty one. As argued in Chapter Four, this phenomenological apodicticity does not exclude fallibility, criticism, or further revision.[86]

The second path to a phenomenological demonstration of a common structure of all concrete lifeworlds is by way of the order of intentional constitution. According to this path, in order for a lifeworld to be constituted *as* a relative lifeworld, it must be constituted as a particular, conditioned apprehension of something which is common. That this is the case was already shown in a preliminary way in our analysis of the phenomenological justification of the relativity of the lifeworld.[87] There it was argued that a 'foreign' or relative appresentation is formed by abstracting from some constitutional layers of the object as apprehended by me, and then possibly modifying this common core by analogy or additions. For example, in the case of the Zulu and the book it was held that the sensible features of the book provided the requisite common nucleus. The phenomenological relativization of the book consists in its losing the sense, 'there for everyone', and receiving the sense 'my (or better, our) apprehension of the common core (here the sensible features), which is there for everyone'. Yet if there were no layer or content constituted as common, then there would be no material for forming the foreign appresentation. The intentional life of the other would then be merely an empty thought, one without *Evidenz*, and the same would be the case for the posited relativity of one's own intentional life.

Husserl argues more generally that we always begin with the naïve experience that the world in which we live is the world '*tout court*', and not the world of this or that particular group. Certain later experiences, especially contact with other cultures or historical periods, leads to the formation of 'foreign' world-appresentations, following the model outlined above. This has a number of important implications for the experience of the original world as well. Firstly, the horizon of this world becomes at least partially thematized so that specific features and characteristics are made to stand out, whereas otherwise we might have remained in the straightforward absorption in the world characteristic of naïve life. Further, the original world is relativized: what was once experienced as *the* world is now experienced as the 'home world', the 'world for us' but not for everyone. A distinction is thereby drawn between features which are shared and those which belong only to this particular world. However, much as in the case of the book, *some* content must be constituted as common if there is to be an appresentation of the foreign lifeworld, and thus if the relativity of our respective concrete lifeworlds is to be more than an empty thought. The divergent concrete lifeworlds are then experienced as different apprehensions of the *one* world, while the content attributed to this one world shifts over time. Yet it is clearly mistaken to attempt to argue for the irreducible relativity of lifeworlds by appealing to phenomenology itself. For one who holds that there are only relative lifeworlds cannot account for how it is possible to have an experience of something *as* a relative lifeworld, and so the end treats the relative lifeworlds as metaphysical 'in-themselves'.

This second argument is actually only a phenomenological version of the formal argument mounted by Husserl against relativism in the *Prolegomena* and discussed in Chapter One: the assertion of relativities presupposes the assertion of something non-relative as a reference point.[88] Our discussion in Chapter One emphasized that relativists often tacitly assume that the subjective cognitive background itself is non-relative, and that this background then serves as the necessary reference point for the relativization of all else. There is a correlate to this revealed by intentional analysis of the constitution of a relative lifeworld as well. For phenomenological relativization requires the addition of a reference to a 'we' or a 'they', and these limited intersubjective groups (their existence and defining features) are not themselves constituted as relative, as 'there' only for some further limited intersubjective group.[89] However, intentional constitution of relativity also requires that some content on the *object*-side must be constituted as non-relative, as 'there' across communities. For failing this, there could be no appresentation of the foreign intentional life and hence no *Evidenz* of limited intersubjectivity itself.

Now Husserl claims not merely that some content of my relativized world must be constituted as shared by the 'foreign' lifeworld, but also that the various relative lifeworlds must be constituted as particular apprehensions of the one, common world. Yet it could be objected that while analysis of intentional constitution shows that there must be *something* (constituted as) common in order for intersubjective appresentation to occur, it does not show that this common content or structure will be the same in all cases, nor that there will necessarily be aspects shared by all lifeworlds. Therefore it does not show that the experience of the 'one' world and of the particular worlds as apprehensions of this one world are phenomenologically necessary.

I think this objection is essentially correct. Analysis of intentional constitution cannot establish the phenomenological *necessity* of the one common world. Rather, here Husserl has to appeal to the contingent *Evidenz* of the one world. That is, the argument must be that even if it is not necessarily the case, it is factually the case that we *always* have experience of some world as 'the' world, as the world which is (constituted as) there for everyone. The idea of the one world and the *Evidenz* of it remains even when the specific content experienced as belonging to this world varies as a result of increased knowledge of others. However, while directedness towards the one world is not shown by this argument to be *necessary*, it is also not simply presupposed. Rather, it is derived from actual (if contingent) experience. For example, Husserl points out that whenever persons from even the most diverse cultures assemble there is always consciousness of some shared ground of experience and directedness towards a common world, and this community has its own *Evidenz*.[90]

Of course this second approach can be supplemented with the first, the approach by way of eidetic analysis, which *does* show that some universal lifeworld structures are necessary.[91] The second approach is not rendered superfluous by the first but provides an important addition to it. This is because the first approach addresses only apodictically necessary lifeworld structures such as space and time, causality, horizonality, persons, and things. It provides a very meager specification of the 'one' world because it omits everything which may in fact be common although only contingently so. By contrast, the second approach is concerned with both the necessary and the contingent content of the common world alike. The analysis of the intentional constitution of relative lifeworlds reveals that *some* content must be shared between every concrete lifeworld and the home lifeworld, and also that the idea and *Evidenz* of the one world persists through changes in the content attributed to it. However, it does not provide a method for determining the nature of this contingent content. This method is provided by the third Husserlian approach.

The third approach is the path to intersubjective consensus through dialogue and *Wechselverständigung*. According to the second approach, we always have an experience of some world as the one world, although the content of this world-idea and world-experience is subject to variation. Further, some of the elements of the common world are constituted as necessary, others as contingent. The *Evidenz* of the contingent elements in particular is far from maximal. Through a dialogue guided by openness to what is different, but also to what is the same, we can learn more about the intentional lives of others and their worlds, and so together with them produce a world-idea whose intersubjectivity is more evident than the one with which we began. As discussed in Chapter Four, this is not to say that dialogue could produce apodictic *Evidenz* as to the intentional lives of others, or as to the non-essential content of the common world; much less that there is a guarantee that expressed agreement regarding what is common (or anything else) will always be the result. However, dialogue and personal contact remain the crucial source of insight into the contingent features of the intentional life of others, and so of *Evidenz* as to what is as well as to what is not intersubjective. Thus this path provides a fuller specification of the common world than the first two, although also a more fragile and tentative one.

I would suggest that the first and third paths to the universal are complementary. However, it could be thought that they are in fact incompatible.[92] The first path – the path of eidetic analysis and reduction to transcendental subjectivity – represents the solipsistic strain in Husserl's thinking. Here it is held that the ultimate determination of everything must be by me and for me, even in the case of the determination of what is universal to the experience of everyone else. By contrast, the third path – the path of *Wechselverständigung* – reflects the (largely undeveloped) dialogical tendency of Husserl's phenomenology. This approach demands *mutual* recognition and grants the other a distinct and equal voice in the determination of the real. The potential exclusiveness of these two paths can be brought out by considering the case of the essential structures of the lifeworld. According to the first path, these are determined solipsistically and apodictically by eidetic analysis. But according to the second path, these should be determined dialogically and tentatively by discourse and consensus among distinct individuals. Clearly, these two paths can produce different results. Further, if the claim of the universality of a lifeworld structure entails the possibility of intersubjectivity regarding it as established by the *second* path, then this universality will not be apodictically established by eidetic analysis. For apodicticity implies the impossibility of imagining a concrete course of experience in which the *Evidenz* of a principle is overturned. But if universality entails the possibility of consensus through discourse, then it is quite possible to imagine a course of experience in which the universality of an 'eidetic' lifeworld structure is overturned: a dialogue in which consensus about the universality of this structure fails to obtain.

However, I think that this perceived conflict between the eidetic and the dialogical approaches is based upon an insufficiently clarified conception of consensus. Here it is important to distinguish between consensus in the phenomenological sense and consensus in the sense of verbal agreement. As discussed in section three of Chapter Four, phenomenological consensus consists in the agreement of my perception of an object or state of affairs and my appresentation of the object as given (or as could be given) in the intentional life of the other. Consensus in this sense can occur or be possible even where expressed agreement is absent. The other's world as appresented by me may be consistent with my own world even though the other fails to see this or refuses to admit it. The claim that some particular judgment is a possible object of consensus implies only that phenomenological consensus is possible, that there is a path from the appresented intentional life of the other to one that is harmoniously consistent with my own. For example, in the case of the Zulu and the book, this path was by way of sensible features and the notion of communication. Whether it is also possible to reach an expressed agreement in a given instance will depend upon numerous empirical circumstances.

While the *Evidenz* of universal lifeworld structures established by eidetic analysis does indeed imply the possibility of *Evidenz* of consensus as obtained by the second, dialogical path, this must be understood as consensus in the sense of harmonious appresentation and not as expressed agreement. Where consensus is thus understood, eidetic analysis produces apodicticity as to consensus as well. For consensus in this sense would fail not if a dialogue ended without resulting in verbal agreement about the universality of a particular lifeworld structure, but only if this dialogue led to the appresentation of the other's lifeworld as lacking the specified eidetic structure. Yet eidetic analysis demonstrates that such an appresentation is unimaginable and impossible, to be excluded on the very same grounds that led to the characterization of this structure as an eidetic one. If, contrary to the apodicticity of the *Evidenz* attained by eidetic analysis, dialogue leads to the imaginability of an appresentation of this kind, then the eidetic *Evidenz* will be overturned as well. In either case, the two paths to specification of lifeworld structures will necessarily lead to compatible and not contradictory results.

More generally, the solipsistic and the dialogical tendencies of Husserl's phenomenology remain complementary. This is because while the other attains a certain degree of independence and a crucial role in the constitution of the real – not only of the world but of the objective self as well – in the final analysis the transcendental self is primary. Even where the other disagrees with me, this disagreement itself and its ground must be capable of being given to me as a phenomenon. Husserl's justification for according this primacy to the self follows from the principle of all principles: my own intentional life is immediately given, whereas the intentional life of the other is appresented on the basis of my own.[93]

Especially in the writings of the 1930's, Husserl embarks upon a fourth path to a justification of universal intersubjectivity, although here more as a goal-idea than as an actual attainment. In these writings he maintains that fulfillment of the spiritual telos of an individual human life, of Europe as a cultural-political unity, and even of humanity as a whole, depends upon the continued pursuit of the ideal of universally valid truth.[94] This uncharacteristically impassioned argument is often couched in terms of an appeal for rationality and 'Europeanism' in the face of the rising tide of irrationalism and nationalism, both political and philosophical. According to Husserl, the crucial feature which distinguishes 'European' rationality from the more natural-pragmatic rationality of other cultures (including those he classes as 'quasi-philosophical', such as the Indian and the Chinese) is its goal-idea of absolute truth, truth which is the same for everyone and for all times, and ultimately grounded.[95] Thus beneath the highly charged and even culturally imperialist-sounding rhetoric, the main *philosophical* import of the *Crisis* attempt to place Europe 'as a spiritual shape' at the telos of human civilization is to claim the universal validity of the universal conception of truth itself.

There is something of a paradox in Husserl's historical-teleological justification of universalism. For while on the one hand he maintains that orientation towards absolute truth is necessary for the fulfillment of human life as such, and hence that the absolute conception is itself universally valid, on the other he insists that the actual possession of this conception is neither essential to a human lifeworld nor in fact to be found in all lifeworlds. Rather, Husserl argues that many lifeworlds possess only the natural, lifeworld conception of truth as limited, pragmatically necessary justification, exactness, and intersubjectivity, and that this alone is universal to all human lifeworlds. Indeed, he is quite insistent about the uniqueness of the absolute, 'scientific' conception of truth to Europe, maintaining that it is a result of the philosophical tradition of the Greeks and to be found only in the European lifeworld, or in other non-European lifeworlds influenced by European thinking. The paradox is that were one to accept the characterization of the absolute conception as specifically European, this would then imply that the claim that this conception is universally valid is phenomenologically indefensible. Consequently, even if it were conceded that Husserl demonstrates that knowledge of absolute truths is possible (e.g., via the phenomenological analysis of truth and intersubjectivity, and the first three arguments above), this would show only that the absolute conception of truth is valid for lifeworlds which employ it, and not for lifeworlds with a 'non-European' rationality, ones in which this conception is absent, meaningless, or rejected. As discussed previously, Husserl himself maintains that the conception of truth must be derived from intentional life itself and not imposed by a philosophical theory with arguments 'from above'.[96] The very first stage of a properly phenomenological justification of a concept is its derivation from actual intentional acts. If the absolute conception of truth is not actually in effect in some lifeworlds then a phenomenological justification will not be possible for them. The attempt to argue for the ethical or spiritual superiority of an historically specific conception of truth is therefore not phenomenological at all, but the reflection of remnants of a *dogmatic* absolutism in Husserl's analysis.

However, I do not think that the 'scientific', universalist conception of truth can be dismissed as itself of merely local validity, nor that any attempt to interpret it teleologically is necessarily dogmatic. For the claim that this conception has universal validity as a telos despite its *de facto* absence from some human lifeworlds could be interpreted undogmatically and phenomenologically as the claim that all natural lifeworlds contain the seeds of this conception and the (sometimes unfulfilled) *tendency* to develop it. This indeed seems to be the import of Husserl's own analysis. For example, he argues in the *Crisis* that although the conception of mathematical exactitude (one aspect of the scientific conception of truth) in fact arose in the specific Greek lifeworld, its motivating sources are to be found in all natural lifeworlds. According to the *Crisis*, the lifeworld basis of geometry and its notion of mathematically exact shapes is the art of measuring, an art to be found in all human cultures in one form and degree of precision or another.[97] Further motivation for the geometric conception is provided by the variability of the precision of lifeworld measurements, a variability apparent at the level of the lifeworld itself. For example, the grocer determines weight in one way and with one degree of precision, the goldsmith in another way and with another degree of precision. The graded sequence of ever more precise measurements motivates the teleological notion of the ideally precise measurement, such as the weight of the object measured with absolute exactness, and so as it is 'in itself'.[98] Thus it could be claimed that there is a natural motivation for and tendency towards the conception of mathematical exactness in all human lifeworlds, even in ones where this conception is absent.

More generally, the *Crisis* analysis suggests that the scientific conception of truth is only an idealized version of the natural lifeworld conception. The requirements for intersubjectivity, justification, and exactitude at the level of the lifeworld are limited and determined by specific pragmatic ends. By contrast, the scientific conception of truth is produced by freeing these requirements from their subordination to practical aims and extending them to the absolute in the interest of pure theory. Further, variations in degrees of intersubjectivity, justification, and exactitude at the level of the pre-scientific lifeworld already establish a graded sequence tending teleologically towards the scientific ideal.

Thus the substantive content of the Husserlian claim that 'European' rationality represents the telos of human civilization is that the motivating basis for and tendency towards the scientific conception of truth are to be found even in lifeworlds where the conception itself is absent. Insofar as this is the case, this claim is not mere dogmatic absolutism, but one which can be grounded (or refuted). Clearly, the existence of the specific preconditions for the development of the scientific notion will be at least in part contingent, and accordingly the demonstration will have to proceed not only by eidetic analysis but also by way of discourse, *Wechselverständigung* and actual contact with other lifeworlds. Husserl may be correct in holding that measuring (the pre-condition for the ideal of mathematical exactitude) is a universal feature of all human lifeworlds, but surely this is a contingent universal feature and not one that can be derived merely from the eidos of the lifeworld (or of the human) as such. The demonstration of the universal existence of the motivating grounds for the affirmation of the ideals contained in the scientific conception of truth will correspondingly be a tentative, dialogical one, and this includes the ideal of universal intersubjectivity itself. However, I believe that the weight of the evidence is on its side.

It would be a misinterpretation of Husserl as well as of the truth to think that this teleology implies that a utopic human civilization would know 'European', universalist rationality alone. For much as scientific truth cannot displace lifeworld truth, but rather complements it and is restricted to its own particular domain, so universalist rationality is not opposed to the various particular rationalities specific to different cultural-historical lifeworlds, but complements them and retains a restricted domain. A properly phenomenological teleology of the absolute is not a totalizing one which tends to the elimination of all relativities. Rather, one of the most important discoveries of Husserl's analysis is that the relative and the absolute are not mutually incompatible but complementary, and even mutually dependent.

The eidetic analysis of the lifeworld provides a first step towards a determination of the common world, but clearly its content extends much further than this. This further content cannot be determined in advance but only through dialogue, exchange of views, and mutual comprehension. The very process of the relativization of the lifeworld therefore constitutes an *increase* in knowledge. Through it, we expand our knowledge of other surrounding worlds. Further, we learn more about our own surrounding world, since we learn to distinguish those elements which are universal from those which belong to this particular world alone. Thus while for relativists such as Carr and Waldenfels the realization of the relativity of the lifeworld is both a beginning and an end, for Husserl the relativization of the lifeworld is only a beginning, a starting-point of an enriched knowledge of others and ourselves, and of the world we share.

NOTES

1. This is the view suggested by David Carr in "Husserl's Lengthening Shadow: A Historical Introduction," in *Interpreting Husserl*, Phaenomenologica, vol. 106 (Dordrecht: Martinus Nijhoff Publishers, 1987), 12.

2. This tendency in Husserl scholarship has also been noted by David Carr in *Phenomenology and the Problem of History: A Study of Husserl's Transcendental Philosophy* (Evanston: Northwestern University Press, 1974), xxiii, n. 18. Even Tugendhat, who discusses the full range of Husserl's writings, fails to give any explanation for the emergence of the lifeworld, or even to see it as problematic (cf. Tugendhat, 238). At the same time, this is not to imply that this question has *never* been addressed. See, for example, Iso Kern, "Die Lebenswelt als Grundlage der objektiven Wissenschaften und als universales Wahrheits- und Seinsproblem," in *Lebenswelt und Wissenschaft in der Philosophie Edmund Husserls*, edited by Elisabeth Ströker, (Frankfurt a.M.: Vittorio Klostermann Verlag, 1979), 68–78; and even Gadamer, "Die phänomenologische Bewegung," *Philosophische Rundschau* 11 (1963): 1–45. The analysis proposed by Kern is similar in many points to the one given here.

3. Cf. *Hua IV* 375 and Carr, *Phenomenology and the Problem of History*, 138. Gadamer also mentions this as the first use by Husserl of *'Lebenswelt'*, but erroneously dates it to 1920. See Gadamer, "Die phänomenologische Bewegung," 24.

4. Gadamer, for one, tends in this direction. *Ibid.*, 19.

5. Cf., for example, *Hua XIV* 321–3; *Hua IX* 491ff.; *Hua I* 165 (*CM* § 59); *Hua XV* 177; *Hua VI* 107 (*K* § 28).

6. *Hua III* 56–60/57–62 (*Id I* §§ 27–9). David Carr also notes this passage as containing a characterization of the lifeworld strikingly similar to Husserl's last. However, Carr fails to notice that the *natürliche Umwelt* of *Ideas I* is already clearly outlined as a concrete, cultural-practical world, and decisively *not* as a world of merely sensible bodies. Cf. Carr, *Phenomenology and the Problem of History*, 35–9, 162.

7. Wilhelm Dilthey, *Der Aufbau der geschichtlichen Welt in den Geisteswissenschaften*, second edition (Stuttgart: B.G. Teubner, 1958), 81–4.

8. "As a person, I am what I am (and every other person is what he or she is) as a **subject in a surrounding world**. The concepts 'I' and 'surrounding world' are inseparably related to each other." ("Als Person bin ich, was ich bin [und ist jede andere Person, was sie ist] als Subjekt einer Umwelt. Die Begriffe Ich und Umwelt sind untrennbar aufeinander bezogen"), *Hua IV* 185.

9. Or, in Husserl's terms, with whom I stand in an *Einfühlungszusammenhang* (a community of mutual empathy). See *ibid.*, 372–3, 375.

10. *Ibid.*, 190–3.

11. The intentional activities involved in the movement from objective constitution at the level of the lifeworld to objective constitution at the level of the natural sciences are laid out in some detail by Husserl for the case of a human being. Cf. *ibid.*, 169ff. For the more general argument, see 182ff.

12. The precise sense of the priority of the lifeworld, as well as the nature of the order of *Seinsgeltung*, and its relation to the more traditional orders of knowledge and of being (which it is intended to supplant), will be discussed further in section 4 of this chapter.

13. *Hua IV* 179–80.

14. Thus Husserl writes in *Ideas II*: "Closer analysis will even show that ... the naturalistic

attitude is subordinate to the personalistic one and gains a certain independence from it through an abstraction, or rather through a kind of self-forgetfulness of the personal I, which at the same time unjustifiably absolutizes the world of the naturalistic attitude, Nature." ("Bei genauer Betrachtung wird sich sogar herausstellen, daß ... die naturalistische Einstellung sich der personalistischen unterordnet und durch eine Abstraktion oder vielmehr durch eine Art Selbstvergessenheit des personalen Ich eine gewisse Selbstständigkeit gewinnt, dadurch zugleich ihre Welt, die Natur, unrechtmäßig verabsolutierend"), *ibid.*, 183–4.

15. Husserl writes not only of the *'Umwelt'* and the *'Erfahrungswelt'*, but also of the *'wir-Umwelt'*, the *'relative Umwelt'*, the *'Heimwelt'* as opposed to the *'Fernwelt'*, and also of abnormal and animal *Umwelten*. See, for example, *Hua XIII* 272, 426, 431–7; *Hua XIV* 96, 103, 116, 192–205, 321; *Hua XV* 177, 214ff., 232, 395.

16. Cf. especially *Hua XIII* 217, 384, 395; *Hua XIV* 112–3, 250–4; *Hua XV* 45–7, 175–7, 215–20, 232–6.

17. Carr, *Phenomenology and the Problem of History*, 201.

18. Carr, "Welt, Weltbild, Lebenswelt: Husserl und die Vertreter des Begriffsrelativismus," in *Lebenswelt und Wissenschaft in der Philosophie Edmund Husserls*, edited by Elisabeth Ströker (Frankfurt a.M.: Vittorio Klostermann Verlag, 1979); reprinted as "World, World-View, Lifeworld: Husserl and the Conceptual Relativists," in *Interpreting Husserl*, Phaenomenologica, vol. 106, 32. Carr also attributes this view of the development of Husserl's conception of the lifeworld to Gerd Brand.

19. Kern, "Die Lebenswelt als Grundlage der objectiven Wissenschaften", 71 and 77.

20. See, for example, *Hua IV* 203 passim; *Hua IX* 56–7, 118–9, 227–30; *Hua XIII* 425ff., 505; *Hua XV* 214–8, 235; *Hua VI* 108–10 (*K* § 28), 306–8. However, Carr is correct in noting that in many passages, including several in the *Crisis* itself, Husserl does not draw this distinction in a clear way. See, for example, *Hua VI* 141 (*K* § 36).

21. It could be objected against this analysis that it begs the question of whether there are any theory-independent contents of perception. However, it should be noted that at least as drawn by Husserl, the distinction between the merely sensible and the concrete lifeworld is a purely descriptive one. It is not derived from the distinction between 'theory-conditioned' and 'theory-neutral' perception, and hence does not presuppose it. Rather, to say that something is sensible is simply to say that it 'is' (i.e., given as) perceived by the senses (e.g., vision, touch, etc., understood descriptively), without at all prejudging whether the senses are themselves conditioned by the theories believed by the perceiver. This phenomenological derivation of the sensible-natural world is clearly elucidated in the *Crisis*, § 28. See *Hua VI* 108ff. (*K* § 28), especially the passage beginning "Here we can now clarify the very restricted justification for talk about a sensible world, a world of sensible intuition, a sensible world of appearances." ("Hier können wir nun die Rede von Sinnenwelt, Welt sinnlicher Anschauung, sinnlicher Erscheinungswelt in ihrem sehr bedingten Recht aufklären.") Of course the notion of sense perception and its specific objects may indeed be somewhat vague even when taken phenomenologically, and accordingly the lines between the *anschauliche Dingwelt* and the concrete lifeworld may be difficult to establish in specific cases. Husserl emphasizes as much by characterizing the *anschauliche Dingwelt* as a product of abstraction, and asserting that we have only very restricted justification for speaking of such a world. However, the precision of this particular distinction is not crucial to the argument. Although the cultural/perceptual distinction is much discussed in the

literature, in terms of Husserl's own analysis and the relativism problematic the more important distinction is that between the concrete lifeworld, which has limited intersubjectivity, and the layer or structure of this world which has universal intersubjectivity, whether this latter is specifically 'sensible' or not.

22. See, for example, *Hua I* 160–3 (*CM* § 58); and *Hua VI* 142 (*K* § 36).

23. Excerpts from some of these manuscripts have been published as *Beilagen* in the volumes on intersubjectivity and in other *Husserliana* volumes. See, for example, *Hua IX* 487–507; *Hua XV* 60–64, 175–185, 214–218, 387–407. For a selected list of additional manuscripts, see the Bibliography. These writings date from the mid-twenties onward. However, even in earlier writings Husserl addresses similar problems arising not from the cultural-historical relativity of the concrete lifeworld but from its perceptual relativity (e.g., its relativity to whether the 'person' is blind, deaf, a jelly-fish, etc.). See, e.g., *Hua XIII* 214–8, 270–8, 381–4; *Hua XIV* 112–9. This concern with perceptual relativity again brings out that the main issue is not whether an aspect of the world is sensible, but whether and the extent to which it is intersubjective.

24. A V 9, manuscript p. 10 a-b; transcription pp. 17–18. ("So sind für den Zulu das, was wir Wissenschaften, wissenschaftliche Werke, Literatur als Bücher, Zeitungen etc. kennen und erfahren, einfach nicht da, obschon die Bücher als Dinge und ev. als mit den und jenen Zaubereien behafteten Dingen da sind – mit welchen Interpretationen sie eben wieder nicht für uns da sind. Nehmen wir, was sich subjektiv-einstimmig, oder <in> historischer Gemeinschaft, national, einstimmig gibt, als zur konkreten Erfahrungswelt dieser Menschheit gehörig, so müssen wir sagen, jede solche Menschheit habe eine andere konkrete Welt.")

25. The portion of the manuscript containing this passage has been published in *Hua IX* as *Beilage* XXVII. The cited passage itself appears on pp. 496–7. ("Nicht mit allen Menschen teilen wir dieselbe Lebenswelt, nicht alle Menschen 'auf der Welt' haben mit uns alle Objekte, die unsere Lebenswelt ausmachen und die unser personales Wirken und Streben bestimmen, gemeinsam, selbst wenn sie mit uns in aktuelle Gemeinschaft treten, wie sie es jederzeit können.... Objekte, die für uns, obschon freilich in wechselnder, bald stimmender, bald nicht stimmender Auffassung da sind, sind für sie nicht da, und das sagt, sie haben von ihnen als diesen Objekten überhaupt keine Auffassungen, keine Erfahrungen: selbst wenn sie sehen und, wie wir sagen, sie diese unsere Objekte sehen.... Adjungieren wir diesem Menschenkreis einen Bantuneger, so ist es klar, daß er angesichts irgendeines unserer Kunstwerke zwar ein Ding sieht, aber nicht das Objekt unserer Umwelt, das Kunstwerk sieht, und daß er auch keine Meinung, keine Auffassung davon – als diesem Gegenstand Kunstwerk – hat, das da ist in 'unserer' Welt als David des Michelangelo mit den diesem Kunstwerk zugehörigen 'objektiven' Bestimmungen.... Danach haben wir verschiedene 'Welten' für die Menschen zu unterscheiden, die Welt des europäischen Menschen, die Welt des Bantu usw., und diese Welten in ihrer personalen ['Wir'-] Beziehung sind selbst wandelbar.")

26. This affirmation has not been sufficiently appreciated in the Husserl literature. See, for example, J.N. Mohanty, "Phänomenologische Rationalität und die Überwindung des Relativismus," in *Vernunft und Kontingenz: Rationalität und Ethos in der Phänomenologie*, edited by Ernst Wolfgang Orth, Phänomenologische Forschungen, vol. 19 (Freiburg and Munich: Karl Alber Verlag, 1986) 53–74; and David Carr, "The Lifeworld Revisited: Husserl and Some Recent Interpreters," in *Husserl's Phenomenology: A Textbook*, edited by William R. McKenna and J.N. Mohanty (Washington,

D.C.: Center for Advanced Research in Phenomenology, University Press of America, 1987), reprinted in *Interpreting Husserl*, Phaenomenologica, vol. 106 (Dordrecht: Martinus Nijhoff Publishers, 1987), 227–246. Both Mohanty and Carr maintain that a phenomenological, non-objectivist analysis necessarily leads to the conclusion that there are many lifeworlds, and sharply criticize Husserl for failing to draw this conclusion himself.

27. For example, even Dilthey's *Weltanschauungslehre* already moves in this direction.
28. This style of objection is generally associated with Davidson. See "On the Very Idea of a Conceptual Scheme," *Proceedings and Addresses of the American Philosophical Association* 47 (1973/4): 5–20. Of course, the argument as sketched here only roughly follows Davidson's actual argument.

   Even Rorty, who argues vigorously in favor of his own notion of incommensurability, is highly critical of talk about multiple worlds, which he links with Kuhn. In a vein strikingly similar to Husserl's, Kuhn holds that what one sees and the world one lives in varies with one's background paradigm: "looking at a contour map, the student sees lines on paper, the cartographer a picture of a terrain. Looking at a bubble-chamber photograph, the student sees confused and broken lines, the physicist a record of familiar subnuclear events"; through education, the student becomes an "inhabitant of the scientists' world"; after a revolution, "scientists are responding to a different world" (Thomas S. Kuhn, *The Structure of Scientific Revolutions*, International Encyclopedia of Unified Science, 2.2 [Chicago: University of Chicago Press, 1970], 112.) Rorty rejects this sort of talk on the grounds that it is too idealist, and he holds that it is better to be behaviorist in epistemology than idealist (Richard Rorty, *Philosophy and the Mirror of Nature* [Princeton: Princeton University Press, 1980], 324ff.). Rather, according to Rorty the only valid sense in which theories, paradigms, or discourses can be said to be incommensurable is that of not admitting a neutral decision procedure in cases of conflict (*ibid.*, 316, 324). But Rorty is incorrect to assert that talk about multiple worlds is necessarily idealist, if by 'idealism' he means the view that worlds are created by and exist only in subjective mental acts. According to Husserl, it is not the being but the being-sense (*Seinssinn*) of worldly objects that is constituted in consciousness, and it follows from this very sense that these objects exist independently of the acts in which their sense is constituted. Thus no question-begging metaphysics is required. And if Rorty objects even to this milder transcendental idealism, he will be in the uncomfortable position of having to defend objectivism (transcendental realism). Indeed, Rorty's unexplained preference for behaviorism over idealism could reflect the remnants of a tacit adherence to realism, despite his alleged pragmatism. Why else would he find talk about multiple worlds so objectionable and talk about decision procedures preferable to the point where the latter should *replace* the former (rather than merely complementing it)?

29. Husserl argues in a general way in *Ideas II* that the experience of an object or objectivity in each case contains an implicit reference to an intersubjective community, as well as the idea of mutual recognition, comprehension, and possible consensus among the members of this community. Thus the conditions for the possibility of experience of an object include not only the conditions for the reidentifiability of the object over a manifold of various perceptual presentations by *me*, but also for its reidentifiability over a manifold of various presentations by many subjects. The object is that which is identical and identifiable throughout the manifold of various appearance-systems of the

members of an intersubjective community. See *Hua IV* 87, 193.

30. In the analysis of the constitution of the other presented in the Fifth Meditation, Husserl maintains that my 'there' (what I would perceive, if I were there) becomes the content of my appresentation of the other's 'here'. See *Hua I* 147 (*CM* § 54).

31. It should again be emphasized that the precise content of the shared core of a fully constituted object need not necessarily be sensible, although it may be sensible in many cases and happens to be so in the two Husserlian examples cited. Moreover, in the context of this discussion these examples function primarily as illustrations of how the *absence* of intersubjectivity is constituted in experience. If one also wanted to read into these examples an implicit argument *for* intersubjectivity (i.e., with respect to the common substratum), this argument could be only that *Evidenz* of the lack of intersubjectivity requires *some* stratum to be constituted as common, and not that specific features (e.g., sensible qualities such as color, shape and weight) must belong to this common stratum. As will be discussed further in what follows, if no stratum of the concrete object were constituted as common, there would be no content for the 'relativized' appresentation of the other's intentional life, and hence the absence of intersubjectivity could not become evident. For a more detailed discussion of this point, see page 183.

32. See *Hua VI* 165–6 (*K* § 47) and Carr, *Phenomenology and the Problem of History*, 26–7, 142–3. According to Carr, the conception of the world as a final horizon rather than a totality of things is dominant only in *Ideas* and the *Crisis*.

33. Husserl points out in *Ideas II* that not only an entire culture, but also various smaller social formations can have their own *Umwelten* (for example, a student association), as the particular horizonal context towards which these groups are communally directed. See *Hua IV* 195.

34. Thus Husserl argues that in the case of animals lacking visual apparatus, the shared core upon which the 'foreign' appresentation is constructed would not include visual qualities. See *Hua XIV* 112–9.

35. Other practical/empirical factors such as the length of time available for discussion and education clearly fall into this category.

36. This point will be discussed further in the next section.

37. Similarly, I argued above that the Zulu could come to perceive the book as a medium for written communication, but not that he would cease to perceive it (or other objects) as embodying ancestor spirits, nor that we would come to perceive them as such. Thus a fully unified world would not be established here either.

38. *Hua XVIII* 126 (*P A/B* 118).

39. We already noted the priority of givenness to intersubjectivity for Husserl's analysis in our discussion in Chapter Two of "Philosophy as Rigorous Science". Here we saw that intersubjectivity itself must be a *product* of *Evidenz* if it is to be a valid desideratum for knowledge. Cf. page 42 above. Further, the priority of givenness is also clear from the principle of all principles of Husserl's phenomenology. Cf. *Hua III* 51/52 (*Id I* § 24) and p. 93, n. 1 above.

40. This distinction is expressed in a particularly clear way in manuscript D 4 of 1921: "We must first distinguish between: 1) objectivity as intersubjectivity, related in apprehension to a 'universe' of subjects, where this universe can be a limited one, e.g., a limited community of subjects; and 2) objectivity in the 'strict' sense, related to the really unlimited 'universe', the totality of all cognitive subjects who stand in a relation with

the present one." ("Es muß aber zunächst geschieden werden: 1) Objektivität als Intersubjektivität, auffassungsmäßig bezogen auf ein 'Universum' von Subjekten, wobei aber das Universum ein beschränktes sein kann, z.B. eine begrenzte Subjektsgemeinschaft; 2) die 'strenge' Objektivität bezogen auf das wirklich unbeschränkte 'Universum', die Allheit aller mit dem Erkennenden in Konnex stehender Erkenntnissubjekte überhaupt"), manuscript p. 6a, typescript p. 11. Here Husserl also concedes that both types of objectivity yield truth: "In general we must distinguish between the true, the genuine, that is truth as the correlate of *Evidenz* in the broadest sense, and the 'objective'. This brings with it the distinction between the merely subjectively and relatively true and the objectively true, and this for all domains of truth." ("Allgemein müssen wir scheiden, das Wahrhafte, Echte, bezw. die Wahrheit als Korrelat der Evidenz im weitesten Sinne und das 'Objektive'. Es ergibt sich damit auch der Unterschied zwischen dem bloß subjektiv-relativ Wahren und dem objektiv Wahren und zwar für alle Domänen der Wahrheit"), manuscript p. 12a, typescript p. 20.

41. Tugendhat also notes that Husserl runs together several different notions of relativity in his discussions of the lifeworld and its truth. However, Tugendhat makes no attempt to indicate any relation among the various notions. See Tugendhat, 248–9.

42. At least two of these kinds of 'relativity' (i.e., limited justification and limited exactness) are clearly not relativity in the usual sense, nor in the sense attacked by Husserl in the *Prolegomena* and "Philosophy as Rigorous Science". I include them here to round out the conception of lifeworld truth that can be derived from the texts, as well as by way of explication of Husserl's own confusing linguistic usage. Indeed, Husserl's frequent use of the term 'relativity' and its cognates to refer to imperfect certainty and justification is a reflection of the tendency of skepticism and relativism in the strict sense to merge in his thinking. Our previous discussions (see Chapters Three and Four) have shown that there is good reason to treat these two themes in tandem.

43. *Hua IX* 497. ("Jedes seiende Objekt ist Korrelat gewisser zu ihm und seiner Objektartung allgemein zugehöriger 'Apperzeptionen', und jeder Unterschied von zusammenstimmenden und nicht zusammenstimmenden, und schließlich von richtigen und unrichtigen setzt schon die betreffende Art und Besonderheit von Apperzeptionen voraus, auf die er sich also zurückbezieht.... Über Wahrheit und Falschheit, über Sein und Nichtsein in unserer Welt können wir miteinander streiten, nicht aber mit dem Bantu, da er als einzelner seines 'Wir' eine andere Umwelt hat.")

This passage suggests that there can be two perceptions which are incommensurable but not in conflict. This is because they are directed to different objects altogether, objects not accessible to both persons, although constituted on a common substrate (as in the case of the European's apprehension of the David, as opposed to the Bantu's). Thus, contra Rorty, in such cases it is inaccurate to speak of a lack of a neutral decision procedure, since there is no conflict to be decided. Conflict itself can occur only where the basic mode of apperception is accessible to both parties, and in general where the conditions for bilateral verification procedures are met.

44. Now it might be objected against our entire reconstruction that Husserl actually excludes justification (and hence truth) from the realm of the lifeworld. For example, in the lectures on phenomenological psychology, Husserl argues that the prescientific world of experience is characterized by a passive, pre-predicative *'Seinsgewißheit'*, a naïve certainty of existence which is not the result of any conscious activity of decision, and whose content is not even made thematic by explicit judgments. Justification,

however, requires critical evaluation, which in turn implies predicative thinking, explicit acts of judgment, and a conscious decision to affirm or deny. Thus in these lectures Husserl concludes that although there is a kind of certainty to the prescientific world of experience, here judgment, justification, and truth have no place at all. (*Hua IX* 62–3.)

But in response to this objection, it should be noted that explicit judgment and justification obviously take place even regarding the objects and states of affairs of the everyday world, and not only in the realm of science. Further, although Husserl clearly has qualms about according the status of 'truth' to everyday judgments with only a pragmatic justification, he eventually does so. Thus in A VII 11 of 1932, he writes: "Even in everyday life human beings attain knowledge, in the ways of experience and its verification, judgment and its verification, although such knowledge in pre- and extra-theoretical life is in the service of the currently dominant, effective interests, whether these be the interests of 'serious life' or life in relaxation, in play. This *unscientific knowledge* is indeed knowledge of truth, and it has the character of a decision to be justified by verification, a deciding of opinions according to truth and falsehood, between which there is no middle alternative. We call this unscientific knowledge *situational knowledge* and this truth situational truth. Its opinion as opinion is horizonally limited, it refers to the current situation, the situation that is obvious to the current knowing subject. But situational truth is nonetheless really truth… " ("Der Mensch ist auch in der Alltäglichkeit erkennend, in den Weisen der Erfahrung und Erfahrungsbewährung, des Urteilens und der Urteilsbewährung, obschon solche Erkenntnis im vor- und außerwissenschaftlichen Leben im Dienst jeweils herrschender und sich auswirkender Interessen ist, sei es Interessen des 'ernsten Lebens' oder denen des Lebens in Erholung, in Spiel. Diese *unwissenschaftliche Erkenntnis* ist in der Tat Erkenntnis der Wahrheit und sie hat den Charakter einer durch Bewährung zu rechtfertigen, einer Entscheidung ihrer Meinungen nach Wahr und Falsch, zwischen denen es kein Drittes gibt. Die unwissenschaftliche Erkenntnis nennen wir *Situationserkenntnis*, die Wahrheit Situationswahrheit, die Meinung ist als Meinung horizonthaft begrenzt, sie bezieht sich auf die jeweilige, für die jeweilig Erkennenden selbstverständliche Situation. Aber Situationswahrheit ist eben wirkliche Wahrheit… "), A VII 11, manuscript p. 41a, transcription pp. 78–9. See also *Hua VI* 126 (*K* § 31); as well as the oft-quoted passage of *Formal and Transcendental Logic*, in which Husserl affirms that even the trader in the marketplace has his truths, by which Husserl presumably means that the principles and practical techniques of the trader are 'true' or justified at the level of the lifeworld insofar as they effectively bring about the desired practical ends. *Hua XVII* 245 (*FTL* § 105).

45. See, e.g., *Hua VI* 22 (*K* § 9 a).

Here one might be tempted to raise against Husserl an objection in the spirit of the arguments of Galileo against the Aristotelians. That is, Husserl asserts that there are no mathematically exact forms instantiated in objects of ordinary sensible perception, but rather that these objects are only approximately and not perfectly determinate. Against this the Galilean would maintain that the shapes of sensible objects are in fact exactly, mathematically determinate, except that they are not perfect lines, circles, or planes, but perfect instantiations of much more complicated mathematical shapes, requiring much more complicated mathematical functions to describe them. (For this sort of argument, see Galileo, *Dialogue Concerning the Two Chief World Systems*, translated by Stillman

Drake, second edition [Berkeley and Los Angeles: University of California Press, 1967], 207–8.)

Yet Husserl's critique of Galileo in the *Crisis* is precisely that this sort of mathematization and idealization of the object replaces the sensible thing as experienced with a logical construct which is not and cannot be given in perception. For once one conceives of the shape of the table as an instantiation of an extremely complex but nonetheless exact mathematical function, the shape as it presents itself at the level of the lifeworld has been left behind by a process of idealization. Cf. *Hua VI* 48–50 (*K* § 9 h); and also page 166. Husserl grants that such an idealization is possible, and even motivated by the varying degrees of accuracy exhibited within the lifeworld itself (*Hua VI* 41–2 [*K* § 9 e]). For example, with improvements in technology, the shape of the table can be measured more and more exactly, suggesting that this increase in precision could at least in principle be eventually extended to the limit of mathematical exactitude. But the assertion of the mathematizability of the sensible world is nothing but a motivated hypothesis, and that it can actually be carried out is in no way guaranteed.

46. *Hua VI* 22 (*K* § 9 a).
47. *Hua XIX/1* 86–7 (*LU A/B* 80–2).
48. *Hua XVII* 207 (*FTL* § 80).
49. In *Formal and Transcendental Logic*, Husserl suggests that even 'scientific' judgments (e.g., the judgments of the logician) are situational in that even these are affirmed only within a particular horizon specifying specific 'practical' aims and methods of verification. Cf. *Hua XVII* 245 (*FTL* § 105). The difference between lifeworld and scientific truths, and hence the non-relativity of the latter, then lies not in the latter's lack of a situational intentional horizon but in the fact that this horizon includes a claim to *universal* as opposed to merely local intersubjectivity.
50. *Ibid.*, 285 (*FTL* § 105). ("Man hat die Wahrheit dann nicht fälschlich verabsolutiert, vielmehr je in ihren – nicht übersehenen, nicht verhüllt bleibenden, sondern systematisch ausgelegten – Horizonten.")
51. See pp. 14–5 above.
52. For a fuller discussion of this example, see pp. 68ff above.
53. See, for example, *Hua IV* 281ff.; *Hua IX* 55ff.; *Hua VI* 48ff., 126ff., 229 (*K* §§ 9 h, 36, 55).
54. *Hua VI* 125 (*K* § 33). These first two senses have also been noted by Carr in "The Lifeworld Revisited: Husserl and Some Recent Interpreters," reprinted in *Interpreting Husserl*, Phaenomenologica, vol. 106 (Dordrecht: Martinus Nijhoff Publishers, 1987), 232.
55. Thus Husserl asks rhetorically in the *Crisis*, "Can reason and being be separated, where cognizing reason determines what is?" ("Ist Vernunft und Seiendes zu trennen, wo erkennende Vernunft bestimmt, was Seiendes ist?") *Hua VI* 9 (*K* § 5).
56. This is not to suggest that there are no theoretical components in the lifeworld. The theory/observation distinction is in any case not a Husserlian one, and is introduced here only to clarify a possible (not strictly phenomenological) objection. The distinction which Husserl employs is that between scientific and lifeworld *Evidenz*. As will be discussed in what follows, both this and the theory/observation distinction are elucidated phenomenologically in terms of degrees of intuitive 'fullness' and foundation relations.
57. *EU* 39–40 (§ 10).

58. Tugendhat, 243.
59. See pp. 163–4.
60. For a more detailed discussion of this issue, see my paper, "Phenomenology and Scientific Realism," *op. cit.*
61. Indeed, here Tugendhat may have been led to this misinterpretation largely by his desire to find in Husserl the roots of Heidegger's position in *Being and Time*, according to which scientific truth is not merely 'less original' (i.e., constituted on the basis of) truth as given pre-theoretically, but also less valuable and less genuinely true: a *distortion* of what things really are. (See, for example, the analysis of *Zuhandenheit* in § 15 where it is held that in *Zuhandenheit*, unlike in *Vorhandenheit*, the everyday thing of experience shows itself as it really is ['sich von ihm selbst sich offenbart'] [*Sein und Zeit*, Gesamtausgabe, vol. 2 (Frankfurt a.M.: Vittorio Klostermann, 1977), 90–7]. For Tugendhat's misguided attempt to read this position back into Husserl, see Tugendhat, 244.)
62. See David Carr, "Husserl's Lengthening Shadow: A Historical Introduction," 12.
63. *Hua VI* 324, 367–8.
64. *Ibid.*, 141 (*K* § 35). ("[Die Lebenswelt] ist die raumzeitliche Welt der Dinge, so wie wir sie in unserem vor- und außerwissenschaftlichen Leben erfahren und über die erfahrenen hinaus als erfahrbar wissen.... Dinge: das sind Steine, Tiere, Pflanzen, auch Menschen und menschliche Gebilde, aber alles ist da subjektiv-relativ, obschon wir normalerweise in unserer Erfahrung und in dem sozialen Kreis, der mit uns in Lebensgemeinschaft verbunden, zu 'sicheren' Tatsachen kommen.... Aber wenn wir in einem fremden Verkehrskreis verschlagen werden, zu den Negern am Kongo, zu chinesischen Bauern usw., dann stoßen wir darauf, daß ihre Wahrheiten, die für sie feststehenden allgemein bewährten und zu bewährenden Tatsachen, keineswegs die unseren sind.")
65. *Ibid.*, 142 (*K* § 35). ("Doch alsbald verschwindet die Verlegenheit, wenn wir uns darauf besinnen, daß doch diese Lebenswelt in allen ihren Relativitäten ihre allgemeine Struktur hat. Diese allgemeine Struktur, an die alles relativ Seiende gebunden ist, ist nicht selbst relativ.") Husserl actually arrives at this solution of the problem of the relativity of the lifeworld far earlier than the *Crisis*. For example, in an early (1915–17) text on intersubjectivity and the problem of perceptual relativity, he argues that if the claim of the sciences to non-relative truth is to hold good, then there must be some properties of intuitable things equally accessible to all subjects. Cf. *Hua XIII* 384.
66. This point is discussed by Husserl in detail for the specific case of geometry in "The Origin of Geometry". Here Husserl argues that when the Pythagorean theorem is asserted to be true for all lifeworlds including those of all past and future generations, it is thereby presupposed that all lifeworlds contain some spatial, sensible bodies. For only on the basis of these latter could the concepts necessary for understanding and proving this theorem (e.g., triangle, distance) be formed. See *Hua VI* 385.
67. Husserl makes the stronger claim in a number of passages. See *Hua VI* 142 (*K* § 35); *Hua IX* 57, 89, 91.
68. Thus Carr writes: "Some of the ideas that populate our world are not merely encountered as items of furniture but constitute, as in the case of science, religion, and philosophy, interpretations *of* reality as a whole. Such ideas can become sedimented in such a way that they affect our 'view', our whole 'sense' of reality.... It becomes harder and harder to distinguish between the world as experienced and the world as interpreted

by this or that theory. The theory has become part of our way of experiencing. Theory in this sedimented and appropriated form may affect the very structure, and not merely the content, of the lifeworld" (Carr, "The Lifeworld Revisited," 243).

69. *Ibid.*, 244.
70. *Hua XVII* 175–7 (*FTL* § 80).
71. Clearly such a position need not be justified empirically, although this seems to be the case in the Carr argument. Another common route would be a quasi-Kantian conception of the subject as 'forming' all perceptions, with the addendum that the relevant subjective faculties are historically, culturally, physiologically, or otherwise variable. This would not help matters much, however, because it would still presuppose a non-relative theory of the subjective faculties themselves, and hence universal lifeworld structures as a basis for intersubjective access to this theory.
72. Bernhard Waldenfels, "Die Abgründigkeit des Sinnes," in *In den Netzen der Lebenswelt* (Frankfurt a.M. Suhrkamp, 1985), 15–33.
73. *Ibid.*, 17.
74. *Ibid.*, 19.
75. *Ibid.*, 23–5.
76. *Ibid.*, 27. A similar argument in favor of the irreducible plurality of spatial structures is given by Mohanty. See Mohanty, 54.
77. See, for example, Waldenfels, 26.
78. Ludwig Wittgenstein, *Philosophical Investigations*, translated by G.E.M. Anscombe, third edition (New York: Macmillan, 1968), § 67.
79. Husserl's own Lectures on Internal Time-Consciousness provide an example of what is involved.
80. Waldenfels is correct to note that the one world-space is a construction. But even the concrete lifeworld itself and its contents are constructions – or more precisely, their *Seinssinn* is a construction. Cf. *Hua VI* 70 (*K* § 14). And in general, there is no opposition between constructedness and intuitive givenness.
81. This is the path taken by Husserl in the lectures on phenomenological psychology, *Hua IX* 64ff. Eidetic analysis of the lifeworld through free variation is also suggested in the *Crisis, Hua VI* 28–9 (*K* § 9 b).
82. *Hua IX* 68–9; *Hua VI* 145 (*K* § 37). In the *Crisis* Husserl also suggests that a certain kind of natural causality – the tendency of properties and events to occur habitually and for reasons – is a necessary structure of the lifeworld. See *Hua VI* 29, 33 (*K* § 9 b, c). Other structures asserted to be essential include horizonality, constitution through noetic-noematic correlations, and (at least for human lifeworlds) rationality in the form of some distinction between truth and falsehood. See *Hua VI* 11 (*K* § 5) for the assertion of the universality of the distinction between truth and falsehood, and *Hua VI* 145–9 (*K* §§ 37–8) for the universality of horizonality and noetic-noematic correlations.
83. *Hua IX* 91.
84. Although not phrased in the language of subjectivity, Heidegger's critique of Husserl clearly moves in this general direction, holding that even the transcendental subject is *phenomenologically* contingent. See *Hua IX* 274–5 and Chapter 4, p. 141, n. 48 above.
85. This analysis of transcendental subjectivity clearly parallels the Kantian one, according to which although the 'I think' can accompany all my representations (and so these have the property of 'mineness'), no specific content can be attributed to this I. Thus for Kant too, the transcendental subject is individuated solely by the 'mineness' of its

representations, and not by the contingent content of these representations. See *Kritik der reinen Vernunft, B* 131ff. for the analysis of the 'I think'; and *B* 158, *A* 350ff. for the impossibility of attributing specific content to this 'I'.

86. See *Hua XVII* 164 (*FTL* § 58), and Chapter Four, section 2.

87. See section two above, especially page 154.

88. See pp. 7 ff. above.

89. Although it does not usually occur, this higher-order relativization of subjective communities themselves is certainly possible. But it can only take place for a limited number of levels, otherwise it would encounter the infinite regress and the disintegration of the relativization itself discussed in Chapter One.

90. Texts in which Husserl argues by way of the *de facto* experience of the common world include *Hua XVII* 383–4; *Hua VI* 166–7 (*K* § 47); A VII 19 (typescript pages 5–6); A VII 31 (typescript p. 3); and B I 12 IV (typescript p. 57).

91. Even the eidetic argument is not *completely* a priori, because it shows only that *if* there is to be experience of a lifeworld, *then* some universal structures are necessary. It does not, however, show that experience of a lifeworld is itself necessary.

92. This seems to be Michael Theunissen's position in *Der Andere. Studien zur Soziologie der Gegenwart* (Berlin: Walter de Gruyter, 1965). Theunissen's critique also tends to obscure the fact that according to Husserl's analysis, it is not the *being* of the other that is constituted but the *being-sense* (*Seinssinn*) and *being-validity* (*Seinsgeltung*).

93. Husserl defends the primacy of the (transcendental) self in relation to the other not only in the Fifth Cartesian Meditation (cf. especially *Hua I* 125–6 [*CM* § 44]), but also in the *Crisis* (*Hua VI* 187–9 [*K* § 54 b]). In this latter passage he makes the important point that this primal subjectivity ('*Ur-Ich*') is termed an 'I' only by way of equivocation. As previously noted, presumably the reason this is an equivocation is that, at least in the first instance, there is nothing that is 'non-I' for this primal subjectivity.

94. The ethical-teleological defense plays an especially important role in the *Crisis* and the Vienna Lectures of 1935. See *Hua VI* 199–201 (*K* § 56); 332, 336–38. However, it is should not be thought to be a completely new line of thinking motivated solely by contemporary events, since similar arguments are also to be found in "Philosophy as Rigorous Science."

95. For the distinction between natural-pragmatic rationality and philosophical-theoretical rationality, and the claim that the latter is to be found only in European philosophy, see *Hua VI* 327–331 (The Vienna Lecture).

96. See page 163 above.

97. *Hua VI* (*K* § 9a), 384 ("The Origin of Geometry").

98. A detailed analysis of this teleology is contained in manuscript B I 12 IV (1926–30), especially transcription pp. 59–60. See also *Hua VIII* 380–91 (*Beilage* X) for a related excerpt from this manuscript.

Conclusion

Phenomenology itself cannot be employed to derive a totalizing relativism, a relativism which everywhere forsakes or denies the universal. Rather, the relativist denial of all universals is only the reverse side of the dogmatic, *un*phenomenological absolutism characteristic of objectivism. The objectivist correspondence theory of truth dogmatically posits the non-relative character of truth, without regard for the possibility of knowledge, or for the nature of the truth that informs actual intentional experience. The relativist rejects the absolutism of objectivism as pre-critical and naïve, but only to substitute a naïveté of his own. For the relativist's conviction of the relativity of all truth arises from a conception of knowledge and reality as 'formed' – and hence relative to – a contingent subjective cognitive background (whether this background be conceived as empirical psychological constitution, historico-cultural world-view, or 'transcendental' faculties). Yet this conception naïvely hypostatizes and absolutizes the subject background itself, and approaches subjectivity with precisely the same pre-critical dogmatism that characterizes objectivism's approach to the object. By contrast, when subjectivity is not treated as some invisible 'thing' – something which exists and possesses a determinate nature independently of any actual or possible givenness in experience – when subjectivity itself is approached as a phenomenon, then it reveals itself to contain universal as well as contingent features.

Of late universalism has come to be accused of violence, of providing a sanction for the trivialization of otherness, and so for brutally enforcing the contingent under the banner of the 'we'. Husserl himself has not escaped this charge. However, the image of relativism as the less violent of the two doctrines is misguided. Even a complacent, pacifist relativism leads to isolationism at best, to an undermining of a central motive for exchange with others: the desire to establish a truth which is shared. Yet the same

203

thinking which holds 'our truths are valid for us, their truths for them' easily degenerates into the much more sinister 'our truths are valid for us, no matter what anyone else thinks'. Thus relativism provides a sanction for the absence of any public debate or attempt to establish consensus. Clearly, a philosophical opposition to violence requires an acknowledgement of the universal no less than a respect for relativity. This is the approach that has been supported in this work.

A final word should be said about the role of limits in this analysis. For ultimately, Husserl's phenomenology is able to provide a positive resolution of the question of relativism only because it everywhere acknowledges such limits. It is the implicit recognition of the phenomenality of knowing itself that justifies and gives rise to Husserl's otherwise highly anachronistic-sounding language of 'apodicticity', the 'absolute', the 'itself', and so on. According to objectivism, reality has no necessary relation to the subject or subjective possibilities of experience, and accordingly knowledge is knowledge of 'things in themselves'. Because it sets too difficult a goal for knowledge, objectivism ends in skepticism. By contrast, Husserl's *Evidenz*-theory of truth is able to establish the possibility of knowledge by acknowledging that knowledge and its objects are themselves 'only' phenomenal, only what is given in experience, and not something that exists apart from it. Further, Husserl emphasizes that the 'strength' of knowledge or *Evidenz* will in many or even most cases necessarily be far from maximal. Correspondingly, the justification Husserl's analysis provides, against relativism, for knowledge of the universal is also of a limited, less than objectivistically absolute nature. This is not only because of the inherent fragility and tentativeness of a consensus to be established through dialogue. Even the path to the universal via eidetic analysis yields an apodicticity which is only phenomenal, a certainty which cannot provide a final guarantee against error and reversals. Thus in contrast to the very strong language employed everywhere by Husserl, his foundationalism is in fact a very moderate, even 'weak' one, one which can be seen to be successful only when and insofar as its emphasis on limits is kept clearly in view. Indeed, with only slight exaggeration one could say that if the Kantian project was to limit reason to make room for faith, the essence of the project of Husserlian phenomenology is to limit reason to make room for knowledge.

Bibliography

I. WRITINGS OF HUSSERL

A. PUBLISHED WRITINGS OF HUSSERL

1. Husserliana Edition

Cartesianische Meditationen und Pariser Vorträge. Edited by Stephan Strasser. *Husserliana,* vol. I. The Hague: Martinus Nijhoff Publishers, 1950.

Die Idee der Phänomenologie. Edited by Walter Biemel. *Husserliana,* vol. II. The Hague: Martinus Nijhoff Publishers, 1950.

Ideen zu einer reinen Phänomenologie und phänomenologischen Philosophie, Erstes Buch. Newly edited by Karl Schuhmann. *Husserliana,* vol. III/1. The Hague: Martinus Nijhoff Publishers, 1976.

Ideen zu einer reinen Phänomenologie und phänomenologischen Philosophie, Erstes Buch. Edited by Walter Biemel. *Husserliana,* vol. III. The Hague: Martinus Nijhoff Publishers, 1954.

Ideen zu einer reinen Phänomenologie und phänomenologischen Philosophie, Zweites Buch. Edited by Marly Biemel. *Husserliana,* vol. IV. The Hague: Martinus Nijhoff Publishers, 1952.

Ideen zu einer reinen Phänomenologie und phänomenologischen Philosophie, Drittes Buch. Edited by Marly Biemel. *Husserliana,* vol. V. The Hague: Martinus Nijhoff Publishers, 1952.

Die Krisis der europäischen Wissenschaften und die transzendentale Phänomenologie. Edited by Walter Biemel. *Husserliana,* vol. VI. The Hague: Martinus Nijhoff Publishers, 1954.

Erste Philosophie (1923/24), Erster Teil. Edited by Rudolf Boehm. *Husserliana*, vol. VII. The Hague: Martinus Nijhoff Publishers, 1956.

Erste Philosophie (1923/24), Zweiter Teil. Edited by Rudolf Boehm. *Husserliana*, vol. VIII. The Hague: Martinus Nijhoff Publishers, 1959.

Phänomenologische Psychologie. Edited by Walter Biemel. *Husserliana*, vol. IX. The Hague: Martinus Nijhoff Publishers, 1962.

Zur Phänomenologie des inneren Zeitbewußtseins. Edited by Rudolf Boehm. *Husserliana*, vol. X. The Hague: Martinus Nijhoff Publishers, 1966.

Analysen zur passiven Synthesis. Edited by Margot Fleischer. *Husserliana*, vol. XI. The Hague: Martinus Nijhoff Publishers, 1966.

Philosophie der Arithmetik. Edited by Lothar Eley. *Husserliana*, vol. XII. The Hague: Martinus Nijhoff Publishers, 1970.

Zur Phänomenologie der Intersubjektivität, Erster Teil: 1905–1920. Edited by Iso Kern. *Husserliana*, vol. XIII. The Hague: Martinus Nijhoff Publishers, 1973.

Zur Phänomenologie der Intersubjektivität, Zweiter Teil: 1921–1928. Edited by Iso Kern. *Husserliana*, vol. XIV. The Hague: Martinus Nijhoff Publishers, 1973.

Zur Phänomenologie der Intersubjektivität, Dritter Teil: 1929–1935. Edited by Iso Kern. *Husserliana*, vol. XV. The Hague: Martinus Nijhoff Publishers, 1973.

Formale und transzendentale Logik. Edited by Paul Janssen. *Husserliana*, vol. XVII. The Hague: Martinus Nijhoff Publishers, 1974.

Logische Untersuchungen, Erster Band. Prolegomena zur reinen Logik. Edited by Elmar Holenstein. *Husserliana*, vol. XVIII. The Hague: Martinus Nijhoff Publishers, 1975.

Logische Untersuchungen, Zweiter Band, Erster Teil. Untersuchungen zur Phänomenologie und Theorie der Erkenntnis. Edited by Ursula Panzer. *Husserliana*, vol. XIX/1. The Hague: Martinus Nijhoff Publishers, 1984.

Logische Untersuchungen, Zweiter Band, Zweiter Teil. Untersuchungen zur Phänomenologie und Theorie der Erkenntnis. Edited by Ursula Panzer. *Husserliana*, vol. XIX/2. The Hague: Martinus Nijhoff Publishers, 1984.

Aufsätze und Vorträge (1911–1921). Edited by Thomas Nenon and Hans-Rainer Sepp. *Husserliana*, vol. XXV. Dordrecht: Martinus Nijhoff Publishers, 1986.

2. *Other Published Writings of Husserl*

Erfahrung und Urteil. Untersuchungen zur Genealogie der Logik. Edited by

Ludwig Landgrebe. With an afterward and index by Lothar Eley. Hamburg: Felix Meiner Verlag, 1985.

"Der Briefwechsel Dilthey-Husserl." Edited by Walter Biemel. *Revista de Filosofia de la Universidad de Costa Rica* (San José), 1 (1957): 101–24.

B. *UNPUBLISHED WRITINGS OF HUSSERL*

The following transcriptions of Husserl's unpublished manuscripts were consulted at the Husserl-Archives of Cologne, Leuven, and the New School for Social Research.

A I 25.   "Evidenz. Apodiktizität und Wissenschaft." 1930.

A IV 2.   "Begründung der Philosophie als universale Wissenschaft." 1926.

A IV 4.   "Die Welt des vorwissenschaftlichen Lebens und die 'Welt an sich'." 1933.

A IV 8.   "Wissenschaft. Naturwissenschaft." 1925–6.

A IV 10.   "Die objektive Welt in der idealisierten Unendlichkeit." Early 1930's.

A IV 12.   "Weg von der geisteswissenschaftlichen Einstellung als Einstellung auf das Faktische der geschichtlichen Welt in die universale eidetische Einstellung, welche das Universum der personalistischen und umweltlichen Möglichkeiten umspannt." 1934.

A IV 14.   "Idee der Wissenschaft. Relativität einer Wissenschaft auf universale 'Voraussetzungen'." 1926.

A V 3.   "Unsere Welt als menschlich-historische Welt." 1933.

A V 6.   "Das Problem der Objektivät der prädikativen Wahrheit." 1932.

A V 9.   "Grundlegende Untersuchungen zur Klärung der Idee Umwelt und 'wahre' Welt und von da aus zur Klärung der personalistischen Einstellung." 1927.

A V 10.   "Zur Beschreibung der Umwelt." 1930 or 1931.

A V 11.   "Tradition. Der autonome Mensch ... stellt sich über alle Tradition, übt eine universale Kritik an aller Tradition." 1930 or 1931.

A V 15.   "Lebenswelt, die immerfort Wissenschaft und der in ihr wissenschaftlich gefaßten Welt vorangeht. Wie ist da letztbegründete Wissenschaft möglich?" 1930–32.

A V 18.   "Wissenschaftliche Leben auf Grund des vorwissenschaft-

	lichens ... Universum der Wahrheit nicht Universum der objektiven Wahrheit." 1934.
A V 22.	"Universale Ethik." Mostly 1931.
A V 26.	"Ist das Ziel einer universalen Erkenntnis nicht überhaupt sinnlos?" 1923.
A VII 2.	"Struktur der Primordialität. Die Stufen der Konstitution des Wahrnehmungdinges." 1934.
A VII 11.	"Probleme der Weltanschauung. Möglichkeit einer Ontologie." 1925 and 1932.
A VII 12.	"Probleme der Weltanschauung." 1932.
A VII 19.	"Welt als All des intersubjektiv Geltenden überhaupt und die 'realen' Welt im besonderen." 1927.
A VII 20.	"Weltanschauung und Ontologie. Methode um die reine Erfahrungswelt zu konstruieren." 1930.
A VII 21.	"Die Erkenntnis der positiven Wissenschaften und die Umwelt. Apriori der Lebenswelt. Von der Endlichkeit in die Unendlichkeit in der Konstitution der Welt." 1927–33.
A VII 23.	"Relativitäten, 'Situationswahrheiten'." 1933.
A VII 31.	"Doxa. Wir Europäer konstruieren die Zweckidee der objektiven Wissenschaft." 1934.
B I 5.	"Epoché hinsichtlich aller Tradition." 1930–33.
B I 7.	"Phänomenologie und positive Wissenschaft." 1925.
B I 7 III.	"Phänomenologie als die absolute, alle Relativität überwindende Ontologie." 1923.
B I 8.	"Relativität der Weltwahrheit, des weltlichen Seins." 1932.
B I 9 VII.	"Versuch von der Idee einer universalen Geisteswissenschaft ... zur phänomenologischen Reduktion zu führen." 1926.
B I 10 I.	"Absolut begründete Wissenschaft." 1932–33.
B I 10 VII.	"Relativität der für uns jeweils seiend-geltenden Welt." 1926.
B I 10 XII.	"Möglichkeit letztbegründeter Wissenschaft." 1926.
B I 12 IV-V.	"Überlegungen zur Klärung derjenigen Evidenz, die in der äußeren (Realitäts) Erfahrung liegt, der in ihr implizierten Horizontevidenzen. 'Evidenzmodus empirische Gewißheit'." 1926–30.
B I 14 VIII.	"Paradoxien oder Antinomien des anthropologischen Relativismus." 1933.
B I 29.	"Problem einer nicht historischen sondern idealen Genesis der Idee strenger Wissenschaft." 1925.

B II 2.   "Absolutes Bewußtsein. Metaphysisches. Gott." 1907–8.

B III 6.   "Das Problem des 'Seins' in einer bloß relativen sinnlichen Welt." 1924–5.

B IV 5.   "Zur '6.' Meditation. 1933, 1934.

D 3.   "Objektivität. 'Objektive' oder Wahrheit an sich." 1920.

D 4.   "Objektivität in Beziehung auf einzelne Subjektivität und Intersubjektivität (Jedermann). Die kategoriale Form der Objektivität. Stufenfolge: das erste 'Objekt' der Leib, das zweite die Nature. Relative Intersubjektivität oder Objektivität und absolute; Sein und Wahrheit im strengen Sinne; subjektive und objektive Werte; 'reale' Objekte; Natur." 1921.

F I 11.   "Grundprobleme der Ethik." 1908–9.

F I 14.   "Idee der 'philosophischen Disziplinen'; vorgetragen als Einleitung in die Grundprobleme der Ethik." 1911.

F I 18.   "Phänomenologie als 'Erste Philosophie'. Absolute Erkenntnis." 1909.

F I 23.   "Aus der Vorlesungen Grundprobleme der Ethik." 1908–9.

F I 26.   "Vorlesungen über Erkenntnistheorie – 1902/3." 1902–7.

K X Heidegger I.   Husserl's notes to *Sein und Zeit*. After 1927.

K X Heidegger II.   Husserl's notes to *Kant und das Problem der Metaphysik*. After 1929.

M III 2 II 7.   Husserl's revisions of chapter 5, Investigation VI of the *Logische Untersuchungen*.

R I   Heidegger. Brief von 10.IX.1917 (Husserl to Heidegger). Brief von 30.XII.1927 (Malvine Husserl to Heidegger).

II. WORKS BY OTHER AUTHORS

Acham, Karl. "Rationalitätsansprüche im Lichte von Wissenschaftssoziologie und Weltanschauungslehre." In *Vernunft und Kontingenz. Rationalität und Ethos in der Phänomenologie*. Edited by Ernst Wolfgang Orth. Phänomenologische Forschungen, vol. 19. Freiburg and Munich: Karl Alber Verlag, 1986, 75–140.

Apel, Karl-Otto. "The Problem of a (Philosophical) Ultimate Justification in the Light of a Transcendental Pragmatic of Language." *Ajatus* 36 (1974): 142–65.

——. "Das Problem der phänomenologischen Evidenz im Lichte einer transzendentalen Semiotik." In *Die Krise der Phänomenologie und die Pragmatik des Wissenschaftsfortschritts*. Edited by Michael Benedikt and Rudolf Burger. Vienna, Österreichischer Staatsdruckerei, 1986, 78–99.

Bachelard, Suzanne. *La logique de Husserl: étude sur logique formelle et logique transcendentale.* Paris: Presses Universitaires de France, 1957.

Barnes, Barry and Bloor, David. "Relativism, Rationalism, and the Sociology of Knowledge." In *Rationality and Relativism.* Edited by Martin Hollis and Steven Lukes. Cambridge: MIT Press, 1984, 21–47.

Berkeley, George. *A Treatise Concerning the Principles of Human Knowledge.* In *The Works of George Berkeley*, vol. II. Edited by A. A. Luce and T. E. Jessop. London and New York: Thomas Nelson and Sons, 1945.

Biemel, Walter. "Husserls Encyclopedia Britannica Artikel und Heideggers Anmerkungen dazu." *Tijdschrift voor Philosophie* 12 (1950): 246–80.

——. "Heideggers Stellung zur Phänomenologie in der Marburger Zeit." In *Husserl, Scheler, Heidegger in der Sicht neuer Quellen.* Edited by Ernst Wolfgang Orth. Phänomenologische Forschungen, vol. 6/7. Freiburg and Munich: Karl Alber Verlag, 1978, 141–223.

Blumenberg, Hans. "Lebenswelt und Technisierung unter Aspekten der Phänomenologie." In *Wirklichkeiten in denen wir leben.* Stuttgart: Reclam, 1981, 7–54.

——. *Lebenszeit und Weltzeit.* Frankfurt a.M.: Suhrkamp Verlag, 1986.

Boehm, Rudolf. "Zum Begriff des 'Absoluten' bei Husserl." *Zeitschrift für philosophische Forschung* 13 (1959) 214–42.

Boyce Gibson, W.R. "From Husserl to Heidegger." *Journal of the British Society for Phenomenology* 2 (1971): 58–83.

Brand, Gerd. "Edmund Husserl. Zur Phänomenologie der Intersubjektivität. Texte aus dem Nachlaß." In *Husserl, Scheler, Heidegger in der Sicht neuer Quellen.* Edited by Ernst Wolfgang Orth. Phänomenologische Forschungen, vol. 6/7. Freiburg and Munich: Karl Alber Verlag, 1978, 28–117.

Brentano, Franz. *Psychologie vom empirischen Standpunkt.* Second edition. Leipzig: Felix Meiner, 1924.

Bruzina, Ronald. "The Enworlding (Verweltlichung) of Transcendental Phenomenological Reflection: A Study of Eugen Fink's '6th Cartesian Meditation'." *Husserl Studies* 3.1 (1986): 3–29.

Caputo, John D. "Husserl, Heidegger, and the Question of a 'Hermeneutic' Phenomenology." *Husserl Studies* 1.2 (1984): 157–178.

Carr, David. *Phenomenology and the Problem of History: A Study of Husserl's Transcendental Philosophy.* Evanston: Northwestern University Press, 1974.

——. "Welt, Weltbild, Lebenswelt: Husserl und die Vertreter des Begriffs-relativismus." In *Lebenswelt und Wissenschaft in der Philosophie Edmund Husserls*. Edited by Elisabeth Ströker. Frankfurt a.m.: Vittorio Klostermann Verlag, 1979, 32–44; reprinted as "World, World-View, Lifeworld: Husserl and the Conceptual Relativists." In *Interpreting Husserl*. Phaenomenologica, vol. 106. Dordrecht: Martinus Nijhoff Publishers, 1987, 213–225.

——. "Phenomenology and Relativism." In *Phenomenology in Practice and Theory*. Edited by William S. Hamrick. Phaenomenologica, vol. 92. Dordrecht: Martinus Nijhoff Publishers, 1985, 19–34; reprinted in *Interpreting Husserl*. Phaenomenologica, vol. 106. Dordrecht: Martinus Nijhoff Publishers, 1987, 25–44.

——. "Husserl's World and Ours." *Journal of the History of Philosophy* 25.1 (1987): 151–167; reprinted as "Husserl's Lengthening Shadow: A Historical Introduction." In *Interpreting Husserl*. Phaenomenologica, vol. 106. Dordrecht: Martinus Nijhoff Publishers, 1987, 1–21.

——. "The Future Perfect: Temporality and Priority in Husserl, Dilthey and Heidegger." In *Dilthey and Phenomenology*. Edited by R. Makkreel and J. Scanlon. Washington, D.C.: Center for Advanced Research in Phenomenology, University Press of America, 1987; reprinted in *Interpreting Husserl*. Phaenomenologica, vol. 106. Dordrecht: Martinus Nijhoff Publishers, 1987, 197–211.

——. "The Lifeworld Revisited: Husserl and Some Recent Interpreters." In *Husserl's Phenomenology: A Textbook*. Edited by William R. McKenna and J.N. Mohanty. Washington, D.C.: Center for Advanced Research in Phenomenology, University Press of America, 1987; reprinted in *Interpreting Husserl*. Phaenomenologica, vol. 106. Dordrecht: Martinus Nijhoff Publishers, 1987, 227–246.

Cobb-Stevens, Richard. "Hermeneutics Without Relativism: Husserl's Theory of Mind." *Research in Phenomenology* 12 (1982): 127–48.

Davidson, Donald. "On the Very Idea of a Conceptual Scheme." *Proceedings and Addresses of the American Philosophical Association* 47 (1973/4): 5–20.

Descartes, René. *Dioptrique*. In *Oeuvres de Descartes*, vol. VI. Edited by Charles Adam and Paul Tannery. Paris: Vrin, 1973.

——. *Passions de l'âme*. In *Oeuvres de Descartes*, vol. XI. Edited by Charles Adam and Paul Tannery. Paris: Vrin, 1974.

——. *Principia philosophiæ*. In *Oeuvres de Descartes*, vol. VIII/I. Edited by Charles Adam and Paul Tannery. Paris: Vrin, 1973.

——. *Regulæ ad directionem ingenii*. In *Oeuvres de Descartes*, vol. X.

Edited by Charles Adam and Paul Tannery. Paris: Vrin, 1974.

Diemer, Alwin. "Die Phänomenologie und die Idee der Philosophie als strenge Wissenschaft." *Zeitschrift für philosophische Forschung* 13 (1959): 243–62.

Dilthey, Wilhelm. *Der Aufbau der geschichtlichen Welt in den Geisteswissenschaften.* Second edition. Stuttgart: B.G. Teubner, 1958.

Erdmann, Benno. *Logik. Logische Elementarlehre,* third revised edition. Edited by Erich Becher. Berlin and Leipzig: Walter de Gruyter, 1923.

Farber, Marvin. *The Foundation of Phenomenology: Edmund Husserl and the Quest for a Rigorous Science of Philosophy.* Cambridge: Harvard University Press, 1943; reprint, Albany: State University of New York Press: 1968.

Føllesdal, Dagfinn. "Husserl's Theory of Perception." Chap. 21 in *Handbook of Perception,* vol. 1. Edited by E.C. Carterette and M.P. Friedman. New York: Academic Press, 1973.

——. "Rationalität in Husserls Phänomenologie." In *Vernunft und Kontingenz: Rationalität und Ethos in der Phänomenologie.* Edited by Ernst Wolfgang Orth. Phänomenologische Forschungen, vol. 19. Freiburg and Munich: Karl Alber Verlag, 1986, 35–52.

Gadamer, Hans-Georg. *Wahrheit und Methode: Grundzüge einer philosophischen Hermeneutik.* Tübingen: J.C.B. Mohr (Paul Siebeck), 1960. Fifth revised and improved edition, in Gesammelte Werke, vol. 1: *Hermeneutik I.* Tübingen: J.C.B. Mohr (Paul Siebeck), 1986.

——. "Hermeneutik und Historizismus." *Philosophische Rundschau* 9 (1961): 241–276; reprinted in Gesammelte Werke, vol. 2: *Hermeneutik II.* Tübingen: J.C.B. Mohr (Paul Siebeck), 1986, 387–424.

——."Die phänomenologische Bewegung." *Philosophische Rundschau* 11 (1963): 1–45.

——. "Vernunft und praktische Philosophie." In *Vernunft und Kontingenz: Rationalität und Ethos in der Phänomenologie.* Edited by Ernst Wolfgang Orth. Phänomenologische Forschungen, vol. 19. Freiburg and Munich: Karl Alber Verlag, 1986, 174–185.

Galilei, Galileo. *Dialogue Concerning the Two Chief World Systems.* Translated by Stillman Drake. Second Edition. Berkeley and Los Angeles: University of California Press, 1967.

Goodman, Nelson. *Ways of Worldmaking.* Indianapolis: Hackett, 1978.

Heidegger, Martin. *Sein und Zeit.* Gesamtausgabe, vol. 2. Frankfurt a.M.: Vittorio Klostermann, 1977.

Hemmendinger, David. "Husserl's Phenomenological Program: A Study of Evidence and Analysis." Ph.D. diss., Yale University, 1973.

Janssen, Paul. *Edmund Husserl: Einführung in seine Phänomenologie.* Freiburg and Munich: Karl Alber Verlag, 1976.

Kant, Immanuel. *Kritik der reinen Vernunft.* In Gesammelte Schriften, vol. III and IV. Royal Prussian Academy of Science Edition. Berlin: G. Reimer, 1911.

Kern, Iso. *Husserl und Kant.* Phaenomenologica, vol. 16. The Hague: Martinus Nijhoff, 1964.

——. "Die Lebenswelt als Grundlage der objektiven Wissenschaften und als universales Wahrheits- und Seinsproblem." In *Lebenswelt und Wissenschaft in der Philosophie Edmund Husserls.* Edited by Elisabeth Ströker. Frankfurt a.M.: Vittorio Klostermann Verlag, 1979, 68–78.

Kolakowski, Leszek. *Husserl and the Search for Certitude.* New Haven: Yale University Press, 1975.

Krausz, Michael. "Relativism and Foundationalism." *The Monist* 67.3 (July, 1984): 395–404.

Kuderowicz, Zbigniew. "Husserl as a Critic of Historicism." *Reports on Philosophy* 2 (1978): 19–29.

Kuhn, Thomas S. *The Structure of Scientific Revolutions.* Second edition. International Encyclopedia of Unified Science, vol. 2, no. 2. Chicago: University of Chicago Press, 1970.

Landgrebe, Ludwig. "Husserls Abschied vom Cartesianismus." *Philosophische Rundschau* 9 (1962): 133–77.

Larmore, Charles. "Tradition, Objectivity, and Hermeneutics." In *Hermeneutics and Modern Philosophy.* Edited by Brice R. Wachterhauser. Albany: State University of New York Press, 1986, 147–167.

Levin, David Michael. "A Critique of Husserl's Theory of Adequate and Apodictic Evidence." Ph.D. diss., Columbia University, 1967.

——. *Reason and Evidence in Husserl's Phenomenology.* Evanston: Northwestern University Press, 1970.

Levinas, Emmanuel. *La théorie de l'intuition dans la phénoménologie de Husserl.* Paris: Alcan, 1930.

Locke, John. *An Essay Concerning Human Understanding.* Edited by Peter Nidditch. Oxford: Clarendon, 1979.

Loux, Michael, translator. *Ockham's Theory of Terms: Part I of the Summa Logicæ.* Notre Dame, Ind. and London: University of Notre Dame Press, 1974.

McCullagh, C. Behan. "The Intelligibility of Cognitive Relativism." *The Monist* 67.3 (July, 1984): 327–340.

Merleau-Ponty, Maurice. *Phénoménologie de la perception.* Paris: Gallimard, 1943.

Metzger, Arnold. *Phänomenologie und Metaphysik: das Problem des Relativismus und seiner Überwindung.* Halle: Max Niemeyer Verlag, 1933; second revised edition, Pfüllingen: Verlag Günther Neske, 1966.

Mill, John Stuart. *An Examination of Sir William Hamilton's Philosophy.* London: Longmans, Green and Co., 1889.

Misch, Georg. *Lebensphilosophie und Phänomenologie.* Leipzig: Teubner Verlag, 1931.

Mohanty, J.N. *Husserl's Theory of Meaning.* Phaenomenologica, vol. 14. The Hague: Martinus Nijhoff Publishers, 1964.

——. "Rorty, Phenomenology, and Transcendental Philosophy." *The Journal of the British Society for Phenomenology* 14.1 (January, 1983): 91–98.

——. "Phänomenologische Rationalität und die Überwindung des Relativismus." In *Vernunft und Kontingenz: Rationalität und Ethos in der Phänomenologie.* Edited by Ernst Wolfgang Orth. Phänomenologische Forschungen, vol. 19. Freiburg and Munich: Karl Alber Verlag, 1986, 53–74.

Okrent, Mark. "Relativism, Context, Truth." *The Monist* 67.3 (July, 1984): 341–58.

Orth, Ernst Wolfgang. "Die Unverfügbarkeit der Rationalität und die Vorrätigkeit des Sinnes." In *Vernunft und Kontingenz: Rationalität und Ethos in der Phänomenologie.* Edited by Ernst Wolfgang Orth. Phänomenologische Forschungen, vol. 19. Freiburg and Munich: Karl Alber Verlag, 1986, 7–9.

Patzig, Günther. "Kritische Bemerkungen zu Husserls Thesen über das Verhältnis Zwischen Wahrheit und Evidenz." *Neue Hefte für Philosophie* 1 (1971): 12–32.

Pöggeler, Otto. "Kontingenz und Rationalität in der phänomenologische Wissenschaftstheorie." In *Vernunft und Kontingenz: Rationalität und Ethos in der Phänomenologie.* Edited by Ernst Wolfgang Orth. Phänomenologische Forschungen, vol. 19. Freiburg and Munich: Karl Alber Verlag, 1986, 10–34.

Putnam, Hillary. "Gibt es dem, was über Wahrheit und Wirklichkeit gesagt worden ist, noch etwas hinzuzufügen?" In *Die Krise der Phänomenologie und die Pragmatik des Wissenschaftsfortschritts.* Edited by Michael Benedikt and Rudolf Burger. Vienna, Österreichischer Staatsdruckerei, 1986, 40–52.

——. *Reason, Truth and History.* Cambridge: Cambridge University Press, 1981.

Ricoeur, Paul. "Husserl et le sens de l'histoire." *Revue de Métaphysique et de Morale* 54 (1949): 280–316.

Rorty, Richard. *Philosophy and the Mirror of Nature.* Princeton: Princeton University Press, 1980.

Sartre, Jean-Paul. *L'être et le néant.* Paris: Gallimard, 1943.

Scheler, Max. *Wesen und Formen der Sympathie.* In Gesammelte Werke, vol. 7. Edited with an afterward by Manfred S. Frings. Berlin and Munich: Francke Verlag, 1973.

Schuhmann, Karl. *Husserl-Chronik. Denk- und Lebensweg Edmund Husserls.* Husserliana Dokumente, vol. 1. The Hague: Martinus Nijhoff Publishers, 1977.

Soffer, Gail. "Phenomenology and Scientific Realism: Husserl's Critique of Galileo." *The Review of Metaphysics* 44.1 (September, 1990): 67–94.

Sokolowski, Robert. *The Formation of Husserl's Concept of Constitution.* Phaenomenologica, vol. 18. The Hague: Martinus Nijhoff Publishers, 1964.

Spiegelberg, Herbert. *The Phenomenological Movement.* Phaenomenologica, vol. 5/6, second edition. The Hague: Martinus Nijhoff Publishers, 1965.

Stapleton, Timothy J. *Husserl and Heidegger: The Question of a Phenomenological Beginning.* Albany: State University of New York Press, 1983.

Ströker, Elisabeth. "Das Problem der Epoché in der Philosophie Edmund Husserls." *Analecta Husserliana* 1 (1971): 170–185.

——. "Husserls Evidenzprinzip. Sinn und Grenzen einer methodischen Norm der Phänomenologie als Wissenschaft. *Zeitschrift für philosophische Forschung* 32.1 (1978): 1–30; reprinted in *Phänomenologische Studien.* Frankfurt a.M.: Vittorio Klostermann, 1987.

——. "Geschichte und Lebenswelt als Sinnesfundament der Wissenschaften in Husserls Spätwerk." In *Lebenswelt und Wissenschaft in der Philosophie Edmund Husserls.* Edited by Elisabeth Ströker. Frankfurt a.M.: Vittorio Klostermann Verlag, 1979, 106–123.

——. "Phänomenologie und Psychologie. Die Frage ihrer Beziehung bei Husserl." *Zeitschrift für philosophische Forschung* 37.1 (1983): 3–19; reprinted in *Phänomenologische Studien.* Frankfurt a.M.: Vittorio Klostermann, 1987.

Szilasi, Wilhelm. *Einführung in die Phänomenologie Edmund Husserls.* Tübingen: Max Niemeyer Verlag, 1959.

Taylor, Charles. "Zur Überwindung der Erkenntnistheorie." In *Die Krise der Phänomenologie und die Pragmatik des Wissenschaftsfortschritts.*

Edited by Michael Benedikt and Rudolf Burger. N.p., Österreichischer Staatsdruckerei, 1986, 150–167.

Theunissen, Michael. *Der Andere. Studien zur Soziologie der Gegenwart.* Berlin: Walter de Gruyter Verlag, 1965.

Trotignon, Pierre. *Le coeur de la raison: Husserl et la crise du monde moderne.* Paris: Fayard, 1986.

Tugendhat, Ernst. *Der Wahrheitsbegriff bei Husserl und Heidegger.* Berlin: Walter de Gruyter Verlag, 1967.

Vallicella, William. "Relativism, Truth, and The Symmetry Thesis," in *The Monist* 67.3 (July, 1984): 452–66.

Waldenfels, Bernhard. "Die Abgründigkeit des Sinnes." In *In den Netzen der Lebenswelt.* Frankfurt a.M.: Suhrkamp, 1985.

Willard, Dallas. "The Paradox of Logical Psychologism: Husserl's Way Out." In *Husserl: Expositions and Appraisals.* Edited by Peter McCormick and Frederick Elliston. Notre Dame: University of Notre Dame Press, 1977, 10–17.

——. *Logic and the Objectivity of Knowledge: A Study in Husserl's Early Philosophy.* Athens, Ohio: Ohio University Press, 1984.

Wittgenstein, Ludwig. *Philosophical Investigations.* Translated by G.E.M. Anscombe. Third edition. New York: Macmillan, 1968.

Index

217

Phaenomenologica

1. E. Fink: *Sein, Wahrheit, Welt.* Vor-Fragen zum Problem des Phänomen-Begriffs.
1958 ISBN 90-247-0234-8
2. H.L. van Breda and J. Taminiaux (eds.): *Husserl et la pensée moderne / Husserl und das Denken der Neuzeit.* Actes du deuxième Colloque International de Phénoménologie / Akten des zweiten Internationalen Phänomenologischen Kolloquiums (Krefeld, 1.-3. Nov. 1956). 1959 ISBN 90-247-0235-8
3. J.-C. Piguet: *De l'esthétique à la métaphysique.* 1959 ISBN 90-247-0236-4
4. *E. Husserl: 1850-1959.* Recueil commémoratif publié à l'occasion du centenaire de la naissance du philosophe. 1959 ISBN 90-247-0237-2
5/6. H. Spiegelberg: *The Phenomenological Movement.* A Historical Introduction. 3rd revised ed. with the collaboration of Karl Schumann. 1982
ISBN Hb: 90-247-2577-1; Pb: 90-247-2535-6
7. A. Roth: *Edmund Husserls ethische Untersuchungen.* Dargestellt anhand seiner Vorlesungsmanuskripte. 1960 ISBN 90-247-0241-0
8. E. Levinas: *Totalité et Infini.* Essai sur l'extériorité. 4th ed., 4th printing 1984
ISBN Hb: 90-247-5105-5; Pb: 90-247-2971-8
9. A. de Waelhens: *La philosophie et les expériences naturelles.* 1961
ISBN 90-247-0243-7
10. L. Eley: *Die Krise des Apriori in der transzendentalen Phänomenologie Edmund Husserls.* 1962 ISBN 90-247-0244-5
11. A. Schutz: *Collected Papers, I.* The Problem of Social Reality. Edited and introduced by M. Natanson. 1962; 5th printing: 1982
ISBN Hb: 90-247-5089-X; Pb: 90-247-3046-5
Collected Papers, II *see* below under Volume 15
Collected Papers, III *see* below under Volume 22
12. J.M. Broekman: *Phänomenologie und Egologie.* Faktisches und transzendentales Ego bei Edmund Husserl. 1963 ISBN 90-247-0245-3
13. W.J. Richardson: *Heidegger. Through Phenomenology to Thought.* Preface by Martin Heidegger. 1963; 3rd printing: 1974 ISBN 90-247-02461-1
14. J.N. Mohanty: *Edmund Husserl's Theory of Meaning.* 1964; reprint: 1969
ISBN 90-247-0247-X
15. A. Schutz: *Collected Papers, II.* Studies in Social Theory. Edited and introduced by A. Brodersen. 1964; reprint: 1977 ISBN 90-247-0248-8
16. I. Kern: *Husserl und Kant.* Eine Untersuchung über Husserls Verhältnis zu Kant und zum Neukantianismus. 1964; reprint: 1984 ISBN 90-247-0249-6
17. R.M. Zaner: *The Problem of Embodiment.* Some Contributions to a Phenomenology of the Body. 1964; reprint: 1971 ISBN 90-247-5093-8
18. R. Sokolowski: *The Formation of Husserl's Concept of Constitution.* 1964; reprint: 1970 ISBN 90-247-5086-5
19. U. Claesges: *Edmund Husserls Theorie der Raumkonstition.* 1964
ISBN 90-247-0251-8
20. M. Dufrenne: *Jalons.* 1966 ISBN 90-247-0252-6
21. E. Fink: *Studien zur Phänomenologie, 1930-1939.* 1966 ISBN 90-247-0253-4
22. A. Schutz: *Collected Papers, III.* Studies in Phenomenological Philosophy. Edited by I. Schutz. With an introduction by Aaron Gurwitsch. 1966; reprint: 1975
ISBN 90-247-5090-3

Phaenomenologica

23. K. Held: *Lebendige Gegenwart*. Die Frage nach der Seinsweise des transzendentalen Ich bei Edumund Husserl, entwickelt am Leitfaden der Zeitproblematik. 1966
ISBN 90-247-0254-2

24. O. Laffoucrière: *Le destin de la pensée et 'La Mort de Dieu' selon Heidegger*. 1968
ISBN 90-247-0255-0

25. E. Husserl: *Briefe an Roman Ingarden*. Mit Erläuterungen und Erinnerungen an Husserl. Hrsg. von R. Ingarden. 1968   ISBN Hb: 90-247-0257-7; Pb: 90-247-0256-9

26. R. Boehm: *Vom Gesichtspunkt der Phänomenologie* (I). Husserl-Studien. 1968
ISBN Hb: 90-247-0259-3; Pb: 90-247-0258-5
For *Band II* see below under Volume 83

27. T. Conrad: *Zur Wesenslehre des psychischen Lebens und Erlebens*. Mit einem Geleitwort von H.L. van Breda. 1968   ISBN 90-247-0260-7

28. W. Biemel: *Philosophische Analysen zur Kunst der Gegenwart*. 1969
ISBN Hb: 90-247-0263-1; Pb: 90-247-0262-3

29. G. Thinès: *La problématique de la psychologie*. 1968
ISBN Hb: 90-247-0265-8; Pb: 90-247-0264-X

30. D. Sinha: *Studies in Phenomenology*. 1969
ISBN Hb: 90-247-0267-4; Pb: 90-247-0266-6

31. L. Eley: *Metakritik der formalen Logik*. Sinnliche Gewissheit als Horizont der Aussagenlogik und elementaren Prädikatenlogik. 1969
ISBN Hb: 90-247-0269-0; Pb: 90-247-0268-2

32. M.S. Frings: *Person und Dasein*. Zur Frage der Ontologie des Wertseins. 1969
ISBN Hb: 90-247-0271-2; Pb: 90-247-0270-4

33. A. Rosales: *Transzendenz und Differenz*. Ein Beitrag zum Problem der ontologischen Differenz beim frühen Heidegger. 1970   ISBN 90-247-0272-0

34. M.M. Saraïva: *L'imagination selon Husserl*. 1970   ISBN 90-247-0273-9

35. P. Janssen: *Geschichte und Lebenswelt*. Ein Beitrag zur Diskussion von Husserls Spätwerk. 1970   ISBN 90-247-0274-7

36. W. Marx: *Vernunft und Welt*. Zwischen Tradition und anderem Anfang. 1970
ISBN 90-247-5042-3

37. J.N. Mohanty: *Phenomenology and Ontology*. 1970   ISBN 90-247-5053-9

38. A. Aguirre: *Genetische Phänomenologie und Reduktion*. Zur Letztbegründung der Wissenschaft aus der radikalen Skepsis im Denken E. Husserls. 1970
ISBN 90-247-5025-3

39. T.F. Geraets: *Vers une nouvelle philosophie transcendentale*. La genèse de la philosophie de Maurice Merleau-Ponty jusqu'à la 'Phénoménologie de la perception.' Préface par E. Levinas. 1971   ISBN 90-247-5024-5

40. H. Declève: *Heidegger et Kant*. 1970   ISBN 90-247-5016-4

41. B. Waldenfels: *Das Zwischenreich des Dialogs*. Sozialphilosophische Untersuchungen in Anschluss an Edmund Husserl. 1971   ISBN 90-247-5072-5

42. K. Schuhmann: *Die Fundamentalbetrachtung der Phänomenologie*. Zum Weltproblem in der Philosophie Edmund Husserls. 1971   ISBN 90-247-5121-7

43. K. Goldstein: *Selected Papers/Ausgewählte Schriften*. Edited by A. Gurwitsch, E.M. Goldstein Haudek and W.E. Haudek. Introduction by A. Gurwitsch. 1971
ISBN 90-247-5047-4

Phaenomenologica

Phaenomenologica

Phaenomenologica

88. D. Welton: *The Origins of Meaning*. A Critical Study of the Thresholds of Husserlian Phenomenology. 1983   ISBN 90-247-2618-2
89. W.R. McKenna: *Husserl's 'Introductions to Phenomenology'*. Interpretation and Critique. 1982   ISBN 90-247-2665-4
90. J.P. Miller: *Numbers in Presence and Absence*. A Study of Husserl's Philosophy of Mathematics. 1982   ISBN 90-247-2709-X
91. U. Melle: *Das Wahrnehmungsproblem und seine Verwandlung in phänomenologischer Einstellung*. Untersuchungen zu den phänomenologischen Wahrnehmungstheorien von Husserl, Gurwitsch und Merleau-Ponty. 1983
                                    ISBN 90-247-2761-8
92. W.S. Hamrick (ed.): *Phenomenology in Practice and Theory*. Essays for Herbert Spiegelberg. 1984   ISBN 90-247-2926-2
93. H. Reiner: *Duty and Inclination*. The Fundamentals of Morality Discussed and Redefined with Special Regard to Kant and Schiller. 1983   ISBN 90-247-2818-6
94. M. J. Harney: *Intentionality, Sense and the Mind*. 1984   ISBN 90-247-2891-6
95. Kah Kyung Cho (ed.): *Philosophy and Science in Phenomenological Perspective*. 1984   ISBN 90-247-2922-X
96. A. Lingis: *Phenomenological Explanations*. 1986
                                    ISBN Hb: 90-247-3332-4; Pb: 90-247-3333-2
97. N. Rotenstreich: *Reflection and Action*. 1985
                                    ISBN Hb: 90-247-2969-6; Pb: 90-247-3128-3
98. J.N. Mohanty: *The Possibility of Transcendental Philosophy*. 1985
                                    ISBN Hb: 90-247-2991-2; Pb: 90-247-3146-1
99. J.J. Kockelmans: *Heidegger on Art and Art Works*. 1985   ISBN 90-247-3102-X
100. E. Lévinas: *Collected Philosophical Papers*. 1987
                                    ISBN Hb: 90-247-3272-7; Pb: 90-247-3395-2
101. R. Regvald: *Heidegger et le Problème du Néant*. 1986   ISBN 90-247-3388-X
102. J.A. Barash: *Martin Heidegger and the Problem of Historical Meaning*. 1987
                                    ISBN 90-247-3493-2
103 J.J. Kockelmans (ed.): *Phenomenological Psychology*. The Dutch School. 1987
                                    ISBN 90-247-3501-7
104. W.S. Hamrick: *An Existential Phenomenology of Law: Maurice Merleau-Ponty*. 1987
                                    ISBN 90-247-3520-3
105. J.C. Sallis, G. Moneta and J. Taminiaux (eds.): *The Collegium Phaenomenologium. The First Ten Years*. 1988   ISBN 90-247-3709-5
106. D. Carr: *Interpreting Husserl*. Critical and Comparative Studies. 1987.
                                    ISBN 90-247-3505-X
107. G. Heffernan: *Isagoge in die phänomenologische Apophantik*. Eine Einführung in die phänomenologische Urteilslogik durch die Auslegung des Textes der *Formalen und transzendenten Logik* von Edmund Husserl. 1989   ISBN 90-247-3710-9
108. F. Volpi, J.-F. Mattéi, Th. Sheenan, J.-F. Courtine, J. Taminiaux, J. Sallis, D. Janicaud, A.L. Kelkel, R. Bernet, R. Brisart, K. Held, M. Haar et S. IJsseling: *Heidegger et l'Idée de la Phénoménologie*. 1988   ISBN 90-247-3586-6
109. C. Singevin: *Dramaturgie de l'Esprit*. 1988   ISBN 90-247-3557-2

Phaenomenologica

Previous volumes are still available

Further information about *Husserliana* and *Phenomenology* publications are available on request.

Kluwer Academic Publishers – Dordrecht / Boston / London